ELIZABETHAN HUMANISM

LONGMAN MEDIEVAL AND RENAISSANCE LIBRARY

General Editors:

Charlotte Brewer Hertford College, Oxford and *N. H. Keeble* University of Stirling

Published Titles:

The Fabliau in English
John Hines

English Medieval Mystics: Games of Faith
Marion Glasscoe

The Classical Legacy in Renaissance Poetry
Robin Sowerby

English and Italian Literature from Dante to Shakespeare: A Study of Source,
Analogue and Divergence
Robin Kirkpatrick

Shakespeare's Alternative Tales
Leah Scragg

The Gawain-Poet
Ad Putter

Donne's Religious Writing: A Discourse of Feigned Devotion
P. M. Oliver

Images of Faith in English Literature 700–1500: An Introduction
Dee Dyas

Courtliness and Literature in Medieval England
David Burnley

Wyatt, Surrey and Early Tudor Poetry
Elizabeth Heale

A New Introduction to Chaucer
Derek Brewer

Marvell: The Writer in Public Life
Annabel Patterson

Shakespeare's Sonnets and Narrative Poems
A. D. Cousins

The Metaphysical Poets
David Reid

The Spirit of Medieval English Popular Romance
Edited by Ad Putter and Jane Gilbert

Women and Dramatic Production 1550–1700
Alison Findlay

The Politics of Early Modern Women's Writing
Danielle Clarke

ELIZABETHAN HUMANISM

Literature and Learning in the later Sixteenth Century

MIKE PINCOMBE

Longman

An imprint of **Pearson Education**

Harlow, England · London · New York · Reading, Massachusetts · San Francisco
Toronto · Don Mills, Ontario · Sydney · Tokyo · Singapore · Hong Kong · Seoul
Taipei · Cape Town · Madrid · Mexico City · Amsterdam · Munich · Paris · Milan

Pearson Education Limited

Head Office:
Edinburgh Gate
Harlow CM20 2JE
Tel: +44 (0)1279 623623
Fax: +44 (0)1279 431059

London Office:
128 Long Acre
London WC2E 9AN
Tel: +44 (0)20 7447 2000
Fax: +44 (0)20 7240 5771
Website: www.history-minds.com

First published in Great Britain in 2001

© Pearson Education Limited 2001

The right of Mike Pincombe to be identified as Author
of this Work has been asserted by him in accordance
with the Copyright, Designs and Patents Act 1988.

ISBN 0 582 28980 7

British Library Cataloguing in Publication Data
A CIP catalogue record for this book can be obtained from the British Library

Library of Congress Cataloging in Publication Data
A CIP catalog record for this book can be obtained from the Library of Congress

10 9 8 7 6 5 4 3 2 1

Typeset by 35 in 11/13pt Baskerville MT
Printed in Malaysia, VVP

The Publishers' policy is to use paper manufactured from sustainable forests.

In memoriam
MIECZYSŁAW DĄBROWSKI

CONTENTS

PREFACE

Anyone who studies Elizabethan literature will soon come across the term 'humanism' and wonder what it means. It is certainly an important term, since everyone uses it, but they do not always – or even often – use it in the same way. What I have tried to do in this book is to give a 'characterisation' of the term 'humanism' as it might have been understood by the Elizabethans themselves. They did not actually use the term in question, but they did use words like 'humanist', 'humanity' and *humanitas*; and by carefully examining what these words mean we can generate a putatively 'Elizabethan' sense for the modern word 'humanism'. I have made no attempt to 'define' the term, however, because it is very hard to set down limits (Latin: *definire*) to its usage. Instead, I have tried to explain and illustrate how a number of closely related senses of the word 'humanity' interact with one another in the later sixteenth century. The word encompassed concepts like literature, grammar, the classics, learning, education, good manners, urbanity, courtesy, gentleness, gentility, human kindness, humanness – and often several at once.

This may sound a daunting prospect, but, in fact, certain semantic configurations pertaining to 'humanity' and its cognates soon emerge, and the purpose of the first part of this book is to set them forth as plainly as possible. The opening chapter offers a brief introduction to the topic, and all readers, at whatever level, are recommended to begin here. More advanced readers will no doubt wish to progress methodically through the following chapters dealing with the Ciceronian origins of Elizabethan humanism, the various conceptions of the 'humanist', the important notion of the 'transference' of humanity from the ancient to the modern world, and a case study of the figure I consider to be the key to Elizabethan humanism: Gabriel Harvey. Scholars will find a great deal of new research and many new interpretations of more familiar material in these pages. However, I am also aware that less experienced readers, particularly those who are interested in one or other of the authors dealt with in the second part of the book, may wish to pass over the 'background chapters' rather quickly; but they are still advised to read Chapter 1 in order to furnish themselves with a basic orientation.

The second part of the book deals quite straightforwardly with five major Elizabethan texts. Each is placed in the context of the explorations undertaken in the first part, though in each case I have examined different aspects of 'humanity' as may best illuminate the text in question. The first three texts – *Euphues, The Shepherd's Calendar, An Apology for Poetry* – all date from the late 1570s, and are all intimately connected in one way or another to the figure of Gabriel Harvey, whose career is examined in the final chapter of Part One. The last two texts – *Doctor Faustus* and *Hamlet* – are both tragedies written for the common stage. These broad similarities speak for themselves, but readers may also discover new relations between these texts as this study persuades them (as I trust it will) of the complex interconnections between the various senses of the word 'humanity'.

A few words on the text might also be useful here. I have chosen to use old-spelling versions of the works under discussion, but, to avoid unnecessary irritation to many readers, I have expanded contractions (except ampersand) and have followed modern conventions regarding u/v and i/j. Texts in languages other than English have been translated, using Tudor translations where possible, and, where none exists, I have made up my own. Here I have used a sort of mock-Tudor English, partly for my own amusement, and partly for the sake of consistency, for why should a sixteenth-century writer sound more approachable in Latin than in English? (In the case of translations from the Latin of English writers, I have used my initials thus [MP] after the first 'quotation'.) Where I have quoted the Latin, I have generally used the form of the word used in a Latin dictionary, so that less experienced readers will find it easier to check if they should wish to do so. I have also tried to keep notes to a minimum (not always with success). In the second part of this book it would have been very easy to refer the reader to all kinds of excellent books and essays which might be of interest, but I have resisted the temptation – the five authors are all well served by modern bibliographies, after all. There is rather more material in the apparatus for the first part, however, since many topics covered will perhaps be unfamiliar even to established scholars.

Lastly, it is a pleasure to thank those who have provided various kinds of assistance during the writing of this book. Amongst academic colleagues, Jonathan Powell and Donald Hill have always been willing to help me with the classical side of my researches; Jenny Richards has been a tireless and stimulating reader of many of the chapters that follow; and Robert Maslen read the entire study and gave me much invaluable advice with regard to final revisions. The Faculty of Arts at Newcastle provided two periods of teaching relief to help me get on with the book at particularly difficult times. And, as always, I am grateful to my wife, Ewa, for her patient support and cheery companionship. It is to her late father, Mieczysław Dąbrowski, that this book is dedicated. Mieczysław was truly a *homo humanus*, and a man much missed by all of us who knew and loved him.

PART ONE

Contexts

CHAPTER ONE

Elizabethan Humanism

Around the year 1601, an unhappy and disappointed scholar called Gabriel Harvey cast a somewhat bitter retrospective look on the 'humanists' who had emerged during the last decades of the sixteenth century. In the margin of his copy of Thomas Twyne's translation of Dionysius Periegetes' *The Survey of the World* (1572), Harvey wrote the following remark (*Marginalia*, pp. 160–1):[1]

> Other commend Chawcer, & Lidgate for their witt, pleasant veine, varietie of poetical discourse, & all humanitie: I specially note their Astronomie, philosophie, & other parts of profound or cunning art. Wherein few of their time were more exactly learned. It is not sufficient for poets to be superficial humanists: but they must be exquisite artists, & curious universal schollers.

As far as Harvey was concerned, at least in the long years of his retirement from public life and letters, humanism was essentially 'superficial' in comparison with other arts which he deemed 'profound' (astronomy was one of his own particular interests). No doubt some humanists were even more superficial than others, but they were all triflers in comparison with philosophers and other genuinely learned men. They are associated not with the library or the lecture-hall, but with the common-room, or, more likely, with the parlour, where 'their witt, pleasant veine, varietie of poetical discourse, & all humanitie' may shine most luminously. They are not 'true poets', even, but ingenious rhymesters out to please.

This may seem an unpromising place to begin a book on Elizabethan humanism, but I believe it provides a salutary perspective on a literary culture which has perhaps too often been taken at its own evaluation. Fifty years ago, C.S. Lewis drew attention to the problem of achieving the right kind of critical distance between ourselves and what we now call 'Renaissance humanism' (1954, p. 20):

> The difficulty of assessing this new temper which the humanists introduced lies in the fact that our educational system descends from them and, therefore, the very terms we use embody humanistic conceptions. Unless we take care, our language will beg every question in their favour. We say, for example, that they substituted 'classical' for 'medieval' Latin. But the very idea of the 'medieval' is a humanistic invention.

And so, we might add, are the ideas of the 'Renaissance' and 'humanism'. Lewis was no friend to Renaissance humanism, but his unsympathetic account of its pedantry and vulgarity in his monumental study of *English Literature in the Sixteenth Century Excluding Drama* (1954) should be read carefully by anyone who is interested in the topic. It provides an enlightening critique of the literary character of Elizabethan humanism which has rarely been matched by later writers, and may profitably be set against a recent tendency amongst some Renaissance scholars to more-or-less openly accept and declare their descent from the old humanists.[2] Naturally, they see the Elizabethan humanist in a rather more positive light than Lewis or I do – or, indeed, than the Elizabethans themselves did.

There is much evidence to suggest that the 'humanist' – the word is an Elizabethan coinage – was regarded as a trifler or dilettante quite as much as a scholar or critic in late sixteenth-century England. Harvey's sceptical remarks on his 'superficial humanists' strike the true Elizabethan note; and we need to change our own ideas about what 'humanism' means in order to accommodate, indeed, where necessary, to emphasise its adverse aspects. This chapter, then, is designed to introduce a range of Elizabethan perspectives – negative as well as positive – on the set of ideas and attitudes we have come to call 'humanism'.

Humanity may have a threefold sense

The word 'humanism' is notoriously difficult to define. In the past century or so, it has acquired so many different senses, and so many nuances within these different senses themselves, that it has consistently succeeded in evading capture by those who wish to pin it down to a more-or-less easily recognisable meaning. Fortunately, the present study is concerned only with how we might best use the term 'humanism' when applying it to the literature and learning of the later sixteenth century in England. Even in this narrowly restricted area, however, we will find that there is a good deal of semantic range, and perhaps a little contradiction. But the attempt to unravel this complex lexical situation seems worthwhile, as the term 'humanism' is one which students of Elizabethan literature will encounter almost everywhere in books and articles devoted to the topic. Unfortunately, it means different things to different critics and scholars.[3] It is possible that the present contribution to the field will only make matters worse by adding to the confusion; but I hope that my novel approach to the question will prove illuminating rather than distracting.

It is well known that the word 'humanism' itself is a late coinage, emerging only in the early part of the nineteenth century. But cognate terms were actually used by the Elizabethans themselves. The word 'humanist' first appeared in 1589; and the now obsolete term 'humanitian' was first used even earlier in 1577. What did the Elizabethans mean by these terms? If we can discover the senses (for there are several) which were assigned to these words in the late sixteenth century, then perhaps we can generate a sense of the term 'humanism' which might have been comprehensible to an educated Elizabethan reader, were we able to go back in time and ask him or her what he or she thought it meant.[4] But we need to go back a stage further, to the word 'humanity', in order properly to lay the foundations of the present study. It is by investigating the various senses attached to this all-important term that we can begin to explore what the Elizabethans might have meant if they had invented the word 'humanism' for themselves. We shall return to this question again and again as we proceed through this study, but let us start with the earliest full definition of the word 'humanity' that I have so far encountered. It comes from a work by the minor Caroline poet Robert Aylett called *Peace with her Four Guarders* (1622). This is not, strictly speaking, an Elizabethan definition; but it sums up the Elizabethan lexical and cultural situation so neatly that it will serve very well as a point of departure for our present investigations.

Peace with her Four Guarders is a series of 'Five Morall Meditations', and the fourth of these is called 'Of Courtesy, or Humanity'. The synonymity of these two terms needs to be emphasised from the start. Since the publication of G.K. Hunter's very influential chapter on humanism and courtship in his study *John Lyly: The Humanist as Courtier* (1962), we have come to accept that 'the Humanist's and the courtier's interests pointed in different directions' (p. 31). But it would be better to say that the real conflict of interests lay between the courtier and the philosopher, not the 'humanist'. Indeed, the first time we hear of the humanist, in the prefatory material to Abraham Fleming's 1589 translation of Virgil's *Georgics*, it is in the pregnant phrase 'courtly Humanists' (sig. A2v). Of course, Aylett and Fleming are the real authorities in the terms of the present study: it is how they and other early modern writers use the words 'humanity' and 'humanist' that matter, rather than how later critics and scholars have chosen to interpret them. And the reinstatement of the courtly aspect of Elizabethan humanism is one of my main aims in this book. However, let us begin by examining the full variety of senses which Aylett mentions in his poem.

For Aylett, 'humanity' is most obviously related to peace because its courteous element is clearly conciliatory. However, he identifies several other aspects (p. 40):

> *Humanitie* may have a *threefold sense,*
> *Mans Nature, Vertue,* and his *education*
> *In humane Arts,* and pure *Intelligence;*
> From whence she seems to have denomination:
>   And therefore *Liberall Arts* by ev'ry Nation,
> Are call'd the *studies of humanity,*
> And breed in man a courteous conversation,
> With *gentle manners* and *civility,*
> Which onely heav'ns bestow on *Muses Nursery.*
>
> And hence it is, that rustique *Boores* and *Clownes,*
> Who want the good of civill education,
> So rude and rustique are in Countrey townes,
> When those, that have with *Muses* conversation,
>   Or neere to *Princes Courts* their habitation,
> Become more *civill, sociable,* kinde,
> Hence 'tis that ev'ry rude and savage nation,
> Where gentle Arts abide not, are inclin'd
> To rustique force, and savage cruelty of mind.

These few lines contain the basic scheme of early modern humanism which Aylett inherited from the Elizabethans, and which they in turn inherited from ancient Roman writers, especially the statesman, orator and philosopher, Marcus Tullius Cicero.

In the next chapter we shall pursue the Ciceronian origins of Elizabethan humanism in some detail; but here it will be sufficient to note how the legacy of his thinking on the word 'humanitas' was made available to Elizabethan writers by means of pedogogical aids such as Thomas Cooper's *Thesaurus linguae Romanae et Britannicae* ('Latin–English Dictionary': 1565). Here the gloss for the word 'humanitas' reads: 'Humanitie: mans nature: gentlenesse: courtesie: gentle behaviour: civilitie: pleasantnesse in maners: doctrine: teaching: liberall knowledge'.[5] His list of examples (almost all from Cicero) indicate that these terms can be divided up under three headings: (1) 'The state of humaine nature commen to us all'; (2) 'Courtesie: gentleness: humanitie'; and (3) 'Liberall knowledge: learning: humanitie'. These correspond, then, to Aylett's threefold disposition: Nature, Virtue, Education. Each of these senses may be said to give rise to a specific inflection of Elizabethan humanism, which, for the purposes of the present study, we may designate as: 'philosophical', 'courtly', 'literary'. These terms require a little explanation.

By 'philosophical humanism', I mean discourse centred on the word 'humanity' which explores human nature in its complex relation to 'divinity' and 'brutality'. This is what allows Aylett to call humanity, paradoxically, 'the summe of *Divinity*' (p. 43). He does not mean that God is human, but rather that the most noble part of human nature is the divine element of the soul, and that, therefore, if humanity is to be cultivated as a positive virtue, then human nature will approach perfection in so far as it approaches the full realisation of its own natural divinity. However, for various reasons, humanity was most frequently coupled with words signifying 'brutality': those aspects of human nature which we share with the animals, usually seen in an adverse light, ranging from stupidity to ferocity. Humanism tended to define itself by how different human beings were from brute creation, rather than by how similar it was to divine being. The main reason for this was because the philosophical aspect of humanism was strongly influenced by the other two inflections, especially the 'courtly'.

'Courtly humanism' is a phrase which needs to be treated with some caution, but it is the only expression which will do in the present circumstances. The Elizabethans inherited from the works of Cicero the notion that *humanitas* was both 'inclusive' – Cooper's 'state of humaine nature commen to us all' – and also (and more importantly) 'exclusive'. It was hard for the upper-class gentleman Cicero to resist the idea that some people might, in fact, be more human than others if they cultivated what made them different from the brutes to a greater degree than their fellow men did. For Cicero, this difference was mainly constituted as reason (*ratio*) and speech (*oratio*); but he also perceived that human beings were naturally inclined to be more sociable than most other animals. Briefly, then, Cicero tended to view *humanitas* as the capacity to live at ease with other people, especially where daily intercourse was marked by a graceful consideration for others ('courtesy'), and, even more importantly, where it was confirmed by witty and elegant conversation, in which the uniquely human virtue of speech could be exercised most fully. Ciceronian humanism is thus 'exclusive', because it is really the property of a social elite which has the wealth and leisure to develop such graces.[6]

For Cicero, and every other Roman writer of the period, human culture had reached its peak at Rome, which was simply referred to as the *urbs* ('city'). Hence Ciceronian *humanitas* is very closely related to *urbanitas* (Ramage, 1973, p. 56). This is one of the most important areas of difference between Ciceronian and Elizabethan humanism. Cicero could never have designated this particular nexus of ideas concerning *humanitas* as 'courtly' (*aulicus*). Cicero's Rome was a republic; and Cicero himself was a staunch republican. But the Elizabethans lived under a prince, and were, on the whole, partisans of monarchy. For them, generally, the royal court seemed to be the acme of 'civilisation'. This word comes from the Latin *civis*, 'citizen'. But the boundary between civil and courtly life was not easy to draw in the Elizabethan period, partly because the court was usually resident in London. For example, the anonymous author of a dialogue called *Civil and Uncivil Life* (1579) reveals that discussion is really centred on the far more familiar and traditional contrariety between 'the Countrey and Courtly lyves' (sig. A4v). Country life is deprecated as 'uncivil' because it lacks the graces which osmotically creep into the minds and hearts of those 'that have . . . neere to *Princes Courts* their habitation', as Aylett puts it (p. 40).

There are one or two exceptions to the general rule that the Ciceronian urbanity is transformed into Elizabethan 'courtliness'. For example, in *Three Proper and Witty Familiar Letters* (1580), Gabriel Harvey locates a typically humanistic dialogue in his home town of Saffron Walden in Essex, which Aylett would probably have dismissed as one of those 'Countrey townes' inhabited by 'rustique *Boores* and *Clownes*' (p. 40). But this is highly unusual. When such conversations take place away from the court or metropolis, they are generally set in a country house to which courtiers or metropolitans habitually retire, such as the 'Rurall Colledge' in which Henry Wotton's courtly speakers discuss various matters in his *Courtly Controversy of Cupid's Cautels* (1578, sig. 2H4r).[7] The reference here is almost certainly to the phrase used by a speaker in Cicero's dialogue *De oratore* ('The Orator': 55 BC) to describe the country villa where the conversations take place: 'suburbanum gymnasium' (1.98). The phrase may call up to the modern mind the image of a fitness centre on the outskirts of town, but Cooper's *Thesaurus* tells us that *gymnasium* means 'schoole' and that *suburbanus* refers to a 'maner or house without the walles of the citie'. For all this, however, the guest's at Crassus's villa in the *De oratore* are not countryfolk but eminent and powerful noblemen of Rome. The situation is similar in Elizabethan England. The usual position is that country people are culturally backward, as represented by the ironical praise of a country squire's library in *Civil and Uncivil Life*: 'Sir Guy of Warwicke, the foure Sonnes of Amon, the Ship of Fooles, the Budget of Demaundes, the Hundreth merry Tales, the Booke of Ryddles, and many other excellent writers, both witty and pleasant' (sig. H4r). On the other hand, John Lyly's *Euphues and his England*, which appeared the following year in 1580, tells a different story. In Lyly's England, there is no such sharp distinction. When Euphues reaches London, he falls into a company of gentlewomen – 'some courtiers, others of the country' – where he amuses himself for the space of a month in 'enterteining of time in courtly pastimes, though not in the court' (p. 84). For Lyly, then, 'courtliness' is not the unique possession of courtiers, but can also be practised by men and women living in London or even in the country. Indeed, when he recounts a love-story between Fidus and Iffida which is meant to have taken place forty years before in the reign of Henry VIII, he affects to apologise for an 'olde wooing' which must seem 'barbarous' to his Elizabethan readers: 'such was the tyme then, that it was straunge to love, as it is now common, and then lesse used in the Courte, then it is now in the countrey' (p. 57). Yet Fidus and Iffida play with great skill and sophistication the courtly game of *questione d'amore* – a sort of quiz on amorous topics – when they are sequestered in the country in Kent. Whatever the original source of Elizabethan courtly behaviour, then, by Lyly's time it had diffused into the general culture of the gentry as a mark of what Cooper calls 'gentlenesse: courtesie: gentle behaviour: civilitie: pleasantnesse in maners'.

On the other hand, we need to be aware of a distinction which was emerging between 'courtesy' and 'courtliness'. Again, Lyly's *Euphues and his England* provides us with a useful illustration. When Lyly goes on to decribe Camilla, the chief ornament of the circle of women whom Euphues meets in London, he uses the word 'courtliness' with some circumspection. Here we learn that Camilla was 'commended for hir gravitie of [i.e. 'by'] the aged' and 'for hir courtlines of [i.e. 'by'] the youth' (p. 85). What makes her 'courtly' is her ready answer, shrill voice and her 'mirth'. This is a word which had sexual connotations in Elizabethan English: 'flirtatiousness'; and Lyly has to make it clear that Camilla did not add 'the length of a haire to courtlines, that might detract the bredth of a haire from chastitie'. On the other hand, she is also the 'picture of courtesie'; and it is clear that this 'courtesy' is the positive standard of social behaviour from which 'courtliness', by virtue of its high spirits and general excitability, tends to lapse in the direction of wantonness. Camilla is praised for 'intermedling a desire of liking, with a disdain of love: shewing hir selfe in courtesie to be familyar with al, & with a certein comly pride to accept none' (p. 84). Lyly's distinctions between 'courtesy' and 'courtliness' are typical of later Elizabethan writers, too. The word 'courtly' tended to resonate in sympathy with the satirical depiction of the court as a place of iniquity and corruption that pervaded Tudor literature (and the 'anticourtly tradition' includes earlier and later writing as well, of course).

Humanity, literature and learning

'Literary humanism', however, is the main concern of the present study, and, since we shall be dealing with this topic in some detail in the chapters which follow, only a brief explanation of this inflection of the word 'human-ity' will be given here. The philosophical origins of the sense of *humanitas* glossed by Cooper as 'doctrine: teaching: liberall knowledge' and 'Liberall knowledge: learning: humanitie' lie in Cicero's insistence on *oratio* as one of the key features which distinguish human beings from the beasts. But all human beings can speak; and Cicero's patrician tendencies towards social exclusiveness prompts him to place an even higher value on the written word than on the spoken, since by no means all Romans could read and write. Hence, indirectly, Cooper's emphasis on the term 'liberal know-ledge'. This kind of knowledge is 'liberal' because *doctrina liberalis* was origin-ally the kind of knowledge which was worthy of pursuit by *liberi*, literally 'free men', or 'gentlemen', as the Elizabethans usually translated the Latin word. The word 'gentleman' can also be traced back to the Roman social hierarchy. A Roman was *gentilis* if he belonged to one of the *gentes*, or 'clans'. He was not necessarily 'mild', any more than the Elizabethan gentle-man was 'gentle' in this modern sense. When Cooper lists 'gentle behaviour' in his glosses of the second nuance of the Latin *humanitas*, he probably means both 'mild' and 'genteel'; but the latter quality was no doubt foremost in his mind.

Furthermore, this 'literary humanism' should be understood to include both 'literature' and 'learning'. Indeed, the two words were synonymous in Elizabethan English. Cooper glosses the Latin *litteratura* as 'Good literature, or learnyng'. However, we shall find it useful to keep the modern distinc-tion between the two terms. They used to be regarded as synonyms because both could mean what we now call 'reading'. The word 'learning' still perhaps carries a trace of the means by which this kind of knowledge is acquired. On the other hand, the word 'literature' gestures towards 'writ-ing', since it is derived from the Latin word *littera*: 'letter of the alphabet'. Of course, not all useful knowledge needs to be written down. Ploughboys did not learn how to handle the team by reading a book. Indeed, *liberal knowledge* tends not to focus on practical sciences like agriculture because they were somewhat tainted by the stigma of labour. The 'liberal arts' were designed to cultivate the mind, not the field. The special cultural value of *litterae*, then, lay partly in their lack of practical application in terms of the struggle for existence which faced most people in Cicero's day, apart from the relatively small group of *liberi* and *litterati*. However, even here we can discern two distinct points of emphasis. The learned aspect of a written text is based in its content, whereas the literary aspect is based in its style. A book on astronomy (the seventh and most advanced of the 'liberal arts') needs only to be clearly written in order to serve its purpose. But it takes on a literary aspect when the writer begins to use the language in a more self-consciously ornamental manner which draws attention to itself as an artistic composition, as opposed to a functional exposition. So, for example, the Greek astronomer Aratus wrote his *Phaenomena* ('The Stars') in verse, and elaborated it with all kinds of rhetorical and poetical figures, such as metaphor and hyperbole and all the rest. In the terminology of Roman and Renaissance rhetoric, he used his *verba* ('words') to trick out and beautify his *res* ('matter').[8] It is this slippage from *res* to *verba* that will eventually bring forth Harvey's critical remarks about 'superficial humanists'. As we see in Chapter 2, the word 'humanity' had a range of senses when applied to the area of literature and learning. At its most comprehensive, it could refer to one of the two great divisions of knowledge: 'humanity' – as opposed to 'divinity' – was the entire corpus of secular arts and sciences. But it could also mean 'pagan literature'; and, more narrowly still, it was sometimes used as a synonym for the word 'grammar', which in Elizabethan times involved mainly learning how to read and write (and speak) Latin. If there was a difference between 'grammar' and 'humanity', it was that the latter was more advanced, with an emphasis on writing Latin *well*. This is where the temptation to place words over matter first creeps into 'literary humanism', and hence the tendency for humanists to deal with the surface of the text rather than with its learned depths.

To conclude these preliminary remarks, we might say that Elizabethan humanism should be seen as complex semantic field which is situated, as it were, on a slope. At its most intellectually elevated, it aspires to the status of a philosophy of life, in which moral behaviour is predicated on an understanding of the natural place of humankind in the world of creation. Let me make it clear that this has nothing to do with the modern philosophical schools which go by the name of 'humanism'. These are founded on the idea that human beings have everything they require to make life in this world perfect without the need for God, or, at least, for the traditional institutions of religion.[9] Nor is it to be confused with the rather over-excitable critical tradition which sees Renaissance humanism as a rebellious cult of humanity which defies the limitations placed upon human endeavour by the doctrines of orthodox divinity.[10] Nor, finally, should it be too closely identified with the more temperate view that Tudor humanism is motivated by a desire to place learning in the service of the 'commonweal' (what we would call the state).[11] Undoubtedly, many men with a university education sought to make a career for themselves in some or other political capacity; but this does not make them 'humanists', or, at least, not in any way that the men so described would have understood.

However, Elizabethan humanism has a tendency to lose sight of its philosophical ends, whether these are conceived as theological or political, or, indeed, in terms of any serious intellectual pursuit. The connection between literary humanity and the drills and exercises of the grammar school led to an emphasis on technical expertise and stylistic flair, not to say flamboyance; and the connection between courtly humanity and the pleasures of witty and often amorous conversation led to a concomitant emphasis on all the more charming and delightful, indeed, 'courtly', aspects of literary composition. From the philosophical perspective of a Gabriel Harvey, this tendency can only seem like trivialisation. The word 'trivial' comes from the Latin *trivium*: 'a place where three roads (*tres viae*) meet'. Hence *trivialis* came to mean 'what you might come across on the street-corner: ordinary, vulgar, unremarkable'. But in the medieval system of the Seven Liberal Arts, the word 'trivium' was used to describe the first three arts in the series: grammar, logic, rhetoric. These are the arts of discourse which needed to be learnt before you could move on to the mathematical sciences of the quadrivium: arithmetic, geometry, music, astronomy. As we shall see, 'humanity' had its own trivium: grammar, poetry, rhetoric. By substituting poetry for logic, the fundamental link between the medieval trivium and philosophical disputation was removed, and a path was laid, by way of poetry's greater emphasis on the pleasures of rhythm and other aural and figurative devices than that of rhetoric, which would eventually become the courtly love-sonnet.

Of course, Harvey's sour remarks on 'superficial humanists' provide only one perspective on Elizabethan humanism. Harvey thought far too well of himself as a polymath, and his own attempts at poetry reveal that the Muses whom he claimed to worship never visited him whilst he had a pen in his hand. However, it may be useful to advance an older literary, or, more precisely, 'belletristic' view of Elizabethan humanism as a means of provoking discussion on the topic at a time when professional academics in the humanities are again tempted by the idea of 'curious universal scholarship' in the form of 'interdisciplinary studies', 'cultural studies' or 'theory'. These schemes, which tend towards a totalisation of human knowledge by means of a certain ordering principle, would have appealed very strongly to Harvey.[12] But such schemes often seem to lose sight of what was probably most important in a sonnet or so many other literary compositions of the late sixteenth century: wit, charm, ingenuity. In the following chapters, we try to find our way back to this element of Elizabethan humanism, via a consideration of its more philosophical and scholarly aspects; and the most useful point of departure for these investigations is an examination of the Ciceronian ideal of *humanitas* and the *artes humanae*.

Notes

1. The fact that Gabriel Harvey signed his copy 'Gabrielis Harveii 1574' has misled at least critics into thinking that this must be the date when the marginal comments were added to it, but see Pincombe, 1993, p. 11 (n. 37).

2. See, for example, Crane, 1993, p. 7; Bushnell, 1996, pp. 185–202. For a general view, see Nussbaum, 1997.

3. The situation is even more complex and misleading when we take the European context into consideration. As Giustiniani remarks: '"Humanism" is one of those terms the French call *faux amis*' (1985, p. 167).

4. See Pincombe, 1993. Some of the material used in this article on 'Some sixteenth-century records of the words *humanist* and *humanitian*' reappears in a revised form in Chapter 2 of the present study, together with several new observations.

5. The ancient Romans derived the word *humanitas* from the word *humus*, or 'earth'. The *humanus* was 'earthly', as opposed to the *divinus*, or 'godly', which is derived from a root meaning 'sky' (cf. *dies*: 'day'). In other words, the *humanus* is *humilis* ('humble, lowly'). Quintilian says that *homo* ('human being') may have been derived from *humus* in his *Institutio oratoria* ('Instructions for Orators': 1.6.34). Harvey, characteristically, refutes Quintilian's authority: 'But this is nothinge, that you speak, Quintiliane' (*Marg.*, p. 112 [MP]). He prefers Nicholas Perrotus's derivation from the Greek *homonoia*, or 'concord'.

6. The literature on Ciceronian humanism is wide and diverse in emphasis. Despite its title, H.A.K. Hunt's *The Humanism of Cicero* (1954) has little to say to the kind of *humanitas* that interests us in this study; but the variety of topics to be considered is well covered in Boyancé (1970).

7. Cit. Bates, 1992, p. 98. Bates's study *The Rhetoric of Courtship* is full of useful illustrative material culled from such unfamiliar sources. Rather surprisingly, Bates makes no allusion in either study to Cicero, although much of the material she has gathered is clearly influenced by Cicero's *De oratore*. Bryson's similar study *From Courtesy to Civility* (1998) also lacks reference to Cicero.

8. Cicero translated Aratus into Latin hexameters. Harvey shows no sign of knowing this, but he would have been impressed.

9. The founding text of this philosophical movement is the book called *Humanism* (1903) by William James and F.S.C. Schiller. Later usage is less specific, so that the 'humanist' is likely to be seen as an atheist by many Americans. In Germany, on the other hand, you can designate yourself as a humanist, as opposed to a Catholic or a Lutheran, for example, for the purposes of church tax.

10.   We might call this 'the School of Marlowe'. For example, in their recent edition of *Doctor Faustus* (1993), David Bevington and Eric Rasmussen discuss the question of Faustus's atheism and Marlowe's orthodoxy or heterodoxy in a section called 'Humanist aspiration' (pp. 22–35).

11.   Hunter calls it 'the myth of state-service as the natural end of a training in the humanities' (1962, p. 15). This political emphasis in studies of Tudor and Elizabethan humanism is largely a postwar phenomenon (see, for example, Caspari, 1954, or McConica, 1965). In recent years, however, now that our conception of politics has become much more diffusely pervasive of all aspects of social life than we thought it was thirty years ago, more complicated cultural models have been suggested to explore the political dimensions of Renaissance humanism (for example, Carlson, 1993; Bushnell, 1996; Stewart, 1997). But here we tend to be dealing more with the politics of the printshop, the classroom or the bedchamber, than with parliaments and councils of state. For 'commonweal humanism', see Skinner, 1978, 2.213–43. Perhaps the best general introduction to English Renaissance humanism is still Martindale (1985); and there is a readable sketch of humanism over the ages in Davies (1997).

12.   Harvey was a 'Ramist', or follower of the French scholar Peter Ramus, whose diagrammatic schemata could be made to produce satisfyingly comprehensive synopses of any art.

CHAPTER TWO

Ciceronian *Humanitas*

Elizabethan conceptions of 'humanity' were very various, but almost every aspect of their thinking on this topic may be traced back to the writings of Marcus Tullius Cicero, and particularly his understanding of the word *humanitas* and related terms. In this chapter, we look at three texts by Cicero which provided the foundations of 'Ciceronian humanism' in late sixteenth-century England.[1] The 'philosophical' aspect of *humanitas* is discussed in Cicero's informal treatise *De officiis* ('Duties': 44 BC); 'literary' *humanitas* is dealt with in his oration *Pro Archia poeta* ('In Defence of Archias the Poet': 62 BC) and the *De oratore*; and the latter work also throws light on the 'courtly' or 'urbane' side of Elizabethan humanism. But let us start with the more philosophical concerns of the *De officiis*.

De officiis: Humanity and bestiality

The *De officiis* is Cicero's last major philosophical work, completed in November 44 BC, not long after his political adversary Julius Caesar was murdered in the Senate House. Cicero did not take part in the conspiracy, but he had made an enemy in Mark Antony, whose troops eventually killed him as he tried to escape Italy. Cicero's head and hands were taken back to Rome and displayed in the Forum. The *De officiis*, then, was written at a time of great anxiety for Cicero, but this seems to have served to concentrate his mind when he came to organise his thoughts, perhaps for the last time, on the bonds of mutual obligation which tie us together in a *societas generis humani*, or 'fellowship of humankind'. The *De officiis* is largely concerned with the proper way to strike a balance between what is good for ourselves (*utilitas*: 'expediency') and what is right (*honestas*: 'honourableness'). Cicero sees no conflict between these two categories, but realises that their true relation is easily obscured by our tendency to allow baser instincts to blind us to our rational understanding that individual interests cannot be separated from the good of the whole community: the *res publica* or 'commonweal'. The real conflict, then, is played out at the level of *humanitas* in the sense of 'human nature'. Cicero explains the origins of this struggle in a passage near the beginning of the *De officiis*, which deserves to be quoted in full. First, Cicero deals with what we have in common with the beasts (1.11; trans. Grimald, 1556, p. 56):

> From the beginning, to every kinde of living creature [*animans*] it is given by nature, to defend himself, his life, and his bodye: and avoyde those thinges, which may seme likely to be harmfull: and seke, and get all thinges, that be necessary to live withall: as feeding, as cooverts, as other of the same sorte. The appetite also of comming together for engendrings sake, and a certayn tendernesse over them that be engendred, is a common thyng to al living creatures.

Then he makes a distinction between humans and other animals:

> But bitween man, and beaste [*belua*], this chiefly is the difference: that a beaste, so farre as he is mooved by sense, bendeth him self to that onely, which is present, and at hande: verie smallie perceiving ought past, or tocome: but man, who is partaker of reason, wherby he seeth sequels, beholdeth grounds, and causes of thinges, is not ignoraunt of their procedinges, and as it wer their foregoings: compareth semblaunces, and with thinges present joyneth, and knitteth thinges tocome: dothe soone espye the course of his holle life, and to the leading therof purveieth thinges necessarie.

It is *ratio* which gives man the edge over beast because it makes him prudent and thus able to form complex social relationships to his own advantage, in which *oratio* plays a leading part by the communication of ideas:

> And the said nature, thorough the power of reason [*vis rationis*], winneth man to man, to a feloweshippe bothe in talke, and also of life [*et ad orationem et ad vitam societas*]: and engendreth a certain speciall favour chieflie to themward, that are of them begotten: and stirreth up the companies of men, that they bee willing bothe to bee assembled together, and also to bee servisable one to an other: and for those causes, that they studie to purveie such thinges, as maie furnish them for their apparaile, and for their sustinaunce: not onelie for themselves, but for their wives, children, and other, whom they holde

dere, and ought to defende. Which care sturreth up also mennes sprites [*animus*], and makes them of more corage to doo their bysinesse [*maior ad rem gerendam*].

In other words, human beings are distinguished absolutely from the beasts not only by virtue of their unique possession of *ratio* and *oratio*, but also by the degree to which they exercise the 'spirit' (*animus*) which is shared by all animals (*animantes*). The word *animus* has many meanings in Latin: 'The minde: the will: sometyme the soule: delectation, or affection, winde or blast, wrath' (Cooper, *Thes.*). Perhaps the modern psychological term 'drive' covers these nuances.

Here, in the last section of the passage, Cicero associates *animus* with a drive to rise above others and do more than these are capable or desirous of accomplishing. On the one hand, the emergence of humanity from mere animality can be seen as a biological advance. (Cicero is never very clear on this point, but elsewhere, as we shall see, he favours an evolutionary model of human history.) Human beings are distinguished from other animals because they are concerned more with their species than with themselves as individuals or as members of a small family unit. The next step, however, is taken only by certain individuals, not by the species at large. This is when a man (it is always a man) distinguishes himself from his fellows by extending his 'care' (*cura*) beyond the confines of the family and outwards towards the whole community. This may indeed make him appear 'superhuman' or 'heroic'. The ancient *heros* was a hybrid: half man, half god. In mythological terms, the *heros* was usually a man who had both mortal and immortal parents, but it is also frequently used to refer to a man who is seen as the defender of his people. Here the connection seems to have been that the heroic man was one who, whilst evidently human, also was driven or motivated by an *animus* which prompted him to do more than most human beings could or would. It made ordinary men *maior ad rem gerendam*: 'greater in terms of what men are meant to do'. This is what Cicero calls, very simply, a *magnus animus*: 'great spirit'.

Cicero's remarks gave rise to a cult of 'magnanimity' in the Renaissance (Greaves, 1954). But Cicero was all too well aware that the *magnus animus* could be destructive as well as protective of human society. On the one hand, the *magnus animus* aspires to a superhuman condition which is similar to divinity. *Honestas*, he remarks, 'seemes to shine brightest: which is wrought with a greate, and loftie corage [*animus magnus*], despising worldly vanities [*humanae res*]' (1.60, p. 74). Here, 'human affairs' are relegated to the level of mediocrity: the wants and worries of the workaday world. The *magnus animus*, however, soars above these, since his overwhelming desire is to achieve *gloria* by heroic acts on behalf of the commonweal. However, as Cicero goes on to point out, if this 'corage' is directed towards personal ends, then the *magnus animus* is little better than a beast (1.62, p. 74):

> But if that hawtienesse of corage which is seene in perels, and travailes, be voide of justice, and doth not fight for a common safetie, but for a private profit: it is to bee reckened faultie. For that not onely is not the propertie of vertue, but rather of brutishnesse [*immanitas*], setting all humanitie [*humanitas*] aside.

He returns to the same idea at the end of the first book. The great spirit must be led by a rational understanding of the inseparability of *utilitas* and *honestas* if it is to be properly put to the service of the commonweal (1.157, p. 109):

> Therfore onlesse thatsame vertue, which consisteth in defending men, that is to saye, the felowshippe of mankinde [*societas generis humani*], dothe meete with the knowledge of thinges: it may seeme a verie bare, and alonewandering knowledge: and likewise greatnesse of corage, severed from common feloushippe, and neybourhod of men [*communitas coniunctioque humana*], muste needes bee a certein savagenesse, and beastly crueltie [*feritas et immanitas*].

Cicero sees the *magnus animus* in itself as a sort of animal energy, then, which must be trained by knowledge. If it submits to reason, then the man who has this great spirit will become a semi-divine hero; but if it breaks the leash, it turns into a wild beast, savaging the very people it is supposed to protect, reducing the world once more to a wilderness, in which knowledge, despised and rejected, wanders like a beggar, wretched and alone.

Cicero is thinking chiefly of the powerful men of this world when he makes these observations. Probably he has Caesar in mind, whom he suspected, not unreasonably, of aspiring to a permanent dictatorship. But he uses other examples to make his point. He notes how Alexander the Great exceeded his father, Philip of Macedon, in military exploits, but how that Philip was much superior in 'myldenesse, and gentlenes [*facilitas et humanitas*]' (1.90, p. 85). In comparison, Alexander was 'full beastlie'. Cicero here has *turpissimus*: 'extremely base'; but Grimald's translation catches the spirit of Ciceronian humanism exactly. The Elizabethans, too, moved with ease in the discourse of *humanitas* and *immanitas* or *feritas* which Cicero established in the *De officiis* and other works. They understood perfectly well the basic historical and pyschological allegories of the 'rise and fall' of humanity, and, as Christians, they also added a theological aspect to Ciceronian humanism. But for the purposes of the present study we are concerned mainly with another inflection of the allegory, in which literature and learning provide the key to *humanitas*. And here we may move on to the work which is most often cited as the Ciceronian text which acts as the 'source' of Renaissance humanism: *Pro Archia poeta*.[2]

Pro Archia poeta: Humanity and poetry

Archias was a Greek from Antioch in Asia Minor, who had attached himself to the cultivated statesman and general, Lucius Licinius Lucullus, whose military exploits he recorded in epic verse. The latter's political rival, Pompey the Great, picked on Archias in order to vex the poet's master. Archias had been granted Roman citizenship by the city of Heraclea; this was contested by the Pompeians, and Cicero stepped in to save Archias from losing his rights as a Roman citizen. Cicero spoke up for Archias because the poet had been the mentor of his youth (§ 2):

> For I am hable to caste my mynde backwarde over the longe intervall of manie yeres past, yea, even unto the daies of my freshest youth, where, serching in my memorie, I see this Archias stand foorth, as the prime mover of my taking up & proceding in these my present studies and occupations.

The 'studies' to which Cicero here refers are those which have equipped him to be an orator; and he tries to win over his audience by suggesting that it is Archias whom they must ultimately thank for any cases Cicero may have successfully pleaded on their behalf in the past. Yet Archias is a poet, not an orator, and Cicero anticipates this objection by explaining that he has never concentrated on oratory to the exclusion of other studies. He concludes: 'For, indede, all those Artes, which pertaine unto humanitie [*artes quae ad humanitatem pertinent*], have a certen common bonde [*commune vinculum*], and, are, as it wer, held together by a certen kinship & affinitie'.

This is the first time Cicero uses the word *humanitas* in the *Pro Archia*. But what does he mean by it? Let us recall Cooper's glosses: 'Humanitie: mans nature: gentlenesse: courtesie: gentle behaviour: civilitie: pleasantnesse in maners: doctrine: teaching: liberall knowledge'. All of these nuances are probably present in Cicero's statement about the interrelationships between the *artes quae ad humanitatem pertinent*. For Cicero, as we have seen, 'mans nature' was defined mainly in contradistinction to bestiality, and the two key terms here were *ratio* and *oratio*: reason and speech. Hence it is the cultivation of these two faculties which allows for a degree of relativity in *humanitas*, which Cicero tends to regard in terms of potentiality rather than as a mere given. The more you develop your intellectual and verbal skills, the more you develop – perhaps increase – your *humanitas*. This is why the verbal arts of poetry in verse and rhetoric in prose are so central to the *artes humanae*. Here is Cicero a little later on the sanctity of poetry (§ 19):

> Therfore, O Judges, and most humane Men [*humanissini homines*], let this name of Poët, be holy unto you, which even the barbarian [*barbaria*] dareth not to spit upon and violate. The very stones of the Wildernes aunswer to his voice; the beastes [*bestiae*] oftentymes are softened, & made still & tame, by hearing of his songe; and shal we that have been educated in the best lerning be deaf, and not moved by the voise of Poëts?

Cicero here sets up two levels of degradation: barbarians and beasts. The Romans inherited the word *barbarus* from the Greeks, for whom the *barbaros* was a non-Greek, a foreigner whose speech sounded in Greek ears like the confused gabble of the brute beasts. The barbarian is the reality behind the bestial imagery endemic in humane discourse from Cicero to the Elizabethans and beyond. A lack of humanity is very often cast in terms of 'swinishness', for example. The *locus classicus* of this metaphor lies in the tenth book of Homer's *Odyssey*, where the sorceress Circe changes Odysseus's sailors into pigs; but countless examples can be found in English literature, too, from Edmund Spenser's epic poem *The Fairy Queen* (1590–1609) to C.S. Lewis's romance for children, *Prince Caspian* (1951).[3] In the terms of Ciceronian humanism, then, the horrifying fantasy of turning into a beast is used as a deterrent: it is meant to stop civilised people lapsing back into barbarism, and the study (in the wider sense of the Latin *studium*, or 'cherishing') of poetry is crucial in this respect. How can the Roman judge and jury call themselves *humanissimi homines* if they do not appreciate the value of poetry? Even the beasts of the wilderness are charmed by music. And he closes the oration with a similar appeal, whose wording also reminds his audience that they are not brutish violators of poetry and learning: 'Let it be seen, then, that Archias has rather been lifted up by your humanitie [*humanitate vestra levatus*], than cast down & violated by your harshness [*acerbitate violatus*]' (§ 31).

The *Pro Archia* also serves to illustrate how *humanitas* was associated with youth. Cicero begins his account of Archias's life as follows: 'From the first tyme, that Archias had left behind him his boyish youthe, and all those Artes, by meanes of which the puerile age is used to be shaped & fashioned unto humanitie [*artes quibus aetas puerilis ad humanitatem informari solet*], he applyed him selfe to the studye of writing' (§ 4). Poetry is one of the arts which set boys in the direction of full humanity in the sense of 'literary culture'. But it always tended to be regarded as 'juvenile' because it was the mainstay of grammar school education. The word 'grammar' comes from the Greek *grammatikē*: 'the art of letters' (*gramma*: 'letter').[4] The Greek *grammatistēs* taught you how to read and write; more advanced study was conducted by the *grammatikos*, who might be a professional teacher or an amateur expert. The Romans had their own words for such things: *littera* ('letter') gave them *litteratura, litterator, litteratus*. But usually they used the word *litteratus* to refer to the amateur, and took over the Greek word as *grammaticus* for the professional. Grammarians taught advanced Greek and Latin language at a surprisingly theoretical level. More importantly for our purposes, they also taught the study of the poets. Suetonius, in his *De grammaticis et rhetoribus* ('Grammarians and Rhetoricians': c. 110) states that the *grammaticus* is ('to speake more stricktlie') an 'Interpreter of the Poëts [*interpres poetrarum*]' (§ 4). Cicero himself, in the *De divinatione* ('Divination': 44 BC), calls grammarians 'Explicators of Poets [*poetarum explanatores*]' (1.116). On the other hand, *grammatica* was still regarded as a sort of game; a phrase (perhaps a euphemism) that was often used to describe the grammar course at school was *ludus litterarum*, 'the game of letters'. Moreover, grammatical studies were pursued by many adults as a leisure activity. Julius Caesar, for example, wrote a book on declensions and conjugations in his spare time whilst crossing the Alps (he dedicated it to Cicero). And Roman gentlemen at large seem to have been genuinely addicted to the discussion of poetry at dinner parties and on other festive occasions (Kaster, 1988). It was the association of grammar and poetry with leisure that made the close connection with *humanitas*, since the term, as we see later in this chapter, was also used to signify a natural inclination towards companionship and festivity. Rhetoric, on the other hand, which was studied by boys after they left grammar school, was not so centrally 'humane' in this respect, because it was meant to be used in the wranglings of the law courts or stormy debates in the Senate.[5]

However, it is because the study of poetry could be seen as puerile, a reminder of days at school, that Cicero has to make an apology for dealing with such a trivial topic. He cleverly flatters his listeners into a position in which they cannot dismiss his digression in praise of poetry without revealing themselves as lacking in *humanitas* (§ 3):

> But, it maye seme a marvel to som, that, in a question of Statute lawe, & in a publique investigation, where it is to be disputed before a Praetor of the Romane people, a moste excellent man, & before such grave Judges, & so great a thronge & assemblie of people; it maye seme marveillous, I saye, that I should use this kynde of speaking, because it is averse, not onely to the customes of the courts of law, but also to forensique & lawyerlike discourse.

Cicero here refers to the traditional division of orations into three kinds: 'deliberative', which is used to persuade an audience to take a particular

course of action; 'forensic', which is used to prove a person guilty or innocent in a court of law; and 'epideictic', or 'display oratory', which is used to
exhibit the orator's powers of expression, usually on set themes such as the
praise of a king. The latter kind was more inclined to use the 'flowers of
rhetoric', especially what we call 'figures of speech', such as metaphors and
similes (Cicero is here rather self-consciously apologising for using the image of the bond). However, as he explains, such language, though it might
seem inappropriate in a forensic oration, such as the one he has prepared in
defence of Archias, is nonetheless well suited to the praise of poetry which
he is about to deliver:

> But I never the less beg of you, that ye will in this case, give me grace, most
> meet and accommodate to this matter, &, I maye hope, in no wise irksom to
> your selves, that, speaking of a consummate Poët, & moste erudite Man, in
> this gathering of most learned men, through your Humanitie [*haec vestra
> humanitas*], and finally, before the Praetor president in this case; I beg, then,
> that ye will permit me to expande upon the studies of humanitie and letters
> [*studia humanitatis ac litterarum*], & to speke a litel more liberallie, and in talking
> fitly of a person, who, devoted to ease & studie [*otium ac studium*], has hardlie
> ever been drawne into the perills of the courts of Lawe, to use a new, and as
> it wer, unused & unusuall kind of speaking.

Here Cicero also plays on a secondary sense of the word *humanitas* in this
passage: 'gentlenesse: courtesie: gentle behaviour: civilitie: pleasantnesse in
maners'. But his direct appeal to his audience's 'humanity' – *haec vestra
humanitas* – is meant to remind them of the literature and learning – 'doctrine: teaching: liberall knowledge' – which binds them to Archias, as well
as to provoke their goodwill to a harmless and vulnerable man. He is
appealing to a basic level of literary education which they have all received,
which is somehow associated with a degree of benevolence; but there are
indications that Cicero may also have had a more advanced level of education in mind, at least ideally, and here we may turn to the *De oratore*.

De oratore (1): Curious universal scholarship

The *De oratore* is a dialogue in three books on the perfect orator. It is set in
the year 91 BC, in Cicero's youth, at a villa in Tusculum – the 'gymnasium
suburbanum' – owned by one of the main speakers, Lucius Licinius Crassus.
Cicero particularly admired Crassus, who was a leading figure in the conservative 'party' of noblemen known as the *optimates*, to which Cicero also
owed allegiance. Moreover, Crassus had taught Cicero rhetoric as a boy, in

which respect he may be considered the rhetorical counterpart to Archias, with whom Cicero studied poetry. Not surprisingly, Cicero gives Crassus many of his own views on oratory, especially his belief that the perfect orator should be well versed in all the *artes humanae*. However, the polymathic ideal as propounded by Crassus is beset with many problems. Is it actually attainable by men whose busy lives as responsible citizens leaves them little time for study? But the most important reservations are not practical, but social, since the connection between polymathy and oratory had long been established by professional rhetoricians, who, as we shall see, were viewed with deep suspicion by the Romans. But let us start with Cicero's own opening statement of the case.

In the prologue to the first book of the *De oratore*, Cicero reminds his brother Quintus, to whom the book is dedicated, of a difference of opinion which has long existed between the two men concerning the relative import-ance of art on the one hand, and, on the other, talent and practice, in the formation of an eloquent orator (1.5):

> I holde, that Eloquence standeth uppon a knowledge of the Artes [*artes*] of the most erudite; wheras thou thynkest it is to be sundered from such elegante and fyne pointes of learning [*elegantia doctrinae*], and made to stand upon a certayne naturall witte [*ingenium*], & exercise [*exercitatio*].

Quintus here represents the typical Roman view. The *ars rhetorica* as it was taught by the Greek masters who had settled in Rome and other parts of Italy was regarded as essentially puerile: a mere propaedeutic to the more important stage of attaching yourself as a 'tiro' to an experienced orator and picking up experience in the courts, the forum and the Senate as you went along. Accordingly, Cicero promises Quintus that he will not 'recall a ragmans rolle of rules & praeceptes from the cradles of our boyish learning longe ago' (1.23).

However, Cicero is more interested in the relationship of true eloquence to the plurality of the *artes humanae* rather than to the particular art of rhetoric which is most commonly associated with speech (1.20):

> For, indede, there is no man hable to be an Orator worthy to be loaded with all prayse, without he must have pursued the knowledge of all Artes, and all matters of the greatest import. For it is fitting that speche should florish [*effloresco*], & overflowe [*redundo*] in the knowledge of thinges [*rerum cognitio*]; which thinges, if they be not grasped & understode, he shal have an elocu-tion, which is rather a vayne and almoste childish talke.

In order to avoid the stigma of childishness, then, the orator needs to acquire and display a wide general knowledge, not just what he has learnt at school. He needs to show that he is familiar with the *rerum magnarum scientia*: 'the knowledge of the most important matters'. By this, Cicero probably means the *artes maximae*: war and statecraft. But he must also mean the *artes mediocres*: 'the middling or ordinary arts'.[6] These include, for example, dialectic, mathematics, music, and 'this studie of Letters [*studium litterarum*], which is professed by them, which we call Grammarians [*grammatici*]' (§ 10). These lesser studies, in fact, seem more appropriate for what Cicero has in mind here. He is not thinking in terms of content, but style. Perhaps it would be useful to know about trench warfare if you were making a speech urging the defence of a border town threatened by an enemy; but Cicero thinks of general knowledge in terms of enhancing the beauty of a speech. The verb *effloresco* refers to the ornamental devices known as *flores*: 'flowers of rhetoric'; and *redundo* signifies the 'overflowing' of a great reservoir of illustrative material with which the points of an argument might be decoratively 'amplified'. In other words, the real use to the orator of a wide knowledge of the *artes humanae* was in providing ornamental detail. Ciceronian humanism, then, as it is represented in the *De oratore* and elsewhere, leads in the direction of Harvey's 'superficial humanists' rather than his 'profound philosophers'.

However, Cicero also knew that his Roman readers would be reluctant to allow his polymathic ideals much sway in practical oratory; and he himself says: 'Yet shal I not laye such a burthen upon the Orator, especially our owne men of Rome, which be taken up by the busy affaires of life in the city, as to beleeve that there is nought they maye not know' (1.21). On the other hand he continues: 'Yet still, the qualitie of the Orator, and the very profession of well-spekinge, semeth to loke for & promise, that all thinges put unto him, shall be spoken of ornately & copiously'. The *perfectus orator* – the perfect speaker in whom nothing at all is lacking – must be accomplished in all three branches of oratory, including epideictic. This is oratory where content may be less important than style, because the epideictic oration is meant to show off (*epideiksis*: 'display') the speaker's talents. A great virtuoso performer of this kind was Gorgias of Leontini. He was famed for the brilliance of his style; but he was also apparently able to speak on any matter proposed to him by a member of the audience. This much we learn from the opening paragraphs of Plato's dialogue *Gorgias*, where it is called a 'show' (447A).[7] This is typical of the Greek *sophista*, or 'skilled man, expert', who travelled from city to city claiming to be able to teach the sons of the rich (for a fee) anything they wished to know. Not all claimed to be omniscient, but many did; and later, especially after attacks on their professional ethics by Socrates, as recorded by Plato in works like the *Gorgias*, they were associated with charlatanry.

Nonetheless, Cicero's *perfectus orator* must be able to speak like Gorgias, as well as the great masters of forensic and deliberative oratory such as Demosthenes and Pericles; and it is here that he needs to be able to draw on a wide range of general knowledge. But the main connection between polymathy and epideictic is not what one would expect: that general reading enables the orator to speak on a particular topic, say mathematics or music, because he actually knows something about the matter in hand. Plato's Gorgias quite candidly admits that he is ignorant of most of the things he is asked to talk about, and that he is able to 'make the vulgare crowd believe he knoweth what he knoweth not' (459E). Rather, as already mentioned, wide reading produces a treasury of interesting facts which can be used to decorate the points of an argument. Interestingly, Cicero declares at the end of his prologue that he will not pay much attention to epideictic oratory (1.22); and he allows only the briefest discussion of panegyric at the end of the second book (2.341–9). Yet the Ciceronian *perfectus orator* is unmistakably sophistic in character. He can speak on any topic, and his wide general knowledge serves to beautify his speeches rather than provide them with content.[8]

Turning to the body of the *De oratore*, we quickly discover that Crassus is also a proponent of an ideal polymathy which threatens to become little more than sophism. Early on in the dialogue, he declares that the orator should be able to speak informedly on any topic: 'What might be in tymes of idlenes, more plesaunt, or more proper to humanitie, than elegant speche & conversation [*sermo*], that is in no thinge rude & unlearned' (1.32). The phrase *nulla in re rudis* means 'ignorant in nothing'; and the sceptical Scaevola interprets this as 'perfect in everie kinde of speche and humanitie [*sermo et humanitas*]' (1.35). He goes on to insist that this must mean that 'the Orator is hable to deal most copiously with speche on all matters to be discussed' (1.41). This includes philosophical topics, but also anything drawn from the *artes humanae*: mathematics, grammar, music (1.44). Actually, Crassus has not quite made this claim (though Cicero has in his prologue). However, he willingly takes up the challenge and confirms the sophistic character of the ideal orator by stating that he must indeed be able to speak on 'whatsoever shall be the matter, which falleth unto him to declare & explain in wordes' (1.64). Finally, he returns to Scaevola's first point and gives it a new and very memorable formulation: 'perfect in everie kynde of speeche, and all partes of humanity [*in omni genere sermonis, in omni parte humanitatis*]' (1.71). This phrase was picked up gratefully by many a Renaissance scholar. We have already encountered a version of it in Gabriel Harvey's comments on Chaucer and Lydgate and their 'varietie of poetical discourse, & all humanitie' (*Marg.*, pp. 160–1). In fact, Crassus's phrase does not necessarily support the sort of polymathic programme with which we are concerned in this investigation of the *artes humanae*. Indeed, Crassus himself seems to have wished not to pursue polymathy too far because of its tendency to collapse into sophism.

Crassus wants to propose polymathy on the basis of a return to true philosophy. In this he follows Cicero, who, in the prologue to the first book of the *De oratore*, explains that 'what the Grekes call *Philosophia*' is 'Procreator & Parent of al laudable Artes' (1.9). The Greek word was still unfamiliar to many Romans in Cicero's day, and he needs to explain it in the *Disputationes Tusculanae* (45 BC) as 'the studye of wisedome' (1.1; trans. Dolman, 1561, sig. B2r). This is what should impel the true orator in his pursuit of the *artes humanae*: to return to the source of all that is important in these various arts. We have already glimpsed this idea of the relationship between philosophy and the arts in the passage in the *Pro Archia* where Cicero states that 'all those Artes, which pertaine unto humanitie, have a certen common bonde, and, are, as it wer, held together by a certen kinship & affinitie [*cognatio*]' (§ 2). They owe their *cognatio*, or 'common descent by birth', through their shared parentage in philosophy and the search for wisdom. Not surprisingly, Crassus, too, uses a version of this formulation when he explains to young Catulus that 'all the learning of these noble & humane artes is bound up in a certaine bonde of kinship' (3.21). He reminds Catulus that this idea is to be found in Plato; and the source has been identified as a passage from his dialogue called *The Sophist* (242D). However, Crassus claims that it was Socrates himself who dealt the crucial blow to the unity of philosophy by trying to separate wisdom and eloquence (as he does, for example, in the *Gorgias*). He explains that there have always been men to whom one aspect of philosophy appealed more than all the others, and that they tend to amuse themselves with their favourite arts when they have time on their hands because they are unable to take part in the active political life of the *res publica*: 'Some have devoted them selves to the Poets, others to the Geometers, and others to Musicians; whilst others still have made for them selves a new study and game [*studium ludusque*], which be Dialecticks; and all have spent their time, nay their very lives, in those Arts, which were invented that the minds of boyes might be shaped towards humanity and manly vertue [*humanitas atque virtus*]' (3.58). Originally, all the *artes humanae* were unified by a common purposes: to shape *pueri* into fully developed *homines*. But once this common purpose has been forgotten, and men pursue a favourite art for the wrong reasons, they tend to arrest their development and become puerile once more, growing to love the idle life of *otium*. Hence, says Crassus, there arose in Greece a class of professional teachers who preferred to steer clear of their political responsibilities as citizens, and to cater instead for the new market for instruction in the specialised study in the various arts. Amongst these somewhat specious 'Doctours of Wisedom [*sapientiae doctores*]' (3.59) he places both Gorgias and Socrates.

Crassus's philosophical purpose in insisting on polymathic knowledge in the perfect orator, then, is to reverse what he sees as an unwelcome specialisation in the arts. However, he does not insist that practical oratory depends on a thorough and detailed knowledge of every aspect of every art. Antonius, whose reputation as an orator is matched only by Crassus's own, has already remarked that polymathy makes too great a demand on the orator, although he has no objection to young tiros dabbling in the humane arts: 'let them read all things, hearken unto all thinges, and busy themselves in all proper studie and humanity [*studium atque humanitas*]' (1.256). This is what they do in any case; but they cannot go too deeply in any of the *artes humanae* because they do not have the time. Crassus meets this point by noting that 'such matters maye be easily learned, if thou wilt take only as muche as needeth, and hast one who can teache thee trulie, and if thow knowest also thy selfe somewhat how to learn' (3.88). The arts have all become very complicated because they have been elaborated by men who take an idle specialist interest in them; but most of these endless ramifications serve no practical purpose. All the orator really needs to study is the fundamentals, and these can be picked up quite quickly by anyone with intelligence: 'unless a man be hable to learn swiftlie, then he shal never be hable to learn throughly, & perfectly' (3.89). In other words, the philosophical aspect of oratorical training might be represented as a centripetal movement towards the unity of *sapientia* which underlies all the various arts and provides them with a set of basic principles, which can be acquired by all who really put their minds to the project.

However, Crassus situates this explanation of the philosophical character of true eloquence in his lengthy remarks on style and ornament. The practical purpose of reading widely in all the arts is that it provides the orators with 'a treasury of choice and rare [*exquisitus*] matter from every parte of learning' (3.92) which is beyond the reach of the ordinary speaker. Hence the orator needs to build up a large store of unusual materials in order to invest his speeches 'with splendid wordes' (3.125). And at this moment, Catulus breaks in with an expostulation which Crassus can hardly have welcomed. Catulus recalls how masters of rhetoric used formerly to regard all the arts as their province, and how Hippias of Elis once boasted 'before all Grece almoste, that there was noe art, in which he did not know everie thinge' (3.127). Not only had he acquired 'all liberall & gentlemanly doctrine' – geometry, music, literature – but also philosophy and politics and even weaving and cobbling. Catulus quickly corrects himself: 'Truly, this felowe went somewhat too farre'; but he then goes on to take the part of Gorgias, admiring his ability and audacity in offering to speak on any topic whatsoever, and observing that 'to him alone of all was set up an Image, not of mere gilt, but of pure Golde' (3.129). Delphi was famous for its oracle of Apollo, so the erection of this golden statue is a rare tribute to a human speaker; but Crassus's attitude towards Gorgias's accomplishments is ambivalent. On the one hand, he is clearly impatient with Socrates's baiting of the sophist in Plato's *Gorgias*, which he puts down to 'too-much abundance of idlenes' (3.122). But earlier in the dialogue, he reacts with something like irritation to the request that he should expatiate on the *ars rhetorica* ('a petty quaestion') because he does not wish to be compared to an 'idle & loquacious Grekeling' such as 'Gorgias the Leontinian' (1.102).

To conclude, the polymathic ideal is a kind of will-o'-the-wisp in the *De oratore*. We expect it to lead to a much more convincing and triumphant establishment of the old connection between philosophy and oratory than the one with which we are finally presented. Sulpicius, for example, who is represented as the most impressive speaker amongst the younger men, simply refuses to accept Crassus's exhortations to the study of philosophy, which he openly dismisses: 'For my parte, thou maist deem, either that I despaire of being hable to learne such thinges thoroughlie, or, which is very sooth, that I contemne & despise them' (3.147). Here we must have regard to the fact that we are dealing not with a treatise but with a dialogue. Crassus returns to the polymathic ideal again and again during the course of the conversation, but no decision is ever finally agreed upon by the collocutors who take part. Moreover, it is clear that Crassus and the others occasionally overstate their own cases in order to make the discussion more lively. Indeed, Crassus and Antonius, though represented as opponents in the discussion, tend to look very similar when we examine their positions over the whole three books of the *De oratore*. We have already seen how Antonius is quite happy that young men should range over 'all proper studie and humanity' (1.256); and he also makes the connection between the *artes humanae* and epideictic. When Catulus remarks that it seems to him harder to speak on abstract themes than to address the practical concerns of legal matters, Antonius corrects him with the observation that 'it is but game to that man, which hath som wit, & training-up, and hath also experience of ordinarie letters & more polished humanitie [*communes litterae et politior humanitas*]' (2.72). General themes are the concern of epideictic or display oratory, and Antonius is making the point that anyone who has been to school can make up, for example, a speech in praise of eloquence. Moreover, Crassus's conclusion that polymathic study provides stylistic ornament rather than real content has already been adumbrated by Antonius in the first book of the dialogue, where he states that such study would be useful only for epideictic orations on general themes drawn from 'the nature of thinges, or humane matters' (1.81). Here a certain style is required: 'this

28

kinde of speaking is bright and rich in wordes'. And from here it is but a short step to the 'festive' elements of Ciceronian humanism.

De oratore (2): Wit and pleasant vein

The first time we encounter the word *humanitas* in the *De oratore* is a very clear illustration of the way in which this term was associated with wit and charm. It occurs in the *mise en scène*, where Cicero relates how Crassus and his party finally left politics behind them and settled down to relax and recreate themselves (1.27):

> Whan all talkynge had come to an end, such was the humanitie that dwelt in Crassus, that when they had bathed them selves, and sat down to board to eat, all the clouwdie melancholy of their former discourse was shaken off, & dispeld, such was the plesauntnes [*iucunditas*] in this manne, so great his gamesome wit [*lepos*].

Crassus's *humanitas* is marked here not so much by his acquaintance with literature and learning as by his desire to please and amuse his guests. Cicero does not tell us what he and they talked about, but no doubt their conversation was much the same as the one recorded in the main body of the *De oratore*. The next day, we are told, Crassus introduces the topic of eloquence in order that 'their spirites might be recreated after the talking of the daye previous' (1.29). And at the midpoint of his brief eulogy, Crassus explicitly associates *humanitas* with witty and charming conversation pursued in hours of leisure, as opposed to the sort of eloquence needed in political life (1.32):

> Naye, let us not still dwell on the Forum, the Benches of the courts, the speakers Platform, and the Senatehouse. What might be in tymes of idlenes, more plesaunt, or more proper to humanitie, than elegant speche & conversation, that is in no thinge rude & unlearned?

We have already seen how the phrase *nulla in re rudis* leads on to the kind of formal oratory that was most dependent on the pleasure it gave to an audience rather than the power it wielded over their minds: epideictic. But here we are more concerned with informal *sermo*, 'conversation'.

Cicero was usually careful to distinguish these two different kinds of eloquence, but he was aware that very little had been written on the sort connected with *humanitas*. In the *De officiis*, Cicero spells out the fundamental difference between the two kinds (1.132, p. 100):

[B]icause the power of speche is greate, and thesame is in two sortes: the one of vehement speche [*contentio*], the other of common talk: let the vehement speche serve for pleadings in judgementes, orations in assemblies, and debating in the Senatehouse: let talke [*sermo*] be used in companies, in disputations, in meetings of familiars: and let it also be at feastinges.

The eloquence suited to *sermo* is the informal kind of speech which Crassus associates with *humanitas* and *lepos* and *otium*, although he does not clarify the connection, presumably because he knew it would be taken for granted. However, in the *De officiis*, Cicero does go into more detail, which is worth recording in full (1.134–6, p. 101):

Let then this familiar talke (in which the Socratians moste excell) be gentle, and nothing obstinate: let ther be therin a pleasauntnesse [*lepos*]. No nor let a man keepe out other, as though he wer entered into his owne possession: but as in other maters, so in common talke, he must think an enterchaunged course oftentimes meete to be used. And let him see, first of all, of what maters he speake: if they be ernest, let him use a sagenesse: if they be merie, a pleasauntnesse. Speciallie let him foresee, that his talke bewray not somme vice in his maners: which then chiefly is wonte to befall: when either in mockage, or ernest, men do bysie themselves to speake raylingly, and spightfully of the absent, to their sclaunder. But this common talke, for the moste parte, is had either of householde maters, or of the commonweale, or of lerning, and teaching artes. We must therfore give good heede: that when the communication beginne to straye to other thinges, to these it be returned: yea howsoever the mater falles oute, that is in hand. For neither all with one mater, nor at every season, nor alike we ar delited. We must marke also, howfarre our talk hath in it a liking: and as ther was a waye to beginne it, so let ther be a measurable meane to end it. But bicause it is verie well taught: that in all our life we flee passions, that is to saye unmeasurable moodes of minde, not ruled by reason: likewise our talk must be voyde of such moodes: leste either anger aryse, or somme greedynesse, or slouthfulnesse, or cowardlinesse, or some such thing appeare. And most of all, we must have regarde: that those, with whome wee keepe talk, we seeme bothe to reverence, and to love.

This, of course, is exactly the kind of conversation Cicero produces in the *De oratore* between Crassus, Antonius and the others. Although he does not use the word *humanitas* in connection with this sort of *sermo*, it is eminently humane in its insistence not only on 'lerning, and teaching artes' and 'pleasauntnesse', but also, for example, on the need to allow everyone a chance to speak. This is *sermo communis*: 'common talke'. Unlike a formal oration, in which one person speaks and the rest (ideally) listen, this kind of eloquence is designed to produce an even exchange of speech between all speakers. Cicero was always aware of the societal aspect of *humanitas*. What makes us human is the use of reason and especially speech by which, as Crassus says, 'we talke amongst our selves, & are hable to expresse our thoughtes in speeche' (*De orat.*, 1.32). Society is founded on that aspect of *humanitas* which combines 'humankind' with 'humankindness'; but it was maintained from day to day by ordinary civil conversation, by means of which people not only communicated their thoughts, but also rehearsed their mutual goodwill and confirmed their trust in the *societas hominum*: 'human and humane society'.

Cicero's comments on *sermo communis* in this passage cast an interesting retrospective light on the phrase which Crassus uses to insist, apparently, on polymathic knowledge in his orator: 'in omni genere sermonis, in omni parte humanitatis' (1.71). If we take *sermo* to mean speech, then Crassus seems to be saying that the orator should be well equipped to speak in all the recognised kinds (such as forensic, epideictic, conversational); and this would imply that the 'parts of humanity' include the various humane arts. But if we consider Crassus's earlier association of *sermo* and *humanitas* with speech which is 'plesaunt' and 'elegant', as well as 'in no thinge rude nor unlearned' (1.32), then the phrase might take on another sense: 'in every kind of conversation and in every aspect of witty and charming speech'. In fact, the context makes it clear that Crassus is mainly thinking of polymathy; but Gabriel Harvey seems to have been alert to the other possibility as well. He admires Chaucer and Lydgate for 'their witt, pleasant veine, varietie of poetical discourse, & all humanitie' (*Marg.*, pp. 160–1). Harvey, then, translates the festive as well as the literary and learned nuances of Ciceronian *humanitas*. This is perhaps to take Crassus's phrase further than its original author intended, but it nevertheless captures the spirit of many other passages in the *De oratore*, especially in the section on the use of wit.

Antonius introduces this section by referring to the two kinds of eloquence which an orator must master: the 'vehement' (*vehemens*) and the 'smooth' (*lenis*). But he does not separate them so completely as Cicero does in the *De officiis*, by allocating them to different kinds of speech, but rather explains how smoothness may be used to mollify the vehemence of a forensic oration: 'Nor is anie speeche more temperatelie well balaunced than that, in whiche the harsh asperitie of contention, is seasoned by the humanitie of the speaker selfe; whilst the intervals of mildnes are given strength & sinewes by a certaine strifeful gravity [*gravitas et contentio*]' (2.212). Antonius introduces an important new element into the discussion here. In drawing attention to the humanity of the advocate, he reminds us of the importance of what the Romans called *conciliatio*. This aspect of oratory dealt with the means by which an advocate made himself agreeable to his audience in order to get them on his side. Not surprisingly, then, the festive kind of *humanitas*, which is meant to please and amuse, is an important element in *conciliatio*. Jokes are especially important, and a young speaker named Caesar, who was famed for his own wit, makes this very plain when he takes over discussion of this part of the orator's skill. At several points he makes an explicit connection between *lepos* and *humanitas*. For example, Socrates surpassed all others in 'witte & humanity [*lepos et humanitas*]' (2.270). Indeed, 'Ther is no occasion in oure lives wher we may not busie our selves with witte & humanitie' (2.271). Later in the dialogue, Crassus praises Catulus for his 'humanitie and witte' (3.29). But he also approves of the way Catulus speaks Latin: 'His speeche is so pure, that it may seem that he almoste alone speaketh Latin'. And with this observation, we reach the heart of the more exclusive kind of *humanitas* which Cicero portrays in the *De oratore* and other of his works. Wide reading and witty expression are perhaps not so very hard to acquire or cultivate; but what really matters is what we might call 'accent'.

De oratore (3): The humane voice

We have already seen in the *De officiis* how Cicero's anthropological theory presents us with three stages of human development. The first men were, as it were, 'subhuman', living like brute beasts in the wilderness; then they developed by the use of *ratio* and *oratio* into their present state, with the race also finally producing a small number of 'superhuman' men who might act like demigods, or, alternatively, might fall back into beastly ferocity. Crassus presents the same basic scheme in the *De oratore*, though with the same mythological application as Cicero had used earlier in the *Pro Archia*. Immediately after his remarks on the pleasures of humane conversation in his praise of eloquence, Crassus states (1.32–3):

> For that one point wherin we moste excell the beastes, is in that we talke amongst our selves, & are hable to expresse our thoughtes in speeche. Who, then, would not marvel at this, yea and rightlie, and deem it a thing to labour in to his uttermost; so that, in that thinge in whych men most excell beastes, so he shall rise above men them selves. But to come now indeede to the sum: what other force or power might have gathered men which were dispersed here & there together in one place, and led them from the beastlie life of the wildernes [*fera agrestisque vita*] to this cultivated state of civil humanitie [*humanus cultus civilisque*]; or whan such civile communities [*civitates*] once wer constituted, to draw up and establish lawes, courts, and rights?

Here the heroic orator leads the brutish prototypes of modern humankind into *humanus civilisque cultus*: 'humane and civil culture'. The emphasis here is still on the 'civic' elements of civility, such as laws and assemblies; and the *magnus animus* of the heroic orator is kept busy maintaining the *res publica* by delivering wise and eloquent speeches in the courts, the Forum and the Senate. Meanwhile, citizens are kept together in the bond of society in more mundane and quotidian ways, as, for example, by civil conversations in which *humanitas* plays a large part. This is *humanitas*, then, seen as a synonym of *urbanitas*.

Part of this anthropological myth of the 'ascent of man' from the wilderness to the city deals with the emergence of a biologically as well as culturally superior human being; and, naturally, the *perfectus orator* is such a person. The orator, of course, needs to have a good voice; but Crassus sees this as only one element in a general physical aptness: 'a slipper tong, a sonable voice, goode lunges, & vigorousnes, and a certaine shapeliness and comeliness of his whole face and bodie' (1.114). A man without these natural gifts of the body might well fail as an orator because he simply did not look or sound right, whereas others were so perfect they seemed like demigods:

> Some men there be, so stammeringe of tong, or unmelodious of voice, or so wilde & rusticall [*vastus atque agrestis*] of face, & in the motions of the body, that though they have witte & arte, yet they maye not be entered amongst the numbers of the Orators; whilst others ther be, so hable & apt in all these thinges, that they seem to be furnished & adorned, not by the giftes of Nature, but rather shaped by som Godde.

Crassus's views on accent fit the same basic scheme. Speaking with the right accent was a crucial part of the orator's equipment because it was the most salient feature of *urbanitas*. As we have already observed, Rome was the *urbs*, and the rest of Italy was merely provincial. Crassus therefore insists that the orator must use 'a certaine Accent [*vox*] proper to the people & Citie of Rome' and avoid 'rusticall harshenes & the singularitie of strangers speeche' (3.44).

For Crassus, then, the orator must speak like a Roman. This means not only that he must speak with a Roman accent, but also that he must use the appropriate Roman expressions. These elements add up to what we might call a Roman 'voice'. Obviously we cannot literally 'hear' this voice in a written text like the *De oratore*, but the term is useful because it catches the essentially dramatic quality of any dialogue. Certainly, in the sophisticated fiction of the *De oratore*, Cicero is trying to make us 'hear' a conversation between cultivated Romans taking place (and the various references to place and setting allow for a rudimentary degree of visualisation as well). All in all, it adds an extra aesthetic dimension to the work which is very much in line with the ideals of Roman *urbanitas*.

To return to the question of accent. In a context where how you pronounced your words was so crucial, your knowledge of *litterae* might be of only secondary importance. Crassus makes this quite clear to Catulus and the others (3.43):

> Oure Romane citisens, doe make less studie of letters, then doe the people of Latium; yet amongst those city-bred gallaunts [*urbani*], whom thow knowest, Catulus, & in whom is lytle or no Litterature, ther is nevertheles none of them but doth easilie passe in mildnes [*lenitas*] of voice, and distinct sounding of wordes, Quintus Valerius of Sora, who of all them that wear the toga, beares the bell for knowledge of letters.

The point here is that Valerius is learned but also provincial (Sora was near Cicero's home town of Arpinum) and therefore lacks the urbane authority of less scholarly men such as Catulus's friends.

We might also turn to Cicero's own remarks on Catulus and his uncle in the *De officiis*. In his remarks on conversation, Cicero says that the tone of voice used on such occasions should be 'clere, and sweet' (1.133, p. 100). And there are plenty of examples that may be followed:

> What was in the Catuli, that ye should suppose them to use a perfite judgement in pronouncing of letters? Howbeit they wer lerned: but so wer other to: yet these wer thought to use the latine toung best. Theyr sounding was sweete: their letters neither to much mowthed, nor drowned: lest either it should be unherd, or over harshe.

Cicero's main point here is that the purity of a speaker's Latin, which includes the way it is pronounced as well as the correctness of usage, does not depend on an education in letters as taught by a paid master of the arts of grammar or rhetoric.

The same priorities are translated into the urbane 'voice' of the *De oratore* earlier in the dialogue when Antonius shows himself anxious to forestall any appearance of professionalism when he commences his own exposition of the perfect orator. He deliberately mimics the complacent self-advertisement associated with teachers of grammar and rhetoric: 'Heark ye, I saie, heark ye! for ye shal heare a man that hath bene to the schole, and hath bene polished by the handes of a master, and by the studie of Greke letters' (2.28). The others all laugh; and Antonius is then free to proceed without the risk of seeming a pedant, or, worse, a mere hireling. This horrifying prospect emerges, for example, in the course of the first day of the dialogue, when Antoninus playfully contradicts Crassus's stipulation that the orator must be well versed in a plurality of sciences, concluding that such knowledge should be regarded as 'set apart from the office and dutie proper unto the Orator' (1.262). Crassus retorts: 'Thou makest of our Orator a mere mechanicall [*operarius*]'. The comparison seems extreme; but Crassus comes back to it the next day, when, Antonius having somewhat recanted his earlier position, he remarks (2.40):

> A nightes rest hath smoothed thy former roughness [*expolire*] and rendered thee a man again, for in our talkinge yesterdaye, thou hast described to us the Orator as a Jack-of-one-Trade, or an oarsman in the galley, or common porter, which is to saye, a fellow rusticall & inurbane, and wanting all humanitie [*inops humanitatis atque inurbanus*].

Polymathy is important to Crassus's own portrait of the orator because it redeems the orator from the stigma of professionalism. There were no professional lawyers in his day: oratory was a skill every citizen was expected to acquire in order to defend his own and his friends' interests in court, perhaps even to defend the *res publica* in the Forum or in the Senate. The true orator had to be in possession of the much more general range of knowledge which furnished a gentleman or nobleman with his claim to full *humanitas*. No galley-slave or porter, indeed, no man who had to work for his living, could easily acquire such an education.

Viewing the *De oratore* in more-or-less dramatic terms allows us to see that Crassus is speaking here with the voice of a particular 'character'. We do not know much about the historical Crassus, although Cicero twice comments on his personal *humanitas* in the course of the *De oratore* (1.27, 3.1). But really Cicero invents Crassus according to a conception of literary *decorum*: 'propriety'. He 'speaks' like the type of a cultivated Roman gentleman. This is the real proof of his own *humanitas*. What he says is also important; and Renaissance humanism returns again and again to certain phrases and ideas put in Crassus's mouth, such as *in omni genere sermonis, in omni partem humanitatis*. But Renaissance writers also occupied themselves with a much more extensive and intimate imitation of the 'voice' with which Crassus and the others speak in Cicero's dialogue. It would not be too far out of the way to say that Elizabethan humanism is at heart a 'posture'. Humanist writers try to impersonate a particular 'character': cultivated, of course, but also wealthy, well respected, probably rather good-looking. It is important that we should keep this fantasy in our minds, too, as we examine the particular inflections given to 'humanity' by individual Elizabethan writers; but in the next chapter we return to the more scholarly aspects of Elizabethan humanism, as it was understood by the Elizabethans themselves, before returning, once again, to the courtly and urbane character which it always seems to take unto itself.

Notes

1. For a comprehensive introduction to Cicero and the Elizabethans, see Jones, 1998.

2. 'If it is true that Italian humanists had no expression closer to "classical scholarship" than *studia humanitatis*, then *Pro Archia* provided with classical scholarship in the Renaissance with its charter of foundation' (Reeve, 1996, p. 22). It was in Cicero's oration on behalf of Archias the poet that Petrarch first came across the phrase *studia humanitatis* in 1333. He started to use it in his own correspondence, and so did his disciples and followers, until the phrase had won wide circulation in learned European circles.

3. In *Prince Caspian* (ch. 14), a group of grammar-school boys are turned into pigs, and no doubt Lewis intends a wry comment on the vulgarity, as he saw it, of Renaissance humanism (as well as a glance at the Gadarene Swine). Less owlishly-inspired juvenile literature also uses the device, as when the obese and vicious son of unpleasantly aspirant parents is given a pig's tail in J.K. Rowling's *Harry Potter and the Philosopher's Stone* (1997, ch. 1). The assimilation of man and pig at the end of George Orwell's *Animal Farm* (1954) belongs to a different kind of writing, but a slight adaptation of the famously revised slogan would not seriously misrepresent Cicero's idea of *humanitas*: 'All human beings are human, but some are more human than others'.

4. For Roman education in grammar, see Bonner, 1977, pp. 189–249.

5. The point is worth emphasising, as we have come to accept the centrality of rhetoric to Renaissance humanism in studies which give the term a political inflection, especially since the seminal essay by Gray (1963).

6. The distinction between the *artes maximae* and the *artes mediocres* is traditional. Earlier, Cicero says that many have excelled 'not merely in ordinarie Artes, but also in almost the Greatest Arts [*non mediocres artes, sed prope maximae*]' (§ 6).

7. Callicles informs Socrates that he has just missed Gorgias, who has 'given a show [*epedeiksato*]'; but Chaerea assures him that Gorgias 'will give a show [*epideiksetai*]' at the drop of a hat.

8. It is worth noting that Archias was the poetic counterpart of the sophist: 'Howe often have I seen this Archias, without the wryting downe of one letter, speke out extemporallie, & without forthought, great numbers of most excellent verses, yea, on matters which were even then most currant! and, what is more, howe, whan he was recalled to that very theme again, which had spoken on before, he would change and vary every word & sentence in his uttering the same' (*Pro Archia*, § 19).

CHAPTER THREE

Humanists and Humanitians

At first glance, it should not be so hard to give a definition of the Elizabethan 'humanist', or 'humanitian', as he was also styled in early modern
English. After all, we can trace a clear line of semantic descent from the
last years of the sixteenth century to the present day, since the traditional
literary-historical characterisation of the humanist as an expert in classical
literature goes back to the 1590s. It is there, for example, in a useful definition of the Italian word *umanista* in John Florio's Italian–English dictionary,
A World of Words (1598). Here the word is glossed (under 'Humanista') as a
'humanist, or professor of humanitie'. Unfortunately, as we have seen, the
word 'humanity' could mean a good many things; but these various senses
have already been adumbrated by our examination of the Ciceronian term
humanitas. Indeed, these early senses of the word should give us a different
view of the Elizabethan humanist as a creature of his own time, rather than
of ours. We shall see, for example, that the words 'humanist' and 'humanitian'
were not ordinarily used to describe what we would call a classicist; and
that 'humanity' was conceived in such a way as to suggest that the humanist
was one who used his knowledge of literature and learning in a way which
makes him seem very much like a courtier. But let us first deal with universalism once again.

Curious universal scholars

The universalist ideals of Ciceronian humanism – *in omni genere sermoni, in
omni parte humanitatis* – survived in the thought of later Roman writers, and
remained an alluring will-o'-the-wisp well into the Renaissance and long

afterwards.[1] Especially important in ensuring their long afterlife was the association which arose during the Renaissance between the *studia humanitatis*, as it was understood by Italian scholarship, and the older Greek notion of the *enkuklios paideia*. The latter phrase means 'standard programme of education'. This kind of *paideia* was called *enkuklios*, or 'cyclical', not because it was conceived as a 'cycle of studies', but because it was the form of education which was 'in circulation' amongst the Greek upper classes (Marrou, 1948, pp. 406–7). Thus, it was a very close equivalent of what Cicero meant by *humanitas*, 'general education', as opposed to the expert study of a particular discipline. On the other hand, the components of Greek and Roman education were very different. We have seen that Roman boys studied grammar and rhetoric, but Greek boys were also expected to study disciplines such as music and geometry. The Romans, however, were suspicious of these arts: music led to sensuality, and geometry was too abstract to be genuinely useful. A hellenising Roman like Cicero might think otherwise; but Cicero also knew that Roman culture was extremely conservative in this respect. In the *Disputationes Tusculanae*, he comments that in ancient Greece, you were expected to know about music and geometry, and that 'neyther could any be counted wel learned being ignoraunt of the same' (1.5, sig. B3r). Still, Cicero kept to his ideal of a wider education, and passed it on to later Roman writers.

One of the most significant of these was Quintilian, who compiled his monumental *Institutio oratoria* ('Oratorical Training') towards the end of the first century AD. Quintilian's importance for the student of Renaissance rhetorical theory is very great; the compendious inclusiveness of the *Institutio* gave him the edge even over Cicero, whose reflections on rhetoric and oratory were dispersed over several uneven texts, and were not presented as methodically as Quintilian's lively synthesis. But for our immediate purposes, Quintilian is particularly significant because it was he who established the connection between Cicero's universalist ideal and 'that worlde of learning [*orbis illae doctrinae*] which the Grekes cal *encyclion paedian*' (1.10.1).[2] These remarks were well known to Renaissance scholars, only their editions of Quintilian read '*encycliopaedian*' rather than '*encyclion paedian*' (whence the modern word 'encyclopaedia'). However, Quintilian's influence is more than matched by a second-century miscellanist called Aulus Gellius, who passed on an important definition of *humanitas* in his *Noctes Atticae* ('Nights in Attica'). This passage is well known to students of Renaissance humanism, but it is worth quoting again in its entirety (13.17):

> Those who have been moste skilled in the latyn tong, and have made right use of latin wordes, have not intended by the word *Humanitas*, what is ment by the vulgar, that is, what the Grekes call, *Philanthropia*: namelie a certaine

favorable & benivolent regard to al men, whomsoever they be: but rather doe they give unto the word *Humanitas*, the same sense that the Grekes do gyve unto theyr word *Paideia*; which is to saye, Erudition & instruction in al good & liberall Artes [*eruditio institutioque in bonas artes*]; for the cherishing of this science, and the learninge of it, is given to man alone of all the animals; and for that reason is it cald *Humanitas*.

Gellius was rather too eager to separate what seemed to him correct and vulgar uses of the word *humanitas*; even Cicero did not go so far. But his emphasis still fairly represents Cicero's position, and the word *paideia* inches us a little closer to the 'encyclopaedic humanism' of Renaissance scholarship.

The final process of assimiliation can be illustrated by examining a number of glosses to the passage in the opening section of the *Pro Archia poeta*, where Cicero comments on the 'common bonde [*commune vinculum*]' which holds together 'all those Artes, whych pertaine unto humanitie' (§ 2). Philip Beroaldus, for example, in his 1517 edition of the text, gives a full explanation, which comes straight from Aulus Gellius (sig. C2r):

> This worde *Humanitas*, doth not signifye merelie benivolence towardes all men, as thinketh the vulgar folke, but what we call Erudition & training-up in all good artes [*erudito institutioque in bonas artes*], or *Paideia*, as the Grekes saye. So it is that they who trulie seek out & cherish these studies of humanitie [*studia humanitatis*] are the most humayne men [*humanissimi*]. Varro saith that the more humayne man [*humanior*] is to be taken as suche on accompt of his erudition & training-up in gentle studies.[3]

Martin Bolerus is even more helpful in his explanation of the *vinculum* metaphor in an edition of 1541 (fol. 9v):

> This is because the Artes are bound together by the bondes of a certaine felowshippe, and stande in need each of the other, for which reson they are called Cyclicall [*cyclicus*]. For that man, which wil busy him selfe in Dialecticke, wil be undone if he knowe not Grammaire; Rethoryk is so closelie akin to Dialecticke, that nether cannot stand without thother; that Astronomer who knoweth not Arithmetrick & Geometrie, we hold of no accompt; & any man that fayleth to applie the tooles of Dialecticke and Rethoryke, whiles he treateth a civil cause in the courtes, will come to nothing.

Here is the 'cyclical' element, then, and the picture is completed by a note on the same passage, and in the same volume, by Francis Sylvius. He refers us to the very similar passage in the third book of the *De oratore* (3.21) where Crassus reminds Catulus of the Platonic origins of the idea of the *vinculum* (fol. 9r):

Ther is also that true saying of Plato, Catulus, which surelie you have heard, that all knowledge of the liberall and humaine artes [*ingenuae et humanae artes*] is contained within a single bond of felloweship. This is the World of learning [*orbis doctrinae*], which the Grekes call *Encyclopaedia*, as saith Quintilian.

A good deal of similar material could be produced to illustrate the process by which these two terms were almost inevitably assimilated by the compilers of such commentaries, as they varied and added to the glosses provided by their predecessors. Certainly, the encyclopaedic notion of the *studia humanitatis* was well established in scholarly texts by the time Elizabethans were learning their grammar in schools up and down the country.

Moreover, the universalism associated with the word *humanitas* only confirmed what was already part of the specifically learned sense of the English word 'humanity'. This sense is first recorded in William Caxton's translation of Jacobus de Voragine's *Legenda aurea* (1483). Here we learn that St Vincent was 'in hys chyldhode sette to studye / where by dyvyne provydence he floured in double science / most profoundly / that is to saye in dyvynyte and humanyte' (fol. 121r b). In its widest application, 'humanity' could mean all knowledge which was not comprehended by the term 'divinity'. For example, in John Lyly's *Euphues: The Anatomy of Wit* (1578), Euphues eventually rejects 'humayne wisedome' in favour of 'devine knowledge'. He cries: 'Farewell therefore the fine and filed phrases of Cicero, the pleasaunt Eligies of Ovid, the depth and profound knowledge of Aristotle. Farewell Rhetoricke, farewell Philosophie, farewell all learninge which is not sponge from the bowels of the holy Bible' (pp. 286–7). Here we have a casual scheme of the *studia humanitatis*: rhetoric, poetry, philosophy. But there were plenty of others. The Elizabethans were well aware that what they called 'humanity' was the composition of a plurality of arts and sciences; but they seem never to have made up their minds what these disciplines were. This point is worth making in the light of the currency gained by Paul Oskar Kristeller's formulations of the *studia humanitatis* as a 'clearly defined cycle of scholarly disciplines, namely grammar, rhetoric, history, poetry, and moral philosophy' (1955, p. 10). This scheme has become an axiom of Renaissance studies over the past fifty years, but it now seems that it does not really fit the documentary record very well at all, even in Italy (Kohl, 1992). Certainly, it makes no sense to apply it to Elizabethan England. Indeed, there was only one scheme which the Elizabethans might agree on with respect to the 'humane arts': it did not matter which they were, or how many, but only that none of them was divinity.

A few examples will suffice to illustrate the variety of arts which were included in the term 'humanity' when opposed to 'divinity'. In his *Apology for Poetry* (ms. c. 1580, pr. 1595), Philip Sidney makes a methical list of the arts which make up 'humaine skill' (p. 163). They include astronomy, geometry, arithmetic, music, natural philosophy, moral philosophy, law, history, grammar, rhetoric, logic, physic and metaphysics. Here we have a loose collection of various schemes such as the Seven Liberal Arts, the Three Philosophies and the Three Professions. But all are contrasted and subordinated to divinity (and poetry). Sidney's friend, Fulke Greville, had even more to add when he asked himself the question, 'What be those Arts then of Humanity?', in his *Treaty of Humane Learning* (ms. c. 1605, st. 51). Military and mechanical arts come into the picture, now, as do agriculture, architecture, trade (st. 120). But in comparison with divinity, they are all 'vaine Idols' (st. 33). However, Greville is writing at the very end of our period; Elizabethan schemes tended to be more conservative. A more typical selection is this list of 'Humaine Artes' from Thomas Nashe's *Christ's Tears over Jerusalem* (1593): 'Logique, Rethorique, History, Phylosophy, Musique, Poetry, are all the hand-maides of Divinitie' (pp. 125–6). And in the second part of his *Catalogue of English Books* (1595), which lists scientific publications, following the divinity books of the first volume, Andrew Maunsell advertises a third part which will deal with '*Humanity*, wherein I shall have occasion to shew what we have in our owne tongue, of *Gramer, Logick, Rhetoricke, Lawe, Historie, Poetrie, Policie*, &c.' (sig. *3v). Alas, this third part was never completed. But the general point to be learnt from these various compilations of the humane arts is that they were, indeed, very various.

But if the typical view of the *studia humanitatis* was so vague, what does this tell us about the Elizabethan humanist as a 'professor of humanity'? Was he a man who could claim expertise in all the various secular arts? In this case, of course, he would seem to have much more in common with Harvey's 'curious universal scholar' than his 'superficial humanist'. Interestingly, there is reason to believe that Harvey himself may have seen the humanist as a universalist at some point, since the word 'humanitian' seems to be used in this sense by his two younger brothers, John and Richard, to both of whom Gabriel acted in his favourite role of mentor. In 1588, John Harvey published a lengthy pamphlet called *A Discursive Problem Concerning Prophecies*. All the Harveys were interested in astronomy; and both John and the middle brother, Richard, had become involved in astrological controversy. In 1583, Richard Harvey produced a set of predictions under the title *An Astrological Discourse upon the Conjunction of Saturn and Jupiter*. This sensational, indeed, apocalyptic pamphlet provoked a good deal of scorn; but John quickly came to his brother's aid with his *Astrological Addition* (1583). Later, however, he took a more considered view, sounding very cautious notes about how far astrological predictions were to be credited, especially those of the more lurid kind. Here his position is that almost all prophecy is impossible to defend 'either according to the grounds and rules of Humanitie, or Divinitie' (sig. A1v). Or again: it cannot be justified 'according to the surest rules, and principles as well of Divinitie, as of Philosophie, and other Humanitie' (p. 1). Here, by the way, we see a typical variation on the basic dichotomy between divinity and humanity. Before the word 'humanity' was coined, and long after, it was 'philosophy' which stood as the secular, often, pagan counterpart to 'divinity'. But here Harvey sees philosophy as a part of humanity, as is confirmed by his question: 'Is there any point, or article either so erronious in divinitie, or absurde in philosophy, or vaine in other arts of humanitie, which has not been maintained, and defended by some divines, philosophers, and humanitians?' (p. 9). A little later, Harvey goes back to the basic bilateral scheme, when he declares that prophecy is a fantasy, 'whatsoever Moses Gerundiensis, or any other *Thalmudist*, or *Cabalist*, or *Rabin*, yea or S. Jerome himselfe, or Osiander, or Melanchthon, or any other later Divine, or Humanitian, hath hitherto published' (p. 16). Andreas Osiander is the divine: he was a theological author, and Harvey is thinking here of his *Conjectures of the End of the World* (trans. George Joye, 1548). Philip Melanchthon is the 'humanitian' counterpart to Osiander in Harvey's view, no doubt, because he was the author of a translation into Latin of the *De praedictionibus astronomicis* ('Astronomical Predictions': 1533) of the ancient Greek scientist Ptolemy.

What John Harvey means by the word 'humanitian', then, is not exactly clear. But he is evidently aware of the plurality of the 'arts of humanity'; and I suspect that for him the humanitian was a man who was generally well versed in secular learning, as was very likely so in the case of his brother Richard in his *Theological Discourse of the Lamb of God and His Enemies* (1590). Richard Harvey was (quite literally) a smaller version of his brother Gabriel: learned, opinionated, pugnacious.[4] It was he, apparently, who started off a vigorous paper war between Gabriel Harvey and Thomas Nashe with the following casual remonstrance in the preface to *The Lamb of God* (sig. A2v):

> It becummeth me not to play that part in Divinitie that one Thomas Nashe hath lately done in humanitie, who taketh uppon him in civill learning as Martin doth in religion, peremptorily censuring his betters at pleasure, Poets, Orators, Polihistors, Lawyers, and whome not?

Harvey refers here to Nashe's remarks on various writers in his first work, *The Anatomy of Absurdity* (1589), and also to the perceived arrogance of 'Martin Marprelate', author of numerous pamphlets against the authority of the bishops in the controversy which bears his name. Both are branded as 'know-alls', rather than as genuinely encyclopaedic scholars – or 'polyhistors'.

This is a useful word for our purposes. It means the same as the word 'polymath': widely learned scholar. John Harvey uses it in a very similar list in his *Discursive Problem*: 'poets, philosophers, polihistors, antiquaries, philologers, schoolemen, and other learned discoursers' (p. 63). Not surprisingly, it is Gabriel Harvey who is credited with the first use of the word in English.[5] And it seems probable that Richard Harvey uses the word 'humanitian' in a 'polyhistorical' sense in his description of Paulus Jovius as a 'humanitian bishop' (*Lamb*, p. 95). Jovius was Bishop of Nocera; but he managed to write books on all kinds of secular topics: Turks, *imprese*, fish, and so on. So perhaps here we have an instance of the humanist as a 'curious universal scholar'.

Later instances of the words 'humanist' and 'humanitian' confirm the impression that a universalist element was important in the way early modern writers conceived of these terms. In his translation of Suetonius's *History of Twelve Caesars* (1606), Philemon Holland describes the Emperor Augustus's grammarian Sphaerus as a 'deep Scholler and great Humanitian as we speake, and whom the Greekes call *Philologon*' (p. 445). We learn what a *philologos* is from Suetonius's own *De grammaticis et rhetoribus*. Here he tells us: 'It semeth that this Atteius took unto him selfe this title, like Eratosthenes, who first made claime unto it, as being well sene in many and sundrie disciplines' (§ 10). Holland says that thanks to Sphaerus, Augustus became '*polumathes*. i.[e.] skilfull in histories, antiquities, etc.'. In other words, Augustus acquired a wide knowledge of the antiquity of his own time; and this antiquarian element was an essential part of the traditional grammatical curriculum, which constantly used old texts, especially legal texts, to establish the correct form or meaning of words.

On the other hand, the modern sense is no doubt present in a somewhat later record of the universal humanist in Fynes Moryson's *Itinerary* (1617). In his chapter of 'Precepts for Travellers', Moryson explains that these tips are intended only for a certain kind of reader (3.3, p. 11):

> I professe to write especially in this place to the Humanist, I meane him that affects the knowledge of State affaires, Histories, Cosmography, and the like, and out of that I write, let other men apply to their use, what they judge fit for them. And if the Humanist judge many things I shall write lesse necessary for him, let him know, that as an Orator and Poet must have some skill in all Sciences, so the Humanist must have some knowledge of all things which fall into practice and discourse.

Moryson's definition of the humanist is clearly based on the Ciceronian ideal of the *perfectus orator*. His wording reveals a debt to Crassus's statement to the effect that the orator should be able to speak on 'whatsoever shall be the matter, which falleth unto him to declare & explain in wordes' (*De orat.*, 1.64). However, his humanist is neither orator nor poet, but rather a man who is interested in 'human ethology'. The full title of Moryson's book is: 'An Itinerary: Containing his Ten Yeeres Travell Through the Twelve Dominions of Germany, Bohmerland, Sweitzerland, Netherland, Denmarke, Poland, Italy, Turky, France, England, Scotland, and Ireland'. It is an account of his travels and reflections on the customs of the people he encounters in various parts of Europe. This is a new sense of the word 'humanist', derived from a new sense of the word 'humanity': 'humankind'. Yet it is still strongly marked by the old encyclopaedic ideal which the Renaissance inherited from Ciceronian humanism.

Literary humanism: grammarians and men of letters

Moryson's polymathic humanist owes something to the Ciceronian ideal of the orator well-seen in the *artes humanae*, but Cicero's orator owes much in his turn to the universalism typically required in the *grammaticus*. We have seen that Cicero himself defines the *grammaticus* as a *poetarum explanator*. The poets needed to be explained not only because they often employed unusual words, or ordinary words in unusual ways, but also because their range of reference could be very wide, extending over mythology, history, philosophy, cosmology – indeed, over the entire *orbis doctrinae*. Encyclopaedic knowledge was therefore required in the *grammaticus* if he was to be able to interpret all-wise Homer. This encyclopaedic element was present in the routines of the Renaissance grammar school, too; and we can tell from notes taken at the lectures on the poets given by the great Italian grammarian Guarino of Verona that a single word could call forth an astonishing quantity of information on various topics (Grafton and Jardine, 1986, pp. 1–28). Elizabethan schoolmasters may have not been so copious, but the margins of school texts were already brimming with this kind of material.

However, grammar was much more narrowly restricted than humanity, though the two words could be used as synonyms. When Caxton compares 'dyvynyte and humanyte', he probably also wants us to understand that 'humanity' means the education devised by pagan grammarians: the *artes humanae* as what we would call 'classical literature'. Such a definition is not uncommon in Elizabethan times. According to the Plymouth schoolmaster William Kempe's *Education of Children in Learning* (1588), there are three schools of learning: Hebrew, Christian and 'the schoole of the Gentiles, which wee may call the schoole of humanitie' (p. 189). This third school included Latin and Greek literature and learning, but also Egyptian, Chaldean and Druidic. On the other hand, 'humanity' was usually restricted to 'classical literature'. The Latin term *humanitas* was used to represent various courses which had formerly come under the term *grammatica* in early Tudor Oxford and Cambridge;[6] and it was not long before the word 'humanity' came to be a synonym of 'grammar' in English as well. For example, Nicholas Udall, in his translation of Erasmus's *Apophthegmata* (1542), glosses the Latin *grammatici* ('grammarians') as 'those that spend their study in humanitie, and whom we cal schole-maisters' (p. 85). The emergence of these words in the late sixteenth century signals a new awareness that humanity might be a kind of 'profession'. And so we arrive at Florio's 'professor of humanity'.

The 'humanist as grammarian' was certainly known to the Elizabethans. For example, in Sir John Harington's treatise on the water-closet, *The Metamorphosis of Ajax* (1596), the word is clearly used to mean 'grammarian'. In 1591, Alexander Hume, master of a grammar school in Bath, wrote a pamphlet which denied the article of the creed which stated that Christ descended into hell. This called forth an angry refutation by Adam Hill in his *Defence of the Article: Christ Descended into Hell* (1592). Hill often returns to the fact that Hume was a mere schoolmaster, with no professional expertise in divinity. He also faults his real faculty: grammar. Hill concludes: 'I must tell you plaine, you speake neither like a Devine nor a Grammarian' (sig. 59v). Perhaps Harington had this passage in mind when he alluded to the controversy a few years later in his *Metamorphosis*, where he, too, is surprised that Hume, as 'a schoole-maister (though being no Preacher)', should speak his mind on matters of doctrine (p. 147). He continues: 'I might repute him as a good humanist, but I should ever doubt him for a good devine'. Hill's 'grammarian' becomes Harington's 'humanist'; but they are both clearly the same man and the same professional figure. Eventually, this sense would be combined with that of the 'humanist as philologer'.[7] By the end of the seventeenth century, the modern literary-historical sense of the word 'humanist' as a classicist was already in place; indeed, it was already being used to refer to a specific group of scholars who were thought to belong to a past era.[8] However, this sense was by no means dominant in the later sixteenth century (in fact, *no* sense was prevalent during this period). This point is worth emphasising, since the grammatical humanist has come to the fore in several recent studies, but he was not so familiar four hundred years ago.

For one thing, humanists were not always 'professors' in the usual academic sense. They might also be 'students' or 'experts' or merely 'amateurs'.

This seems to have been what was meant when Richard Stanyhurst first introduced the word 'humanitian' to the English language in the 'History of Ireland' which he contributed to Raphael Holinshed's famous *Chronicles* in 1577. In his list of the famous 'learned men' of Ireland, Stanyhurst includes: 'Olifer, or Oliver Eustace, a student of the civile and Cannon law, a good humanitian, & a proper philosopher'.[9] It is hard to believe that Eustace could have simultaneously professed all these disciplines at once, although it is not impossible that he professed them one by one in the course of a rather varied career (though not in this order). But it is more likely that he had been a 'student' of all of them at school, university, and, perhaps, the Inns of Court; that he did well in all of them; and that he was remembered for having done so. But he may not have been a great expert in any of these disciplines. Unfortunately, we do not know enough about this man to come to any firm conclusions, but it seems quite probable that for Stanyhurst the 'humanitian' was a 'student of humanity' rather than a 'professor'.

Moreover, the word 'humanity' was never restricted to 'grammar', even in its more obviously 'literary' as opposed to 'learned' sense. Cicero used the word *humanitas* to refer to writings in his own vernacular as well as those written in Greek; and it is clear that some Elizabethans used the word 'humanity' in a similarly inclusive sense, indeed, more so, since Christian as well as pagan authors could be regarded as purveyors of *litterae humaniores*. For example, Harington, in the preface to his translation of Ariosto's *Orlando Furioso* (1591), notes that Moses and David were brought up in the pagan schools of the Egyptians and Chaldeans, and concludes: 'If then we may by the example of two such special servants of God spend some of our young years in studies of humanitie, what better and more meete studie is there for a young man than Poetrie?' (p. 198). But the poetry Harington has in mind includes that produced not only by pagan writers but also by Christian poets like Ariosto and Harington himself. In fact, Harington's phrase 'studies of humanitie', with its emphasis on poetry, gestures towards to the literary emphasis of the *studia humanitatis ac litterarum* in Cicero's *Pro Archia*.

A genuinely Ciceronian interpretation of the literary sense of the word 'humanity', then, would be defined in terms of what the eighteenth century called *belles lettres*. This phrase is now used (if it is used at all) to designate a category of 'light prose'. But originally it was a synonym of the phrase *bonae litterae*; and in other literary cultures similar terms, such as the Polish *literatura piękna* or the Hungarian *szépirodalom*, are still used in bookshops to direct purchasers to works which might well be included in sections called Classics in anglophone countries. This belletristic sense of the word 'humanity' would include any writings in whatever language and from whatever period, provided that they were 'beautiful' or 'good'. Naturally, there would be a tendency to locate such writings within a 'classical tradition', because anyone who was interested in literature as such would have been to grammar school, at least, and there imbibed a sense of literary values based on the study of Latin and Greek poetry and prose. But this aesthetic did not exclude works written in the modern vernaculars as long as they were good enough to be compared with what you had read and admired at school. In other words, there was no reason why English works should not be included in a consideration of 'humanity'. This is certainly what Gabriel Harvey had in mind in his pamphlet *Pierce's Supererogation* (1593) when he drew up a list of the best English authors in verse and prose and called them 'the gentlest Spirites, that English Humanity affourdeth' (sig. Y4r). What else is 'English Humanity' than 'English Literature'?

Harvey's phrase is very important for our understanding of Elizabethan humanism, since it implies that the 'humanist' need not be a grammarian, but rather a 'man of letters', in a very general sense. It allows Elizabethan humanism to proceed from the grammar school to literary culture at large, and to acquire 'courtliness'. It will be noticed that Harvey's English authors are described as superlatively 'gentle', by which he probably means 'genteel' rather than 'kind'. All the male writers whom Harvey lists are gentlemen, and several are knights: Sir Geoffrey Chaucer, Master Edmund Spenser, Sir Thomas More, Sir John Cheke, Master Roger Ascham, Master John Astley, Sir Philip Sidney and Sir Edward Dyer. But Harvey allows a woman to end this procession of gentle literary genius. He does not name her, but he means Sidney's sister, and fellow poet, Mary, Countess of Pembroke: 'the Gentlewooman of Curtesie, the Lady of Vertue, the Countesse of Excellency, and the Madame of immortall Honour'. Harvey pictures English Humanity as a kind of court with Mary Pembroke, rather than Elizabeth, as its queen, the 'Verticall Starre' to whom all 'divine Poets, and sweet Oratours' pay their homage. And in doing so, he merely produces a more rhapsodic variation on the theme of courtly humanity that was still strongly represented thirty years later in Aylett's *Peace with her Four Guarders*.

Indeed, all the senses of the word 'humanity' which we have so far discussed – universalist, grammatical, literary – are relatively rare in comparison to the basic synonymity of 'humanity' and 'courtesy'. This was by far the most common sense of the word as it was used by Tudor writers. In fact, 'humanity' was regarded by many late medieval and early Tudor writers as a specifically courtly virtue. In the prologue to Henry Bradshaw's *Life of Saint Radegund* (1525), for example, we are given a description of a Hallowmas feast in a lordly hall, where household and guests 'passe the eventide / after good humanite / In myrthes / in disportes / and liberalite' (sig. A3r). The word 'humanity' seems also to have been used with special reference to 'courtesy in speech'. Alexander Barclay's translation of Domenicus Mancinus's *Mirror of Good Manners* (1518) notes that 'true humanite' is used to keep friends by 'fayre pleasant wordys' (sig. H2v). And in the third of John Fisher's *Three Dialogues* (1558), Will thanks God that 'backbityng, sclaunderyng, or liyng' are not part of the dinner conversations in his household: 'At out table let there be suche humanitie / As becometh his people both livyng and diyng' (sig. F3r). Or again: Hugh Rhodes in his *Book of Nurture* (1577), which is a courtesy book for children and servants, makes the following observation: 'To prate in thy maysters presence, / it is no humanitye: / But to speake, when he talketh to thee, / is good curtesye' (p. 86). This last record is particularly significant. Not only does the word 'humanity' have nothing to do with literature, but the very idea that a literary education might be a courtly requirement never enters the English writer's mind. The word 'humanity' is simply used as a substitute for 'courtesy'. And it is against this background that we need to set our next object of enquiry: 'courtly humanists'.

Courtly humanists (1): Abraham Fleming

The word 'humanist' seems to have been coined by Abraham Fleming in his translation of Virgil's *Georgics* in 1589. The grammatical context is made clear by Fleming's declaration that he has made his version 'to do some good for Grammar Schooles' (sig. A2r). In fact, it was intended as a crib. However, Fleming was also aware that his translation might fall into the hands of more sophisticated readers, whom he asks to bear with the imperfections of his work (sig. A2v):

> The translators meaning is, when occasion serveth, to make this interpretation of his run in round rime, as it standeth now upon bare metre: partly to discharge his sufficiencie, and partly to please the readers fantasie: desiring them to beare with such shifts as they shall see used heere and there for the conveiance of the poets sense in plaine words applied to blunt capacities, considering the expositors drift to consist in delivering a direct order of construction for the releefe of weake Grammatists, not in attempting by curious devise and disposition, to content courtly Humanists.

Fleming's humanists, then, are at the other end of the scale from his 'Grammatists'. This is another coinage, though much less successful, as apparently the word 'grammatist' has never been used since. Its meaning, however, is clear: it represents the Latin word *grammatista*, or 'smatterer in grammer: a meane grammarian' (Cooper, *Thes.*).[10] Given this grammar-school context, it would be very easy to assume that Fleming's humanists are schoolmasters, like Harrington's Hume. But this seems not to be the case. For one thing, Fleming is anxious lest the humanists fault him as a vernacular poet, rather than as a translator; and this is not something one would expect of a grammarian. Moreover, even if we allow that a grammarian would, indeed, be concerned that a crib should accurately convey the sense of the original Latin, Fleming's humanists are only interested in 'curious devise and disposition'. The word 'curious' has two closely related senses here. On the one hand, it means 'carefully made' (Latin *cura*: 'care'). On the other hand, it can also mean 'finical'. If you spend too much care on a thing which does not really deserve so much attention, 'curiosity' becomes a vice associated with waste and idleness. This, I suggest, is what makes Fleming's humanists 'courtly', but the point will need some explanation.

Fleming's translation of Virgil's *Georgics* was printed together with his second version of the Roman poet's *Bucolics*; and certain remarks in the 'Argument' of this text may throw some light on the 'courtliness' of Fleming's humanists. Here, Fleming alludes rather impatiently to 'foolish rime (the nise observation whereof many times darkeneth, corrupteth, perverteth, and falsifieth both the sense and signification)' (sig. A4v). In fact, Fleming uses unrhymed fourteeners in both these new translations of 1589. That is what he means by 'bare metre': his lines scan (roughly), but they are not rhymed. He seems to suggest that the necessities of finding rhyme-words to go at the end of each line may produce distortions in the usual word order of English which might confuse the schoolboy reader. On the other hand, his own fourteeners are rather opaque. Here is the famous opening of the first eclogue: 'O Tityrus thou lieng under shade of spreading beech, / Doost play a countrie song upon a slender oten pipe' (sig. B1r). This extended vocative is not an English construction, but it does loosely follow the order of Virgil's Latin: 'Tityre, tu patulae recubans sub tegmine fagi / silvestrem tenui musam meditaris avena' (*Bucolics*, 1.1–2). Had Fleming wished to follow the Latin word for word, he would then have had to write: 'O Tityrus, thou spreading lying under shade of beech, / Country slender song dost play upon oaten pipe'. Clearly, this would have resulted in gibberish; and in Fleming's earlier translation of the *Bucolics* in 1575, made at a time when he was not so much concerned with prosodic experiment, these lines read much better: 'Thou Tytire' lying at thine ease, under the broade beeche shade, / A country song dost tune right well, in pipe of oate straw made' (sig. C1r). This is still not Elizabethan poetry at its best, but at least he is writing English.

But 'curious device and disposition' is exactly what humanists admired in Latin poetry. Take, for example, John Sturm's *De nobilitate litterata* ('The Literary Education of the Gentry': 1549). Sturm was one of Europe's greatest Protestant scholars and therefore particularly admired in Elizabethan England. The German writer, commenting on the structure of the first four lines of Virgil's first eclogue, observes 'how trimly are they handled, how cunningly are they framed and set togither' (trans. Browne, 1570, sig. E1v).[11] Sturm argues that these lines are constructed 'in manner of a circle: for even as in words, so likewise in things there is *cyclus* and *ergasia cycloeide*, that is to say a circle, or a circlelik handling and setting forth of the matter' (sig. E2r). He even adds an explanatory diagram:

This may not look like a very helpful way of analysing Latin verse to us, but to men like Sturm it was self-evident that the complex syntactic and thematic structures of Virgil's poetry could be made visible and obvious. What Fleming's 'courtly Humanists' want is the same complexity to be put into English verse. Anyone who had been to grammar school would have been familiar with the intricacies of Latin metre, compared to which the metrical principles of English poetry seemed crude and simple, as Attridge reminds us (1974, p. 89):

> One difference would be immediately apparent to him: lines of English verse had no metre, as he understood it; there was no complex pattern of syllables of different types, and hence no intellectual pleasure to be gained from observing how the pattern was kept and the rules obeyed, and no resulting sense of admiration for the skilful poet who, following the extensive and detailed precepts established by tradition and authority, had made from the loose and disordered flux of words a carefully constructed artefact.

Fleming's humanists, then, want to see 'curious device and disposition' in his translation of the *Georgics* because they appreciate metrical complexity as an essential part of poetry written not only in Greek or Latin, but also in English. But why does there seem to be a connection between Fleming's 'courtly Humanists' and a specifically English poetics? The answer may be found, I suggest, in another text published in 1589: George Puttenham's *Art of English Poesy*.

Courtly humanists (2): George Puttenham

Puttenham's text is exactly what its title states it to be: a detailed description, with copious illustration of every point, of the way poetry is written in English. It is an *ars*: a manual by which a particular skill may be learnt. Moreover, Puttenham's art of English poesy is an avowedly courtly art: it is devoted to the skills required by 'our Courtly Poet' (p. 186). And according to Puttenham, courtiers prefer English 'rhyme' to classical 'metre', despite the reservations of men like Fleming. The Elizabethans knew that when Rome was overrun by Germanic invaders in the middle centuries of the previous millennium, the Latin writers of late antiquity began to compose rhymes under the influence of their Germanic overlords. The learned tended to regard this as a lapse into barbarism. For example, Sturm's friend Roger Ascham, in his immensely influential book on teaching Latin called *The Schoolmaster* (1570), laments that 'all good verses and all good learning' were destroyed by the Goths and Huns, who substituted their own 'rude beggarly ryming' for the rich beauties of classical metre (p. 289). Puttenham is not so appalled by the alteration. True, he has nothing good to say about mediaeval Latin rhyming verse, even at its most 'curious', as in the celebrated poem by 'Hugobald the Monke, who made a large poeme to the honour of Carolus Calvus, every word beginning with *C*, which was the first letter of the kings name, thus, / *Carmina clarisonae Calvis cantate camenae*' (p. 15).[12] This is dismissed, understandably, as a mere 'phantasticall devise' (p. 16). Later on, he observes, when Italy was restored to some measure of order, and Greek scholars from Byzantium arrived in the country, the ancient metres were restored: 'Which neverthelesse did not so prevaile but that the ryming Poesie of the Barbarians remained still in his reputation, that one ['metre'] in the schole, this other ['rhyme'] in Courts of Princes more ordinary and allowable' (p. 12). In other words, Germanic poetics, so despised by Ascham, are still preferred by courtiers, though scholars may amuse themselves with metrical revivals of sapphics and asclepiads and so forth. For Puttenham, the question of 'the Grammaticall versifying of the Greeks and Latines, and . . . whether it might be reduced into our English arte or no' (p. 116) was relatively unimportant, despite the somewhat intemperate criticisms of Ascham and his numerous followers in the metrical camp (including no doubt Fleming). Such issues were 'scholastical toyes': diversions which served to pass the time amongst academically minded poets. But against these, Puttenham sets what he calls 'courtly trifles'.

Not suprisingly, Puttenham, who was interested mainly in poetry as a courtly art, is a great supporter of rhyme. He is by no means overwhelmed by the achievements of the ancients and their metre with its somewhat specious 'musicall numerositie in utterance' (p. 72). Really, he says, there is not much more to their art than this musicality: 'Take this away from them, I meane the running of their feete, there is nothing of curiositie among them more then with us, nor yet so much'. In other words, English rhyme is capable of greater 'curiosity' than Greek and Latin metre, which Puttenham regards as a point in its favour. As if to prove this, Puttenham presents his readers with diagrams of the various stanzas, some of them very complicated indeed. These ineluctably remind us of Sturm's diagrams, as, for example, the simple '*distick*' (p. 89):

$$
\begin{array}{l}
\underline{\hspace{6cm}} \\
\underline{\hspace{6cm}} \Big) \\
\underline{\hspace{6cm}} \\
\underline{\hspace{6cm}} \Big)
\end{array}
$$

But the truly 'courtly' measure of curiosity lies in the figure poem (p. 95):

> Your last proportion is that of figure, so called for that it yelds an ocular representation, your meeters being by good symmetrie reduced into certaine Geometricall figures, whereby the maker is restrained to keepe him within his bounds, and sheweth not onely more art, but serveth also much better for briefenesse and subtiltie of device; and for the same respect are also fittest for the pretie amourets in Court to entertaine their servants and the time withall, their delicate wits requiring some commendable exercise to keepe them from idlenesse.

These poems – which take the shape of eggs, pyramids, lozenges, and so forth – are commended because they are difficult and therefore require more 'art' in their execution.[13] On the other hand, they are also deemed 'fittest' for amorous young ladies at court, so the difficulty is of a delicate and perhaps not very laborious kind. Puttenham, with mischievous piety, asserts that such tasks keep these amorets from 'idlenesse', by which he probably means flirtation or more advanced kinds of sexual dalliance. In other words, writing poems in the shape of a pillar is an activity akin to sewing a particularly complicated flower into a sampler. The difficulty is trivial.

Moreover, these figure poems could still deal with love matters; and Puttenham relates with evident fascination and delight how the Lady Kermesine wrote these verses, pieced out in 'letters of rubies & diamants entermingled', in the shape of a lozenge and gave it to the Emperor of Tartary, Temir Cutzclewe, on his return from conquering the nearby kingdom of Corasoon (p. 98):[14]

Sound,
O Harpe,
Shril lie out
Temir the stout
Rider who with sharpe
Trenching blade of bright steele
Hath made his fiercest foes to feele.
All such as wrought him shame or harme,
The strength of his brave right arme,
Cleaving hard downe unto the eyes
The raw skulles of his enemies,
Much honor hath he wonne,
By doughtie deedes done
In Cora soon
And all the
Worlde
Round.

Kermesine admires Temir's virility as it is violently expressed on the battle-field; and it is worth recalling at this point that Christopher Marlowe's *Tamburlaine* had been presented on the London stage only a year or so before Puttenham's *Art* was published in 1589. The Scythian's adversaries frequently describe him as 'Barbarous and bloody Tamburlaine' (Part 1, line 855); but Zenocrate is won over to his manly vigour, though without quite the relish shown by Kermesine. But my point here is that Puttenham proposes as an example of the most curious kind of courtly poetry a piece whose context bears all the marks of barbarism: violence, passion, opulence. Surely this emphasis on the brutal and concupiscent goes counter to any traditional idea of *humanitas* or 'humanity'? In the next chapter we shall see that Roger Ascham certainly thought it did, in his surprisingly harsh criticisms of the Tudor court; but here it may be enough to conclude that courtliness is not always the same as courtesy.

Courtly humanists (3): Gabriel Harvey

Puttenham's example of Kermesine and Temir Cuzclewe is amusingly deviant in terms of the usual conception of literary humanity in its courtly and amorous context. The connection between literary humanism and love poetry may be put down pretty squarely to the courtly inflection of the word 'humanity' which we touched on earlier. It was sanctioned by none other than Count Baldessare Castiglione in his immensely influential courtesy manual *Il Libro del cortegiano* ('The Book of the Courtier': 1528). This is a courtly dialogue on the character and attainments required of the perfect courtier; and at one point, Ludovico da Canossa – 'Count Lewis' in Sir Thomas Hoby's 1561 translation – proceeds as follows (p. 80):

> [Let us] retourne againe unto oure Courtier, whom in letters I will have to bee more then indyfferentlye well seene, at the leaste in those studyes, which they call Humanitie, and to have not only the understandinge of the Latin tunge, but also of the Greeke, because of the many and sundrye thinges that with greate excellencye are written in it. Let him exercise hym selfe in poets, and no lesse in Oratours and Historiographers, and also in writinge both rime and prose, and especially in this our vulgar tunge. For beside the contentation that he shall receive thereby himselfe, he shall by this meanes never want pleasaunt interteinments with women which ordinarylye love such matters.

Here we see a very good example of the tendency for humanity to drift towards courtliness. Count Lewis clearly understands the primary sense of 'humanity' as 'grammar': Latin and Greek. Moreover, the particular disciplines singled out by name are 'literary': poetry and oratory, and, to a lesser extent, history. He does not mention philosophy, say, or medicine or architecture. This makes the transition from literary compositions in the ancient languages to ones written in the modern vernaculars all the smoother; and from there it is but a small step to the accommodation of *litterae humaniores* to the courtly ends of 'interteinments with women'. Indeed, since the English word 'court' (like the contemporary terms *courtiser* in French and *corteggiare* in Italin) meant both 'to act like a courtier' and 'to pay court to a woman' (Bates, 1992, pp. 25–9), the sixteenth-century connection between humanity and flirtation seems almost inevitable.

Certainly, this association underlies Gabriel Harvey's conception of the 'humanist'. We have already seen that he thinks of the humanist as a 'superficial' writer in comparison with the universal erudition of the true poet; and that his expertise in 'witt, pleasant veine, varietie of poetical discourse, & all humanitie' owes as much to the festive as to the universalist dimension of Ciceronian *humanitas*. But in another marginal comment, written, it would appear, about the same time as the one in his copy of *The Survey of the World*, Harvey's humanist reveals he has an amorous side as well. In the notable review of English writers which he wrote on the back page of his copy of Thomas Speght's edition of *The Works of Our Ancient and Learned Poet Geoffrey Chaucer* (1598), Harvey considers the popularity of the authors he likes most (*Marg.*, p. 232):

> Amongst which, the Countesse of Pembrokes Arcadia, & the Faerie Queene ar now freshest in request: & Astrophil, & Amyntas ar none of the idlest pastimes of sum fine humanists.

No names are mentioned, but Harvey is referring to the two poets who were most esteemed by their Elizabethan contemporaries: Sir Philip Sidney and Edmund Spenser. Here it is Sidney who most concerns us, as the author both of *The Countess of Pembroke's Arcadia* (1593) and *Astrophil and Stella* (1590). The first is a prose epic, the second a collection of sonnets and other short lyrics, and this is why 'Astrophil' runs the risk of being described as an 'idle pastime'. Love poetry was traditionally regarded as idle and vain; and Harvey's humanists are attracted to it because it was also a chance for them to display their verbal skills. Can there be any doubt that the 'fine humanists' of this passage are the same as the 'superficial humanists' we have already encountered? They are 'fine', I suggest, because they are more concerned with what we might call the 'finery' of the text than the body of content it surrounds: superficial *verba* as opposed to profound *res*. In other words, they are like Fleming's 'courtly Humanists' with their interest in 'curious device and disposition', or, again, like Puttenham's 'pretie amourets in Court' with their delight in the complexities of the figure poem.[15]

Harvey does not, in principle, have anything against love sonnets. He likes Sidney's *Astrophil and Stella*, and praises its humanity in another marginal comment written in his copy of Speght's *Chaucer*. Harvey praises Chaucer as excellent in 'every veine, & humour'; and proceeds to assert that there is 'none so like him for gallaunt varietie, both in matter, & forme, as Sir Philip Sidney: if all the Exercises which he compiled after Astrophil, & Stella, were consorted in one volume, Works in mie phansie, worthie to be intituled, the flowers of humanitie' (*Marg.*, p. 226). The poems to which Harvey refers would appear to be the lyrics which were added as a sort of appendix to the main sonnet sequence in *Astrophil and Stella*. Perhaps Harvey thought they were sufficiently different in character to be collected as a separate volume called 'The Flowers of Humanity', which would suggest that the sonnets themselves were somewhat weightier and more serious (although that is not obvious). In any case, Harvey might seem to come very near to calling Sidney a 'humanist' in this note. However, Harvey's humanists, whether seen as superficial or fine, are characterised by the trivial ends to which they direct their artistic and general knowledge as poets and scholars. Sidney may well have written a few love sonnets, but he had also written the *Arcadia*, which Harvey placed on a level with the encyclopaedic epic poetry of Homer.[16] But humanists are only interested in lighter productions which display wit and charm and a certain technical facility.

Harvey's ambivalent attitude towards humanity is instructive. It describes a tendency in Elizabethan humanism which we need constantly to keep in mind. The *studia humanitatis* did seem to imply the need for a wide range of knowledge in the writer who would cultivate 'humanity', yet this polyhistorical impulse was offset by the pervasiveness of the courtly ideal of *sprezzatura*, which required that such curious universal scholarship should be kept hidden or treated lightly. As a consequence, Elizabethan humanism occupies a wide range of positions between secular polymathy and amorous trifles, with a tendency to slip from the former to the latter rather than the other way around. In the next chapter we look at the way in which this same tendency can be seen to work in one of the great myths of Renaissance humanism, which explained how modern literary cultures were informed by those of ancient Greece and Rome: *translatio humanitatis*. First we shall look at the positive side of this myth in two works by the mid-Tudor writer Sir Thomas Smith; but we then see how easily this position was reversed by his more well-known friend and colleague Roger Ascham.

Notes

1. For later developments, see Grafton, 1985, pp. 31–47.

2. However, Quintilian does not seem to know the literary sense of the word *humanitas*; for him it means 'kindness' or 'courtesy'. For example, he criticises the schoolboy's habit of applauding every speech made by one of his friends as 'a most unwurthie kynde of humanitye, as thei call it' (2.2.10).

3. The allusion to Varro is also in Aulus Gellius; and cf. *De lingua Latina* ('The Latin Language'), where Varro states that we have pots which both hold our food and also look attractive: 'since the one satisfieth the mere man, and the other his humanitie [*quod aliud homini, aliud humanitate satis est*]' (8.31).

4. Nashe calls him 'Pigmey Dicke' in *Have With You to Saffron Walden* (1596: p. 82).

5. See Harvey's *Letterbook*, p. 166. Actually, he uses the word in its Greek form: πολυ'ιστωρ.

6. For the situation at Cambridge, see Leader, 1988, pp. 108–68 and 235–42 ('Early Humanism'). For Oxford, see Fletcher, 1986, pp. 157–200, and McConica, 1986, pp. 693–721. Literature was taught mainly at the college level, rather than in university lectures, providing a kind of alternative curriculum (see Fletcher, 1986, p. 180). See also Curtis, 1959, and Kearney, 1970.

7. It is interesting to note that the first record of the word 'philologer' in the *Oxford English Dictionary* (*OED*) is in the sentence from Harvey's *Discursive Problem* already cited; and that the two other early modern records quoted establish a very clear connection with humanism: 'that renown'd Humanitian and Philologer' (1659); '*Philologer*, and Humanist, a Man of Letters' (1706).

8. *OED* ('humanist', 3) dates the earliest instance of such usage around 1670.

9. Richard Stanyhurst, 'The History of Ireland', in Raphael Holinshed, ed., *The Chronicles of England, Scotland and Ireland* (London, 1577), fol. 24b. Stanyhurst also mentions 'Robert Joise, borne in Kilkennie, a good humanitian' (fol. 41b) and 'Andrew White, a good humanitian, a pretie philosopher' (fol. 44a).

10. Suetonius tells us that the difference between the *grammaticus* and the *grammatista* is that the former is an 'absolute maister' and the latter 'but meanly learned' (*De gram.*, §4).

11. Browne translates these lines thus: '*O happie art thou Tityrus, / that under Beechen tree, / Thy song in Pipe of slender Ote, / doste sounde with voyce so free*' (sig. E1v).

12. The poem goes on for 146 lines . . . For the amusing alliterative antics of Hucbald (840–930) and other poets, see the chapter 'Formal mannerisms' in Curtius, 1948, pp. 282–91.

13. One is tempted to see a mannerist influence in Puttenham's poetics. Shearman notes, for example, the importance of *difficultà* to Italian artists of the sixteenth century, and the *virtù* required to overcome such obstacles with *grazia* (1967, pp. 19–22). But he also observes that it was important for the effort expended on such labours to be *invisible*, whereas Puttenham wants his eggs and lozenges to show 'more art' rather than less. This complicates the picture of Puttenham as a courtly theorist, since, as Shearman observes, it was through Castiglione's *Courtier* that the mannerist terms just cited gained general circulation, along with the more familiar term *sprezzatura* ('carelessness, insouciance, nonchalance').

14. The words 'shrillie' and 'Corasoon' are split in half in the original, presumably to make the figure more symmetrical.

15. It is perhaps worth noting that Harvey's much-admired Spenser wrote a set of sonnets called *Amoretti* (1595). The word *amoret* could mean 'amiable girl' (Spenser has a character by this name in *The Fairy Queen*); but it also was a word for 'love sonnet'.

16. In his fulsome praise of Sidney in *Pierce's Supererogation*, Harvey exclaims, 'if Homer be not at hand . . . you may read his furious Iliads, & cunning Odysses' in Sidney's *Arcadia* (sig. G3v).

CHAPTER FOUR

The Translation of Humanity:
Thomas Smith and Roger Ascham

Ciceronian *humanitas* provided Elizabethan humanism with many, if not most, of its basic concepts and positions, but it was unable to supply the Elizabethans with one of their most important cultural myths: 'The Renaissance'.[1] It was an axiom of Elizabethan humanism that literature and learning – *bonae litterae* – were destroyed when the Germanic nations swept across the ancient world in the middle centuries of the first millennium. It was only with Petrarch and his followers in Italy that the *studia humanitatis* were rediscovered and 'reborn'. However, the relation between the *humanitas* of the old Mediterranean world and the new nation states of central Europe and the Atlantic seaboard could also be seen as a cultural equivalent of the political *translatio imperii*, or 'transference of sovereignty'. After the fall of Troy, sovereignty moved westwards to Rome, whose imperial destiny was legitimated by the myth that Aeneas, the founder of the Roman dynasty, was himself a princely Trojan refugee. After the fall of Rome, sovereignty moved westwards again, and northwards, to suit the imperial ambitions of the various modern European states. The legendary basis for the second phase of the *translatio* was already in place in the form of myths which claimed that Aeneas was not the only Trojan prince who escaped the fall of his city to found a new nation. For example, Britain takes its name (so the legend went) from Aeneas's great-grandson, Brutus, who landed at Totnes in Devon around 1100 BC. Cornish was thought by some to be a descendant of the tongue of the Trojan colonists (the county was supposed to take its name from Brutus's lieutenant Corineus). And the old name for London, as every Elizabethan schoolboy knew, was Troynovant: 'New Troy'. This legendary British history was coming under attack in the sixteenth century, but it still held a powerful grip on the literary imagination of Tudor and Elizabethan writers, partly, one suspects, because it well accorded with the idea of what we may call a *translatio humanitatis*. Here is a typical statement of the theme from Gabriel Harvey's *Pierce's Supererogation* (sigs. B4v–C1r):

> It is not long, since the goodlyest graces of the most-noble Commonwealthes upon Earth, Eloquence in speech, and Civility in manners, arrived in these remote parts of the world: it was a happy revolution of the heavens . . . when Tiberis flowed into the Thames; Athens removed to London; pure Italy, and fine Greece planted themselves in rich England; Apollo with his delicate troupe of Muses, forsooke his old mountaines, and rivers; and frequented a new Parnassus, and another Helicon, nothinge inferiour to the olde, when they were most solemnely haunted of divine wittes, that taught Rhetorique to speake with applause, and Poetry to sing with admiration. But even since that flourishing transplantation of the daintiest, and sweetest lerning, that humanitie ever tasted; Arte did but springe in such, as Sir John Cheeke, and M. Ascham: and witt budd in such, as Sir Phillip Sidney, & M. Spencer.

This passage captures very well the mythic dimension of the *translatio humanitatis*. Harvey does not mention the tedium of the grammar-school exercises on which the translation of humanity was really based; but he sees it as a mysterious relocation of England at the centre of the literary cosmos. Nor is it merely literary. The useful phrase 'Eloquence in speech, and Civility in manners' reminds us that Harvey saw the process in terms of a *translatio humanitatis ac litterarum* in the usual sense of the Ciceronian formulation. But most importantly for our present purposes, Harvey sees the translation of humanity and letters as having occurred fairly recently. The references to mid-Tudor scholars such as Cheke and Ascham would suggest that humanity arrived in England in the 1530s and 1540s. We do not have space in this study to touch on the interesting figure of Sir John Cheke, but we shall look in detail at the works of Roger Ascham, especially his seminal treatise *The Schoolmaster* (1570). But let us begin with the third member of what was actually a trio of brilliant young Cambridge scholars: Sir Thomas Smith. Ascham's comments in *The Schoolmaster* on the persistence of 'Gothic' ignorance well into his own day are well known, but Smith's more positive account of the *translatio humanitatis* deserves wider attention as well.

Sir Thomas Smith and the *translatio humanitatis*

Sir Thomas Smith was an extraordinary man. Nowadays he is best known as a 'commonweal humanist' by virtue of two works on economics and politics: *A Discourse of the Commonweal of This Realm of England* (ms. 1565; printed 1581) and *De republica Anglorum* ('The Commonweal of England':

1583).[2] Nor was his counsel on such matters merely academic: Smith held important positions in government under Edward VI and Elizabeth I. He was (in the words of his biographer): 'A Tudor Intellectual in Office'.[3] But he was also a 'polymathic humanist', a genuine polyhistor with interests in 'astronomy, architecture, natural phenomena, drugs, and medicines' (Dewar, 1964, p. 15). Not surprisingly, he was much admired by his younger kinsman Gabriel Harvey, who, upon Smith's death, wrote a sequence of elegies called *Smithus; vel Musarum lachrymae* ('Smith; or, The Tears of the Muses': 1578). One by one the Muses of the several arts come on to lament the loss of their well-beloved son, and Calliope notes that Smith was 'Much-Knowing' (sig. D3r [MP]).[4] Finally, Smith was also a 'grammatical humanist': he was much concerned with the establishment of *humanitas* in English literature and learning at a more-or-less academic and scholarly level. This is the Smith who mainly concerns us here, and especially as the author of two books published in Paris in 1568: *De recta et emendata linguae Graecae pronuntiatione dialogus* ('The Correct and Improved Pronunciation of Greek'); and *De recta et emendata linguae Anglicae scriptione dialogus* ('The Correct and Improved Writing of English'). Both texts tell us much about contemporary attitudes towards the *translatio humanitatis*.

The *De linguae Anglicae scriptione* is a dialogue between two characters called Smithus and Quintus. Unsurprisingly, Smith (for so I shall translate his name) does most of the talking; but it is Quintus who initiates the conversation by remarking on a discussion on the topic of English orthography he has had with a certain Obstinatus, who justifies the lack of system in the way English is spelt on the grounds of custom and tradition. This allows Smith to launch into a spirited attack on intellectual conservatism. He believes that English orthography was once a perfect art, but that it has since degenerated due to the disturbances brought on by waves of invasions from the Saxons to the Normans. In other words, the history of English follows the same pattern as the history of Latin and Greek: it is involved in the general decline and fall of an ancient tradition of literature and learning. But Smith begins his discourse by going back to the very earliest days of literary *humanitas*.

He explains that the writing was originally hieroglyphic: 'certaine Characters and rude likenesses of Beastes, Foules, and Serpentes' (p. 44). But then 'sharpe minds' perceived that an alphabetic system would be more efficient; and so the art of letters was devised. Smith notes the improvement, and goes on to observe how different cultures have adapted various alphabets in order to make them fit their own languages more exactly (p. 46):

> The Latines, though in the first place, they toke on and accepted the letters [*litterae*] of the Grekes, there being mingled amongst them settlers and

Colonistes of the Arcadians and Troyans, from whiche they chefely learned their humanitie [*humanitas*]; yet, because their own soundes were different, they also toke on other divers letters, more proper to these soundes, and yet agreeing in manie other places with those of the Grekes.

Humanitas ac litterae: the familiar Ciceronian collocation is given a new variation here. Smith takes us back to the very dawn of Roman culture, when the Latins did not even have letters, far less literature; and these letters are clearly viewed as part of the *translatio humanitatis* from Greece (and Troy) to Italy.

Smith continues: 'Those rude Ages were contented to be tought, and cast away their wretched & penurious Acornes, which they were used to feed on, once Corne was by them discovered'. The allusion here is to another important literary *topos*: The Golden Age. According to ancient mythology, there have been several races of humankind, each with its own age: Golden, Silver, Bronze, Iron. We live in the Iron Age, which is marked by wickedness and impiety of every kind. But in the Golden Age, under the rule of Saturn, men and women lived in peace and plenty. According to the first book of Ovid's *Metamorphoses* (8 AD), the men and women of the Golden Age lived in ease (*otium*). They did not need to work because they lived on the fruits of the land: cherries, strawberries, brambles – and 'acornes dropt on ground from Joves brode tree' (1.105; trans. Golding, 1564–7, p. 23). Ironically, it was Jove who put an end to all this. He killed his father Saturn and introduced burning summer and freezing winter. Men and women of the Silver Age now had to build houses where they had once lived in caves; and to cultivate the land to grow corn, where once they cheerfully subsisted on berries.

There are two ways of looking at this alteration. Usually, the passage from the Golden to the Silver Age is represented as a loss of innocent bliss. It can be seen, particularly, as a fall from leisure to work: *otium* to *negotium*. On the other hand, it could also be represented as a necessary first step towards full humanity. After all, the men and women of the Golden Age could be seen, retrospectively, as pursuing a life not much different from that of the beasts of the field. This would have been Crassus's view. He sees the early phase of human history as marked by the 'beastlie life of the wildernes', from which men and women were led by the heroic orator to 'this cultivated state of civil humanitie' (*De orat.*, 1.32–3). Smith also sees the myth in this light (p. 18):

Great Jupiter, Father of Goddes & men, so the Poetes saye, compelled mortals to the learning of Artes; and thou seest, Quintus, how all Artes be brought to perfection by litle & litle, and slowlie, by intervals of times and whole Ages;

61

whereas, if in the meane time, they had not so proceded, they would have remained rude & simple by the like proporcion; as the first men lived in content upon Acornes.

But later on they progressed to bread; and they came to drink beer and wine as well as water. So, too, he argues, should English writers proceed to a more sophisticated orthography; and he produces the example of the early Latins to show that the predecessors of the illustrious Romans also had to work towards perfection rather than simply make do with what they had. Here, then, we see the positive aspect of the *translatio humanitatis ac litterarum*.

But Smith is also very much aware that just as a system of orthography may be perfected by the addition of new letters to cover different sounds, so it may be impaired by the reverse process. Once he has completed his survey of the sounds of English and their correct representation by the letters taken from the Roman and Greek alphabets, Smith reveals that there is still a deficiency: 'Certaine English soundes ther be, which even now, are merely vagrant, and wander without a seat or home' (p. 136). Smith turns out to have made a close inspection of certain ancient Anglo-Saxon books, where he has noted the use of the letters thorn (þ) and edh (ð) to represent the sounds now written *th* in modern English. Why have these sounds been lost? Quintus has read that when Greece and Rome first began to feel the impact of the barbarian invasions, there was an exodus of scholars to Britain (p. 140):

> Godly men, which were lovers of ease & pietie & good letters, fled unto this Ilande, as being most remote from all those evils, whiche were than felt keenly in the main land & Continent; so that for long tyme afterwardes, Greke & Latine letters flourished amongst us, whilst in the meane time, in Rome and Athenes, and in all partes of Italie and Greece . . . their own verie tongs began, by litle & litle, to growe barbarous & perish awaye.

Ease, piety, letters: Ciceronian *humanitas* is itself given a Golden Age inflection by the addition of *pietas* to *otium* and *litterae*. It was at this period that the English alphabet was perfected, with the invention of letters like edh and thorn to represent sounds which did not occur in Greeek and Latin.

But the survival of ancient humanity in Anglo-Saxon England did not last long. Eventually, the tidal wave of barbarism reached the distant British Isles. Smith now picks up the tale (pp. 140, 142):

> Scithians, whom we now call Scottes, seized & occupied one parte of our land, and Pictes, Danes, Northemen, and Swethlanders, like a Tempest, or a

Clowde of Locustes, overwhelmed all the land, and for longe yeres vexed it; being at the first, peoples which knew not Christ, and were extremely barbarous; for they drew off [*haurire*] from us our Christian faith & all good letters, which by meanes of these troubles & vexations, by litle & litle, began to perish awaye amongst us also.

Quintus relates how *litterae* were 'translated' to England by refugees from the collapse of the Roman Empire; now Smithus tells us that they were taken away again, together with the true Christian faith, by invaders who were both pagan and barbarian. It was a commonplace of Reformation humanism, of course, that Roman Catholicism was a degenerate form of Christianity, not much better than paganism; in other words, it was the equivalent in divinity of the 'Dark Ages' of humanity. As far as Smith is concerned, English letters, in the strictest sense, have never recovered from these attacks, because the old Anglo-Saxon characters have not yet been restored to their rightful place, but still wander without a home. Nor will they be rehabilitated until unregenerate conservatives like Obstinatus cease to cling so stubbornly to long-established convention.

This resistance to innovation is also the great impediment which stands in the way of Smith's reforms in the *De linguae Graecae pronuntiatione*. Smith's interest in the reform of Greek pronunciation goes back to the mid-1530s, when he and Cheke, having read Erasmus on the topic, adopted his views and began to use the new way of speaking Greek in their own lectures at Cambridge. It seems that the younger scholars, and one or two older ones as well, were also won over to the new pronunciation, which was supposed to be more like the one used by the ancient Greeks themselves. But it also met with a great deal of resistance, and eventually the chancellor of the University, Bishop Stephen Gardiner, spoke against it and banned its use in an edict of 1542. The *De linguae Graecae pronuntiatione* is Smith's response, in the form of a carefully argued letter to Gardiner. However, Gardiner was not impressed and told Smith to press on with his new career as a civil lawyer, and to abandon such 'trivialities' (cit. Danielsson, 1978, p. 213). Smith took the hint, and dropped the matter; but he kept his papers and published them a quarter of a century later.

The central concern of *De linguae Graecae pronuntiatione* lies in the revival of the ancient pronunciation of Greek. It is thus a typical document of the Renaissance recovery of antiquity; and Smith tells the usual story of the 'organic' rise and fall of the ancient tongues (p. 46):

The Latine & Greke tongs, first brought forth rough & hardy Orators, and uncouth & as it were, unkempt [*horridulus*] words; presently, however, in the prime of age, these bore all that we have which is soft, witty, swete, choice,

pleasaunt, pure, and trim; therupon folowed hoary eld, & the tongs were seen
to bear forwithered fruit: wordes folish & idle, figures inept, speche stammer-
ing like a folishe boy, or gabling halfe-barbarouslie. At the laste, Turckes &
Scithians, Gothes & Vandals, Quadians & Heruliyans, and all the great flood
of the barbarous nations, like a winters storm, crueller still then Boreas bitter
blast, rooted them up by stock and by braunch, yea, even the very trunckes
of these two tongs were torn up and cast downe.

Smith extends his georgic metaphor of language as a kind of fruit tree by
explaining how words were nonetheless stored: 'Learned men, longe time
ago, busily gathered up the words of olden tyme, each in his proper season
in the long year, as it wer, of those antique ages, in bookes, like thriftie
householders, who take their berries, & corne, & Vintage, to cellars, &
grain-houses, & caves, and there store them up'. The classical canon is thus
a great storehouse of the preserved fruits of classical Latin and Greek,
permanent now and immutable, whatever might have happened to the
languages in the aftermath of the barbarian invasions. So, Smith argues,
when we read Sophocles or Plato or Isocrates, we should read them not
with a modern Greek pronunciation, far less a modern French or Italian
one, but in a way which as closely as possible reproduces the ancient pronunciation which was used by the writers themselves. It is not, perhaps, a
particularly good argument (Gardiner made short work of it). But it speaks
with force and sincerity to the Renaissance humanist's reverence for antique literature and learning.

Smith wants what he and others see as the original pronunciation of
classical Greek to be revived; and he uses as a precedent the success with
which classical Latin has been substituted for medieval Latin in scholarly,
diplomatic and political writing. Smith praises the Italian scholar Laurentius
Valla for rediscovering the storehouse of pure Latinity and restoring correct
usage in his *Elegantiae linguae Latinae* ('Refinements of the Latin Tongue':
1441–9); then he alters the allegory to fit Christ's revival of Lazarus (p. 54):[5]

He raised from the grave the first born brother, not merely four dayes dead
& buried, but four hundreth yeares, and brought him back to the light; an
ordinarie citisen & private man, this Valla settled this brother rightfully in the
estate of his fathers, and in his special seat & as it were castle, of his honour
& dignitie; and he, who had passed him selfe off as his younger brother, and
for so manie yeares, and with the common consent of nighe all the worlde,
fiercely had seized & occupied the schools and lecturehalls, the lawcourtes &
Tribunalls, bokes & Houses of the Muses, and al publique platformes; him, I
saye, this Valla did prove of adulterous & base birth, spoiling him of all
honour & dignitie; and were it not, that he hid him selfe in the formulationes
of Lawyers, and in certaine olde libraries, under the shadowe of use, and

former majestie, as though behind the ladders stuffed into the booths, indeede, he would nowadayes be no where to be sene.

These are brave words. In fact, the new Latin (or the old, pristine Latin, as Smith saw it) had not triumphed quite so completely at Cambridge. More precisely, not everyone wished to see the great medieval writers dismissed in the brusque way proposed by Smith.[6] They might themselves write in a more or less 'Ciceronian' style, but they were quite happy to read Aquinas and Sacroboscus and Rogerus Baconus in the non-classical Latin in which their treatises were originally written. Moreover, they were suspicious of innovation, especially when it seemed (as it often was) motivated more by stylistic than by intellectual considerations. What Smith prizes most in classical Latin seems to be 'all that we have which is soft, witty, swete, choice, pleasaunt, pure, and trim' (p. 46).[7] But he makes no mention of its value as an instrument of cogitation.

Smith, of course, presents any resistance to his own proposals as an indication of the lingering influence of the savage younger brother. He says it is absurd that a 'barbarous custome should be helde Sacrosanct in a schole of humanitie & learning [*humanitas & doctrina*]' (p. 100). Moreover, he intimates that the ferocity with which the younger brother usurped literary and intellectual culture in the first place has left its mark on his opponents. Smith cites the Greek philosopher Epictetus to the effect that there are always two ways ('handles') in which you can treat a person with whom you are not in agreement: kindly or spitefully. He explains (p. 106):

> This Wiseman judgeth, that what stands betwixt Philosophers and those who are entirely *Apaideutoi*, or devoide of learning, and rudely ignorant of all humanitie and good letters [*humanitas ac bonae litterae*], is this: that Philosophers alwayes take any matter by the Right & better handle, and so feel less vexations, and bear all thinges with Equanimitie, and an even grace ... Contrariwise, saith he, they which be inurbane & rustical, and *Apeirokaloi*, which is to say, Ignoraunt of bewtie, usually seise that other handle, whence issues scoffs, strifes, emnities, hostile thoughts, and deadlie hates.

It is crucial, Smith concludes, to conduct debate with 'humanitie & grace' (p. 108). We would all agree; and Harvey underlined this phrase, adding in the margin: 'The handle of humaniti [*ansa humanitatis*], not savageri, is to be grasped'.

For Smith, then, the *translatio humanitatis* is not exactly a cultural *fait accompli*; at least, he is not truly certain whether such an event has yet taken place in England. It is rather a rhetorical *topos* ('standard theme') to be used in literary controversy. Smith finds it convenient to manipulate the familiar narrative of the decline and revival of ancient *humanitas* in order to make his opponents look boorish; but he fails to make his case for the old pronunciation on this basis. This can be simply demonstrated by his inability to prove that the ancient pronunciation was more refined than the modern. Smith has to argue that the Greeks became degenerate in the last centuries of antiquity: 'more barbarous in manners, tong, & race'. Therefore, they cannot possibly have been 'more urbane & exquisite, in their care & cultivation of the true and natural sounde of Greke letters' (p. 142). But words do not have a 'natural sounde' (as he concedes elsewhere).[8] Smith asserts that it is better to pronounce certain combinations of letters as diphthongs because it makes speech have a 'fuller, richer, & fatter sounde' (p. 152). Gardiner flatly contradicts him: diphthongs are marked by 'coarseness and lack of refinement' (cit. Danielsson, 1978, p. 211). Ultimately, Smith fails to make his case because he has no real evidence. Perhaps this accounts for the impatience with which he occasionally treats his opponents. His genuine desire to embrace the civil aspects of *humanitas* as well as the eloquent and learned ones makes him adopt a persona which displays more gentleness and consideration than he appears to have possessed in life: 'Smith was mercurial in temperament, rash and impetuous, incredibly insensitive to other people' (Dewar, 1964, p. 6). In other words, Smith embodies in his own person the conflicts and tensions which surrounded the *translatio humanitatis* in mid-Tudor England. His own tendency to be hasty and intransigent was one of the reasons why other men such as Gardiner resisted him and his partisanship of the new learning. So it is even with Roger Ascham, who is usually regarded as a most genial writer: 'everyone's friend' (Lewis, 1954, p. 279). So he is for the most part. But talking about *humanitas* often brings out the worst in the humanist: it is too close to his heart for him always to be witty and charming when he sees it threatened or scorned.

Roger Ascham: Ciceronian and Valerian *humanitas*

Sir Thomas Smith is still a relatively unfamiliar figure to most students of Elizabethan literature; but with Roger Ascham we come to the only Elizabethan humanist who has achieved any kind of lasting posterity in literary history. His reputation rests now almost entirely on a single work: *The Schoolmaster*. This unfinished treatise on 'The Bringing Up of Youth' and 'The Ready Way to the Latin Tongue' displays a markedly Ciceronian humanism. For example, it is peppered with allusions to the *De oratore*; and the prelude, in which Ascham relates how the book came to be written, is even modelled on the *mise en scène* of Cicero's dialogue. Ascham was present at a dinner in Sir William Cecil's chamber in 1563, when the court lay at Windsor Castle. Most of the other guests were important statesmen, but this was no council meeting (p. 175):

> M. Secretarie [Cecil] hath this accustomed maner, though his head be never so full of most weightie affaires of the Realme, yet, at diner time he doth seeme to lay them alwaies aside: and findeth ever fitte occasion to taulke pleasantlie of other matters, but most gladlie of some matter of learning: wherein, he will curteslie heare the minde of the meanest at his Table.

Negotium is followed by *otium*: 'What might be in times of idlenes, more plesaunt, or more proper to humanitie, than elegant speche & conversation, that is in no thinge rude nor unlearned' (Cicero, *De orat.*, 1.32). The talk turns to good and bad schoolmasters; and so the seed of Ascham's book was sown. And the *humanitas ac litterae* exemplified in the conversation over dinner at Windsor spills over into Ascham's digressive, anecdotal, familiar style in *The Schoolmaster*. It really does read like a genial scholar talking informally about a topic close to his heart.

However, Ascham's humanism is not merely Ciceronian; it is also characterised by an emphasis on 'clemency' derived ultimately from Valerius Maximus's *Facta et dicta memorabilia* ('Memorable Deeds and Sayings': 31 AD). This is a collection of almost one thousand historical anecdotes arranged under various headings. It was a commonplace book, then, intended for use by Roman orators and students of rhetoric. Not surprisingly, Valerius was an invaluable treasure-house of useful material to later writers as well, especially in the Middle Ages and Renaissance, from which period 'more manuscripts of the *Memorable Deeds and Sayings* survive than of any other Latin prose text, save the Bible' (Bloomer, 1992, p. 2). The fifth book of the *Facta et dicta* begins with a chapter headed 'Humanity and Clemency'. Now clemency is not a nuance which is much to the forefront of Ciceronian *humanitas*; but there is good reason why it should be in Valerius's view of the world. Ciceronian *humanitas* takes its character from the old Roman upper class, when 'the *homines* were those who held the highest power in the state, and so realised the most free and independent kind of *humanitas*' (Rieks, 1967, p. 69). But Valerius dedicated his book to the emperor Tiberius, by which time 'an abyss had suddenly yawned between the monarch, a mighty superman raised almost to the level of a god, and the people, who were now merely subjects' (ibid.). It is now that the philosophical sense which Cicero gives the word *humanitas* in the *De officiis* comes to the fore. The elevation of the *divus imperator* produced a corresponding abasement of all Roman citizens as 'merely human'. Not surprisingly, the fullest development of the inclusive sense of *humanitas* was elaborated (by Seneca) under the degenerate god-emperors Caligula and Nero (Rieks, 1967, pp. 89–137). This *humanitas* was applied to such almighty men when they condescended to acknowledge that they shared a common nature with their subjects, or with the rest of the world in general.

Valerian *humanitas* may be seen as a particular virtue of the powerful, then; and the concept found its way into the literature of Renaissance thought, particularly, though in moderated form, into the language of patronage, where it combined to a certain extent with Ciceronian humanism as well. Typical is the Oxford scholar Laurence Humphrey's insistence in his *Optimates* (Latin, 1560; trans. anon., 1563) that as the nobleman is superior in rank to his inferiors, so should he be 'more lowly, humble, and gentle [*humaniorem*]' (p. 148, sig. H6v). In particular, he should display his humanity in affable conversation with such persons: 'Curtesye [*humanitas*] requireth easie speech, civile companye, friendly pleasant and courteous talke' (p. 262, sig. Q6v). Here is the voice of Cicero, of course; but a line or two earlier Humphrey has noted that nothing makes a nobleman more amicable than 'mercy or curtesye [*humanitas ac clementia*]'. One can almost see Humphrey at work with his commonplace book open at the heading 'Humanitas'. Here he adds a little Cicero, there a little Valerius, harmonising the different shades of meaning that attach themselves to the word *humanitas* in these two very different writers. Indeed, Humphrey may have other senses of the word in mind as well, such as the rather vague definition given by Sir Thomas Elyot in his *Book Named the Governor* (1531).[9]

Elyot was an early commonweal writer, who busied himself mainly with useful translations and compilations of ancient moral philosophy; he also made a Latin–English dictionary. But his most famous work deals with the skills and virtues required in men of the governing class. Elyot devotes a chapter (1.8) to 'The Three Principal Parts of Humanity', which begins quite usefully (p. 147):

> The nature and condition of man, wherin he is lasse than god almightie, and exellinge nat withstanding all other creatures in erthe, is called humanitie; whiche is a generall name to those vertues in whome semeth to be a mutuall concorde and love in the nature of man.

However, Elyot goes on to state that these three parts – benevolence, beneficence, liberality – actually make up not 'humanity' but 'benignitie or gentilnes'. Perhaps it was Elyot's facility with synonyms and shades of meaning that led him to lexicography; but the relative vagueness with which he uses the word 'humanity' is typical of his time. He reminds us that Cicero states that the most honourable virtues are 'mercy and placabilitie'; and that the opposite vice is 'ire, called vulgarely wrathe, a vice moste ugly and ferrest from humanitie' (p. 136). Here Elyot makes a plausibly Valerian connection between mercy, placability and humanity. And in the same passage in which Humphrey combines Ciceronian and Valerian notions of conversational and clement *humanitas*, he also notes that as the nobleman is ranked higher than others, so he should treat them with all the more 'lenitye & curtesye [*placabilitas & humanitas*]'.

Ascham's Latin correspondence is full of praise for this kind of *humanitas*. But when he actually comes to define the word *humanitas*, he strikes out on his own course. It occurs in a letter of 1553 to one of his lifelong patrons, Sir William Paget. Ascham is writing to thank Paget for persuading Queen Mary to renew a valuable annuity; he is understandably generous in his praise:[10]

> But in a universall Chorus of praises of your Wit, & Learnyng, Experience, & Industrie, and in the most courtious sweetness of manner, no Vertue of yours shineth out more brightlie, than that, which, since it is most proper to humankind, is called Humanitie [*humanitas*]. This Vertue takes its name from the word *Homo*, yet, trewlie, it is cherished by GOD, to whose Goodnesse it seemeth particularlie to belong; and ever when I perceive, how by verie Nature, your own will is disposed to deal kindlie with all men, I esteme & judge this prayse to belong not to your Humanitie, but to a certaine Divine Nature [MP].

Ascham liked the paradox that *humanitas* was really a token of divinity. He also uses it in letters written at the same time to other patrons: Gardiner and Cecil. Perhaps we should see a Valerian source for the conceit.

Cicero frequently uses the notion of a divine gift to distinguish exceptionally talented men from the common rout, but the exaltation of the emperors to the status of a *divus* is far in advance of anything the republican Cicero could have contemplated; and 'mere humanity' took on a quite different conceptual complexion:

> Mere existence became quite important to the indivual once more, protection against the overwhelming forces of fate and state. A new solidarity based on human vulnerability was experienced. The component of *philanthropia*, of the *clementia* within *humanitas*, which was not decisive in Cicero's time, now came to the fore. It meant an indulgent leniency, a benevolent forbearance, a friendly condescension on the part of the powerful towards those who were hopelessly and often guiltily cast down before them: Winner and Loser; Survivor and Corpse; Magnate and Supplicant – *divus princeps* and *homo*.
>
> (Rieks, 1967, p. 69)

Valerius's anecdotes all tend to emphasise this gap; but several make it clear that *humanitas* is not simply a gesture of kindness, but an acknowledgement of humankind on the part of the mighty, however much they may be flattered as 'divine'. We learn, for example, how Lucius Cornelius buried the body of an enemy general: 'believing that his Victory would be the less envied both by Gods and Men, when there was so much of Humanity mix'd with it' (5.1.2, p. 204). But the most famous act of clement *humanitas* is the behaviour of Julius Caesar towards the corpse of his rival Pompey the Great, after he had been treacherously murdered by the Egyptian boy-king Ptolemy, who presented Pompey's head to Caesar as a token of his loyal esteem. Caesar wept, and buried the head with great ceremony: 'For if the mind of that divine Prince had not been so tender, He that a little before was accompted the Pillar of the Roman Empire (so Fortune turns the scales of Humane Affairs [*mortalium negotia*]) had lain uninterr'd' (5.1.10, p. 209). In fact, Caesar was deified only after his death in 44 BC, but Valerius manages to convey the impression that this official apotheosis was a mere ratification of his innate divinity (Caesar claimed descent from Venus); and his *divinitas* is clearly proved here by his *humanitas*.

However, Ascham's application of the paradox to Paget and the others lacks the gravity it has in the *Facta et dicta*. Ciceronian humanism has many affinities with comedy, not least its emphasis on wit, but also in its conviviality and festiveness. Valerian humanism, on the other hand, is predicated on the existence of a tragic world of death and disorder. Caesar displays his *divinitas* and *humanitas* at once by not acting like a tyrant or a savage or a beast. He could have crowed over his fallen adversary and stuck his head on a pole for birds to peck at. Lesser men, it is suggested, would have insulted Pompey's corpse. But the temptation does not arise in Caesar's case because he is 'divinely humane'. Hence the force of Valerius's rather audacious use of Rome's great enemy Hannibal as an example of *humanitas*. When Marcellus was killed, Hannibal buried him decently: 'And therefore the sweetness of Humanity penetrates into the very breasts of rude Barbarians, mollifies the cruel and severe eyes of Enemies, and bends the most insolent pride of Victory' (5.1. ex. 6, p. 213). Was the 'barbarian' Hannibal a *divus princeps* as well?

Ascham grafts this tragic aspect of Valerian *humanitas* on to Cicero's myth of progress towards a *humanus cultus civilisque* in his *Report and Discourse of the Affairs and State of Germany* (1570). This he wrote in 1553, on his return from three years spent on diplomatic business at the court of the Holy Roman Emperor, Charles V. Here he records his impressions of the main characters in the troubled political drama to which he was witness, and also offers many interesting reflections on the lessons to be learnt from various events. The political philosophy he brought with him was clearly based on Cicero's teachings in the *De officiis*, although he cites as his source a letter written by another man of letters and diplomat: 'old Syr Thomas Wiat' (p. 128). According to Wyatt: 'the greatest mischief amongest men and least punished is vnkyndnes'.[11] By 'unkindness' we should understand 'unnatural behaviour', in other words, a sundering of the bonds of common humanity upon which civil society is founded. Left unchecked, unkindness leads to the atrocious acts of cruelty which stand at the heart of Tudor tragedy, as exemplified in a play roughly contemporary with Ascham's *Report*, Thomas Sackville and Thomas Norton's *Gorboduc* (1561, pr. 1565). Here we see Britain reduced to ruins as a result of actions which go 'against all course of kinde' (1.1.11). Ascham, too, reports how he has 'sene here by experience' the tragic effects of unkindness between the various princes involved in the tumults he witnessed. What particularly appals him is the ease with which supposedly enlightened Christians can degenerate to brutal inhumanity.

Ascham makes it plain that it was the Turks who started off the spiral of depravity by treacherously slaughtering the population of Tripoli; but he also concedes that the Christians were no better once roused (p. 131):

> This Turkish crueltie was revenged this last yeare in Hungary, when lyke promise of lyfe was made, and yet all put to the sword[,] the Christians bidding the Turkes remember Tripoly. To such beastly crueltie the noble feates of armes be come unto betwixt the Christen men and the Turkes.

Ascham goes on to relate how the Turks slowly cut a Christian prisoner to pieces, feeding the bits to hungry mastiffs. The men who were sent to ransom him were forced to endure this gory spectacle; they returned with the news, and, when three Turks were captured by the Hungarians, the original torment was varied with devilish ingenuity. They were cut up and fed to the pigs: 'because ye Turkes will eate no swines flesh, you shall see if swine will eate any Turkishe fleshe'. This is worse than anything in *Gorboduc*; though one is reminded of the scene in *Tamburlaine* where the Turkish emperor Bajazeth is commanded by his Scythian conqueror to eat his own flesh (Part 1, 4.4). But in Ascham's account, we see Christians behaving with exactly the same 'beastly cruelty' that they conventionally deplored in their Muslim adversaries.

Here Ascham has reversed the import of Valerius's example of Hannibal, which opened up the possibility that Romans and barbarians might be united (at least at the princely level) by a common *humanitas*. Now we see that ordinary Turks and Christians are united by a common *inhumanitas*. Fortunately, Ascham still found a model of *humanitas* to admire in this ugly imbroglio: 'John Fredericke Duke of Saxony'. Frederick is a Protestant 'defender of Luther . . . and as true a follower of Christ and his Gospell' (p. 153). This alone is probably enough in Ascham's eyes to ensure that he could never be party to such appalling crimes as those perpetrated by the

Turks and the Christian, indeed, Protestant Hungarians. But his portrait also owes much to ancient panegyric. He is a man of huge stature: 'yet he is a great deale bygger in all kyndes of vertues, in wisedome, justice, liberalitie, stoutnes, temperancy in hym self, and humanitie towardes others'. His humanity, then, stands in contradistinction to the appalling lack of clemency in these other men; he is a Ciceronian 'great spirit'. Moreover, his example has a positive influence on other men of power. He was captured by the Catholic Charles, who was advised by 'bloudy counsellors' that all the Protestants in his dominions would be cowed into reconversion if the duke were to be executed on the walls of Wittenberg, the cradle of Lutheranism. But Charles was so impressed with the calm nonchalance with which Frederick read his death warrant (he was playing chess) that he changed his mind. His 'naturall clemency' was woken by Frederick's 'merveilous constancie'; and he then 'shewed him more humanitie then any Prince that ever I have read of ha[th] hetherto done to his prisoner' (p. 154).[12]

The Schoolmaster: Courtiers and barbarians

The Schoolmaster is generally regarded as the great classic of Elizabethan humanism. For example, it put the question of quantitative metre versus qualitative rhyme at the centre of poetic debate in England for the next thirty years. Hardly anyone touched on the matter without referring directly to Ascham or paraphrasing his comments on 'rude beggerly ryming' (p. 289).[13] Even more perdurable were Ascham's comments on the typical themes of medieval romance. His scathing remarks on 'open mans slaughter, and bold bawdrye' (p. 231) are familiar even now to most students of Elizabethan literature. They are often interpreted in terms of the scholar's disdain for popular literature, especially popular literature, which had secured a place for itself amongst the aristocracy and was even 'received into the Princes chamber'. But Ascham's distaste for this kind of writing is also informed by his experiences in Germany, which left their mark on *The Schoolmaster* and the account it gives of the relationship between humanism and courtiership. Ascham thought that the court was particularly susceptible to a collapse into barbarism because it was the centre of wealth and power. The horrified comparisons of Turks and Christians in his *Report of Germany* bear witness to his intuition that barbarism could not simply be used as a way of separating the pagan East from the Christian West. Rather, barbarism was a culture based on the unregenerated bestial instincts of human nature. It is the culture in which Cicero's *magnus animus* runs wild and reverts to 'brutishnesse' (*De offic.*, 1.62, p. 75). And Ascham suspected that it was precisely this sort of decadence, though operating at a much less obviously tragic level, which informed literary culture at the English court during the mid-Tudor period, as is amply demonstrated by his comments on English literature in *The Schoolmaster*.

But let us make a first approach to the humanistic aspect of Ascham's *Schoolmaster* by examining certain remarks on Latin composition (which is the main topic of his treatise). Ascham only uses the word 'humanity' once in his book, but that instance is highly revealing. It occurs in his remarks on 'epitome'. This literally means 'cutting away', and it is used by Ascham to refer on the one hand to abridgements of texts, and, on the other, to a stylistic exercise which needs to be applied to writing which is 'over full of words, sentences, & matter'. Ascham's aversion to this kind of style probably has Ciceronian origins. He relates how 'Tullie himselfe had the same fulnes in him; and therefore went to Rodes to cut it away' (p. 262). Indeed, we can see a hint of oriental opulence here. The full style was called 'Asiatic' in classical antiquity, as it was thought to have been imported from Greek speakers from Asia Minor after the death of the Athenian orator Demosthenes in 413 BC. According to Ascham, Cicero used epitome to reform his stylistic excesses: 'in binding him selfe to translate *meros Atticos Oratores* [the worthy Attic orators], and so bring his style, from all lowse grosnesse, to soch firme fastnes in latin, as is in Demosthenes in Greeke'. Cicero, then, reverses the decadence of oratory since the death of Demosthenes by abandoning Asianism and reviving its discarded oratorical opposite: 'Atticism'. Athens was located in Attica, hence it was regarded as the source of stylistic *urbanitas* in Greek.

Ascham provides an example of a modern writer who could benefit from the same exercise: the Portuguese humanist and Roman Catholic divine Hieronymus Osorius. Ascham generally admired Osorius as a Latinist, and thought that if only he could temper his penchant for the full style he would be unrivalled amongst modern writers.[14] However, this stylistic reform is bound up with much larger issues of reformation (p. 261):

> If Osorius would leave of his lustiness in striving against S. Austen, and his over rancke rayling against poore Luther, and the troth of Gods doctrine, and give his whole studie, not to write any thing of his owne for a while, but to translate Demosthenes, with so straite, fast, & temperate a style in latine, as he is in Greeke, he would becume so perfit & pure a writer, I beleve, as hath bene fewe or none sence Ciceroes dayes.

Osorius, Ascham implies, is prevented from leading the restoration of Ciceronian style to its former glory because his Roman Catholicism holds him back, much as Cicero himself needed to be cured of his Asianism before he could reach the acme of eloquence. Indeed, the cure is exactly the same: a course in translating Demosthenes.

But it is not merely Osorius's adherence to the old religion that stands in his way. His 'lustiness' is also a problem. Ascham declares that Osorius is afflicted by a certain 'lustines of nature', by which he means a certain exuberant vigour ('fulnes') which is normally associated with youth, but interferes with the self-command expected in an older man:

> This fulnes as it not to be misliked in a yong man, so in farder aige, in greater skill, and weightier affaires, it is to be temperated, or else discretion and judgement shall seeme to be wanting in him.

The idea is traditional; but Ascham probably goes directly to Cicero's *De oratore*, where Antonius condones the redundance of Sulpicius's earlier orations on account of the speaker's youth (2.89). However, this exuberant vigour needs to be controlled as boys turn into men and come into the fulness of power and authority; otherwise, they risk lapsing into the unruly or tyrannical *magnus animus*, albeit on a smaller scale. This is why Ascham makes the connection between Osorius's style, religion and character. His natural 'lustines' is unrestrained by the corrupt laxity of the Roman Church, which thus allows and even encourages 'rancke rayling' and stylistic 'grosnesse'.

Yet Ascham recognises that, but for this defect, Osorius is to be admired for his 'excellent learning, great wisdome, and gentle humanitie' (p. 262). Here the word 'humanity' occurs in a typically Ciceronian collocation of learning and politeness. It is the *humanitas* to which Cicero appeals in his listeners in the *Pro Archia*, and the *humanitas* which Smith hopes to find in Gardiner in the *De linguae Graecae pronuntiatione*; and phrases like *humanitas ac litterae* occur not infrequently in Ascham's Latin correspondence. Ascham goes on to regret that Osorius cannot bear his doctrinal disagreements with Protestant writers with 'mere conscience in a quiet minde inwardlie', but has to resort to 'contentious malice with spitefull rayling openlie'. The vehemence of *contentio* only releases the disruptive energies produced by deeply held doctrinal differences; therefore, the *humanitas* which presides over *sermo communis* is required to mitigate the potential violence of such encounters and to prevent the descent into mere polemic. Ascham deplores excessively contentious writers as bestially inhumane: 'bloodie beastes, as that fat Boore of the wood; or those brauling Bulles of Basan'.[15]

The boar is particularly interesting because it features prominently in Ascham's account of the effect of the religious changes on his beloved Cambridge. He remembers with great fondness how Dr Nicholas Medcalfe, the Master of Ascham's old college, St John's, in the 1530s, was a great furtherer of the 'newe learning (as they termed it)' (p. 279). This useful and much-used phrase escapes precise definition, but we may be sure that what Ascham means is the combination of the new *studia humanitatis* and the new reformed religion which attracted so many of the best young minds in 1530s Cambridge. Yet Medcalfe supported the new learning 'though he were a Papist'. Ascham once fell foul of the university authorities for speaking aginst the Pope 'amonges my companions'. A remark let out in private conversation, then, led to 'open threates' from Medcalfe against those who dared support Ascham's election to a fellowship. But actually, Medcalfe secretly made sure that Ascham was elected, covering his manoeuvre by making a show of 'great discontentation thereat' (p. 280). Here, then, Medcalfe exercises his true *humanitas* – in both the literary and moral senses – under cover of *contentio*.

However, the flourishing state of letters and manners at St John's was brought to a sudden end by 'that grevous change that chanced. An. 1553' (p. 281). Ascham means the accession of the Roman Catholic Queen Mary, and, more especially, her subsequent marriage to Philip of Spain:

> For, whan *Aper de Sylva* [Latin: 'the boar from the wood'] had passed the seas, and fastned his foote againe in England, not onely the two faire groves of learning in England were eyther cut up, by the roote, or troden downe to the ground and wholie went to wracke, but the yong spring there, and everie where else, was pitifullie nipt and overtroden by very beastes, and also the fairest standers of all, were rooted up, and cast into the fire, to the great weakning even at this day of Christes Chirch in England, both for Religion and learning.

These two fair groves of learning are Oxford and Cambridge, which Ascham alludes to by means of a traditional metonymy. The grove or garden outside Athens called the Akademia in which Plato used to teach philosophy was used to refer to any place of learning, usually, following Horace, in the plural form: 'The Groves of Academe'.[16] However, he develops this metonym as a metaphor in very interesting ways in this passage. The trees of the grove become scholars, some of whom are used as firewood, that is, burnt at the stake like Latimer and Ridley. And the metaphor of the grove calls up the association with the 'boar of the wood': '*Aper de Sylva*'. This foul beast whose natural habitat is the wild forest overturns and destroys the groves of learning, not only by extirpating its best scholars, but also corrupting all the others by allowing barbarism to creep back into the schools: '[Y]ea, I know, that heades were cast together, and counsell devised, that Duns, with all the rable of barbarous questionistes, should have dispossessed of their place and rowmes, Aristotle, Plato, Tullie, and Demosthenes'.

This scenario should by now be quite familiar. Smith took the view in the 1540s that barbarism was pretty much on the retreat; and Ascham seems to have felt that the new learning had effectively triumphed. But the triumph was short-lived; and Ascham describes the decay of learning in Marian Cambridge as part of a wider decay in manners and morals. He tells us that university life came to be marred with 'contention' and 'factions', which is always a tell-tale sign of the lapse from true *humanitas* in Ascham's eyes. But the first thing that comes to his mind suggests that he associated this corruption with the court: 'than began simplicitie in apparell, to be layd aside: Courtlie galantnes to be taken up' (p. 282). This leads on to a list of other vices: 'frugality in diet' and 'honest pastimes' (like his much-loved archery) were replaced with 'Towne going to good cheare' and 'unthrifty and idle games' played in nocturnal corners (presumably dice, but perhaps fornication is also hinted at). These are the staple elements of 'prodigalism', the all-pervasive network of ideas and themes and tales connected with the parable of the Prodigal Son. But the initial position of 'Courtlie galantness' indicates that Ascham believed these vices to have their source in the court, or, rather, in people's perceptions of the court. For Ascham, the return to Roman Catholicism was a return to barbarism in three ways: the violent barbarity of the treatment meted out to outspoken Protestants; the return of the 'barbarous questionistes' to the schools from which they had been displaced by classical authors; and the lapse into unruly sensuality amongst the fellows and especially the students of the university. In a word, they began to act as if they were courtiers.

For Ascham, then, scholarship and courtiership were largely irreconcilable. He has a clear picture of the scholar as a man who cherishes the Ciceronian ideals of *humanitas ac litterae* and attempts to live by them. But when learning and society are corrupted by an unregenerated Roman Catholicism, then scholars such as Osorius tend towards discursive barbarism by writing violent polemics, and ordinary students tend towards a sort of sensual and concupiscent brutishness which Ascham associates, rather boldly, with the court. The courtier, as he is described in the pages of *The Schoolmaster*, often appears as a kind of a ruffian. Ascham expresses grave reservations about the wisdom of the tradition that persuaded gentlemen to send their sons to court in order to finish their education and find themselves a place in the world. He concedes that there are 'manie faire examples in this Court, for yong Jentlemen to folow' (p. 206). But on the whole, the court is peopled by less worthy models for imitation. Ascham depicts a generally corrupt courtly culture centred on what he ironically terms 'Grace of Court' (p. 207). This consists in an eagerness

> to dare to do any mischief, to contemne stoutly any goodnesse, to be busie in every matter, to be skillful in every thyng, to acknowledge no ignorance at all. To do thus in Court, is counted of some, the chief and greatest grace of

all: and termed by the name of a vertue, called Corage & boldnesse, whan Crassus in Cicero teacheth the clean contrarie, and that most wittilie, saying thus: *Audere, cum bonis etiam rebus coniunctum, per seipsum est magnopere fugiendum* [*De orat.*, 2.93]. Which is to say, to be bold, yea, in a good matter, is for it self, greatlie to be exchewed.

Courtliness, then, at least as Ascham had observed it during his fifteen years as a courtier himself, is directly opposed to Ciceronian *humanitas*. What they call 'Corage & boldnesse' is actually a perversion of the *magnus animus* which Cicero delineates in the *De officiis* (though without its tragic effects). It also involves a perversion of Ciceronian universalism, in that the courtier pretends to be 'skillful in every thyng'; but, more importantly, it works against civil conversation. The courtier must 'be able to raise taulke, and make discourse of every rishe [rush, i.e. trifle]: to have a verie good will, to heare him selfe speake'.

All these 'graces' add up to the portrait of the courtier as an aggressive but pusillanimous and rather buffoonish character, a courtly inflection of the *miles gloriosus*, or 'Braggart Captain', of Greek and Roman comedy (p. 207):

> Moreover, where the swing goeth, there to follow, fawne, flatter, laugh and lie lustilie at other mens liking. To face, stand formest, shove backe: and to the meaner man, or unknowne in the Court, to seeme somwhat solume, coye, big, and dangerous of looke, taulk, and answere: To thinke well of him selfe, to be lustie in contemning of others, to have some trim grace in a privie mock. And in greater presens, to beare a brave looke: to be warlike, though he never looked enimie in the face in warre: yet some warlike signe must be used, either a slovinglie busking, or an overstaring frounced hed, as though out of everie heeres toppe, should suddenlie start out a good big othe.

In Ascham's view, which was an expert one, the courtier is a travesty of the chivalrous knight. His model is 'som Smithfield ruffian' (p. 208). Though little more than back-stabbers, courtiers like to appear threateningly soldierly. They even have their hair frizzed to look like the snaky-headed Fury. But this 'brave looke' is a sign of barbarism not true martial valour, which is expressed only on the field of battle by these 'warlike signs' of physical fury. They are misplaced in conversation, and in the daily round of courtly life at large; and that is why we know that brave looks are really the symptoms of a personality which, in Ciceronian terms, has not yet developed very far towards genuine, or, to put it another way, complete *humanitas*.

For Ascham, then, the court was not a place where humanism might be expected to flourish. It was too incorrigibly 'barbarous'. Despite the example of learned and pious princes such as Edward VI and Elizabeth, the rank and file of the court persisted in cherishing its unregenerately 'Gothic' literary culture. Like Smith, Ascham is a partisan of the humanist myth of the Dark Ages: a long period of intellectual obscurity which extends from the collapse of classical antiquity to the restitution of its learning and to some extent its supposed values by Petrarch and his disciples in the fourteenth century. Unlike Smith, Ascham saw this restitution as secondary and subordinate to the rediscovery of primitive Christianity and the supersession of the Roman by the Reformed Church. But the old religion was strong, and so was the literature and learning associated with it. We have already seen how Ascham shakes his head at the memory of the return of the 'rable of barbarous questionistes' at Cambridge during the Marian interlude. He seems to have been equally exasperated by the survival of the Gothic literary tradition at Mary's court (pp. 230–1):

> In our forefathers tyme, whan Papistrie, as a standyng poole, covered and overflowed all England, fewe bookes were read in our tong, savyng certaine bookes of Chevalrie, as they sayd, for pastime and pleasure, which, as some say, were made in Monasteries, by idle Monkes, or wanton Chanons: as one for example, *Morte Arthure*: the whole pleasure of which booke standeth in two speciall poyntes, in open mans slaughter, and bold bawdrye . . . This is good stuffe, for wise men to laughe at, or honest men to take pleasure at. Yet I know, when Gods Bible was banished the Court, and *Morte Arthure* received into the Princes chamber.

Books like the '*Morte Arthure*' – the sequence of chivalric romances written by Sir Thomas Malory in the late fifteenth century – were still very much in vogue at the early Elizabethan court. And Ascham clearly believes that Elizabethan courtiers relish depictions of 'open mans slaughter, and bold bawdrye', since they not only are inclined to displays of impotent martialism, but also profess the art of 'Palmestrie, whereby to conveie to chaste eares, som fond or filthie taulke' (p. 208).[17]

There is also a hint of courtly defection in Ascham's famous account of the superiority of classical metres to native 'rhyme'. This position was to become the keystone of Elizabethan neoclassicism, so it is worth exploring in detail. Ascham recalls how he used to discuss the writing of English verses according to the metres used in Greek and Latin poetry with colleagues at Cambridge in the 1540s (p. 289):

> [We] wished as Virgil and Horace were not wedded to follow the faultes of former fathers . . . but by right *Imitation* of the perfit Grecians, had brought Poetrie to perfitnesse also in the Latin tong, that we Englishmen likewise would acknowledge and understand rightfully our rude beggerly ryming, brought first into Italie by Gothes and Hunnes, whan all good verses and all

good learning to, were destroyd by them: and after caryed into France and Germanie: and at last receyved into England by men of excellent wit in deede, but of small learning, and lesse judgement in that behalfe.

Ascham's account of the fall of classical antiquity and its aftermath makes an interesting contrast with Smith's in the *De linguae Anglicae scriptione*. Smith tells us how *humanitas* was carried first westwards from Greece and Troy to Italy, and later northwards to Anglo-Saxon England; Ascham sends barbarism in its pursuit over this second phase of the translation. Puttenham, as we have seen, followed this course, too, when he relates how 'the ryming Poesie of the Barbarians' was still honoured and cherished 'in Courts of Princes' (*Art*, p. 12). But a situation which the courtly Puttenham regarded with complacence utterly appalled the scholarly Ascham, who insists on the inhumanity of 'barbarous' poetry. Like Smith, he also uses the acorn as a metaphor for old literary conventions which need to be dismissed, but more vehemently. Ascham continues (p. 289):

> But now, when men know the difference, and have the examples, both of the best, and of the worst, surelie, to follow rather the Gothes in Ryming, than the Greekes in trew versifying, were even to eate ackornes with swyne, when we may freely eate wheate bread emonges men.

Ascham adds a new detail to the acorns metaphor which moves it far away from the myth of the Golden Age. Eating acorns is now associated with pigs rather than with the children of innocence and bliss. Ascham is probably thinking of St Jerome (Helgerson, 1976, p. 55). Perhaps, also, the parable of the Prodigal Son is at the back of his mind. The Prodigal Son was reduced to herding pigs, and dreams of eating pigswill (Luke 16.16). But the most obvious comparison is with the figure of Gryllus. The Greek historian and moralist Plutarch (46–120) wrote a short dialogue about one of Ulysses' companions called Gryllus, who complained at being turned back into a man after having spent a day or two transformed into a pig by Circe's wand.[18] The Greek word *grullos* comes from the verb *grullizo* ('grunt'), and this hint of bestial inarticulacy fits well with the metaphor of the acorns.

Ascham's is a polemical sketch: early English poets lacked *humanitas* to a degree which allows Ascham to compare them to pigs. Not surprisingly, Ascham goes on to temper this severe judgement somewhat (p. 289):

> In deede, Chauser, Th. Norton, of Bristow, my L. of Surrey, M. Wiat, Th. Phaer, and other Jentlemen, in translating Ovide, Palingenius, and Seneca, have gonne as farre to their great praise, as the copie they followed could cary them, but if soch good wittes, and forward diligence, had bene directed

to follow the best examples, and not have bene caryed by tyme and custome, to content themselves with that barbarous and rude Ryming, emonges their other worthy praises, which they have justly deserved, this had not bene the least, to be counted emonges men of learning and skill, more like unto the Grecians, than unto the Gothians, in handling of their verse.

As far as Ascham was concerned, the *translatio humanitatis* had not yet been fully achieved in Elizabethan England. Poets might well have the right mental material – 'good wittes' (what Cicero calls *ingenium*) – and they might try hard to write good verses, but because these verses rhyme, they cannot be considered as *litterae humaniores*. Ascham associates rhyme with the Goths, with barbarism, and finally with swinishness, thus running throught the gamut of insults which humanists offered to those writers and readers whose literary culture and values did not square with their own.

This is Ascham at his most small-minded; he seems less 'The School-master' and more 'The Pedant'. Observe how his list of English poets begins with the customary nod to Chaucer, but then concentrates on translated works; indeed, it concludes not with English poets, but with Latin ones, who are clearly much more important than their unnamed translators. Ascham mentions Thomas Phaer, who turned seven books of Virgil's *Aeneid* into rhymed fourteeners (1558); but he does not think it necessary to name Arthur Golding as the translator of Ovid's *Metamorphoses* (1564–7), or Barnabe Googe as that of Palingenius's *Zodiacus vitae* ('The Zodiac of Life': 1565), or to identify Jasper Heywood, John Studley, Alexander Neville and Thomas Nuce as translators of Seneca's tragedies during the 1560s. The English poets are able to write as well as they can only because their 'copie', that is, their Latin originals, was too robust for them to ruin utterly by their barbarous rhyme. But when Ascham comes to praise 'men of learning and skill' in the matter of metrics, he betrays a want of literary sensibility which is quite astonishing in one whose judgement is otherwise usually quite sound. Ascham derides a fellow Cambridge scholar who wrote Latin plays 'which he called Tragedies', but which do not deserve the title, he says, because 'he began the *Protasis* with *Trochaeis Octonariis*' (p. 284). Thomas Watson, on the other hand, is singled out for special praise because he refused to let the text of his own play circulate 'bicause, in *locis paribus, Anapestus* is twise or thrise used in stede of *Iambus*'. This is the sort of dainty and fastidious concern with externals which Fleming would later condemn in his 'courtly Humanists', of course, and the scope for such exquisite posturings was immensely wider in scholarly circles, since the technical aspect of ancient metre was so much more complicated. Yet the same Watson is also praised by Ascham for the following rendering of the first lines of Homer's *Odyssey*: 'All travellers do gladly report great prayse of Ulysses, / For that he knew many mens maners, and saw many Cities' (p. 224). Ascham offers these verses, together with the Greek original, and Horace's Latin version, as 'an Example to good wittes, that shall delite in learned exercise'. This sums up the limitations of his own view on the reformation of English versification and poetry generally. For Ascham, *humanitas* was still too closely confined within the four walls of the schoolroom or lecture-hall ever to be truly 'translated' into English literary culture at large. A timid man, who throughout his career as a minor courtier longed to return to the safe haven of his Cambridge study, Ascham himself becomes more aggressive as he retreats behind the walls of grammatical erudition. Clearly, there is an element of inhumanity in comparing Chaucer or Wyatt or Phaer to pigs because they use rhyming verse. But herein lies the central paradox of Elizabethan humanism: the nervous concern of the humanist with his own literature and learning leads him so frequently and often thoughtlessly to apply a cultural allegory of bestiality which makes himself seem 'inhumane' in the wider ethical sense of the word.

Unfortunately, Ascham's view was shared by many later Elizabethan writers, especially the so-called University Wits, who were active mainly in the period between the late 1570s and early 1590s. These were men who often came from commoner families, or from the lowest echelons of the non-landed gentry, so it is not surprising that they should perhaps overvalue the education in *humanitas* which had given them some prominence as writers, and by which they hoped to secure some remunerative position and so become 'gentlemen'. In the next chapter, we review the career of a man who is not usually placed amongst the University Wits, but who surely needs to be seen in the same context: Gabriel Harvey. He is an egregious character in many ways, but in others he may be considered the archhumanist of the Elizabethan period.

Notes

1. The word 'Renaissance' was not known to the Elizabethans; like 'humanism', it dates from the nineteenth century. But the concept of a rebirth or revival of letters was common enough in the period.

2. The *Discourse* was written in 1549, and the *De republica* in 1565. Both remained in manuscript until after Smith's death in 1577.

3. See Mary Dewar, *Sir Thomas Smith: A Tudor Intellectual in Office* (London, 1964).

4. Calliope is the Muse of Epic, but she praises Smith for his excellence in rhetoric, languages, geometry, arithmetic, law, physic: 'Ohe / Smithus multiscius'.

Dr Pandotheus, the authorial figure in Smith's *Discourse of the Commonweal*, is another polymath: 'This man speaketh very naturally of every thinge, as a man universally sene, that had joyned good Learninge with good witt' (p. 37).

5. This passage is copiously underlined by Gabriel Harvey in his copy of the *De linguage Graecae* (reproduced in facsimile by Danielsson). But this particular allegorisation seems to have left no trace in his own writings on the topic.

6. For grammatical conservatism, see Jensen, 1996.

7. These are the qualities of the daintier kind of *litterae humaniores*. Harvey echoes Smith's phrases when he describes himself as a 'silly humanitian of the old world' in *Pierce's Supererogation* (sig. T1v). Then, writers 'esteemed every thing fine, that was neat, & holesome'; but now men must have 'the fiercest Gunpouder, and the rankest pikesawce'.

8. In the *De linguae Anglicae*, he accepts that the words *littera* and *gramma* are wrongly applied to sounds as well as signs: 'But touching their meaning, it skilleth not whether we use them to speake of utterance, or writing' (p. 28).

9. Despite the similarity of their titles, Elyot's *Governor* seems to have surprisingly little connection with Castiglione's *Courtier* (but cf. Major, 1964, pp. 60–76). Elyot's governor belongs to the scholarly and polymathic tradition of humanism, rather than to the courtly one with its emphasis on more trivial accomplishments. Elyot says that anyone who has been to grammar school can 'write an epistle or a flatering oration in latin' (p. 55). But the real orator – and the governor must be able to speak well – must be acquainted with 'a heape of all maner of lernyng: whiche of some is called the worlde of science, of other the circle of doctrine, whiche is in one worde of greke *Encyclopedia*' (p. 56).

10. *Letters*, ed. Giles, no. 161 (vol. 1, pt 1, p. 390). This letter is translated as no. 54 in Vos's edition.

11. I have not been able to find the source of this remark in Wyatt's writings. Perhaps it was really a 'saying' that Ascham had heard, rather than read.

12. This is an anecdote which might fit very well into a new *Facta et dicta*. But the Valerian element is still intermingled with a Ciceronian emphasis on the fact that Frederick is a 'lover of learnynge' with a library 'furnished with bookes of all tongues and sciences'.

13. Harvey is already showing impatience with Ascham's monopoly of critical authority on the topic by 1580 (*Three Letters*, p. 622); but William Webbe can still reverently allude to Ascham's comments on 'this tynkerly verse which we call ryme' in his *Discourse of English Poetry* (1586, p. 240). See Attridge, 1974, pp. 93–100.

14. Ascham was particularly impressed by Osorio's Ciceronian orations *De gloria* ('Glory': 1552) and *De nobilitate* ('Nobility': 1552). He sent copies of one or other of these texts to Sir William Paget, Sir William Petre and Cardinal Pole

(ed. Vos, 1989, p. 207). But Ascham's ardour cooled when Osorius wrote a public letter to Elizabeth in 1563, urging her to return to the Roman communion.

15. The boar comes from Psalms 80.18; the bulls from Psalms 22.12. In Psalms, the boar destroys the vines which the Lord has planted out of Egypt in Israel. Is there a hidden pun on the name of Osorius's bishopric in the Portuguese city of Silva?

16. The phrase represents *silvae Academi* in Horace's *Epistles* (2.2.45). Cicero displays his allegiance to Academic philosophy when he sets the first conversation of the *De oratore* under a plane tree (1.28), which, as one speaker explicitly remarks, is similar to the one under which discussion takes place in Plato's *Phaedrus*. Ascham's friend Sturm continued the allusion by setting his dialogues on Aristotle's *Rhetoric* under some cherry trees, as Ascham noted with approval in a letter from Austria of 29 January 1552 (Giles, vol. 1. no. 135; Vos, no. 46).

17. It is worth pointing out that Ascham is here merely restating what he had already pointed out twenty years earlier, in the aftermath of the scandal over the pronunciation of Greek, in the address to his book on archery, *Toxophilus* (1545). Here we learn: 'In our fathers tyme nothing was red, but bookes of fayned chevalrie, wherin a man by redinge, shuld be led to none other ende, but onely to manslaughter and baudrye . . . These bokes (as I have heard say) were made the moste parte in Abbayes, and Monasteries' (pp. xiv–xv).

18. The story is known best to students of Elizabethan literature in the version at the very end of the second book of Spenser's *Fairy Queen*: 'The donghill kind / Delights in filth and foule incontinence: / Let Grill be Grill, and have his hoggish mind' (2.12.87).

CHAPTER FIVE

The Arch-humanist:
Gabriel Harvey

Gabriel Harvey has a special place in the history of Elizabethan humanism, since he is the first person publicly to declare himself a 'humanitian'. This declaration occurs in *Pierce's Supererogation*, where Harvey calls himself a 'silly humanitian of the old world' (sig. T1v). The phrase appears in a passage reproving his erstwhile friend John Lyly for casually abusing Harvey in his pamphlet *Pap with an Hatchet* (1589). The 'old world' to which Harvey refers is the time he and Lyly spent together as young university men newly arrived in London, living as fellow residents in the Savoy in the late 1570s. This was when Lyly wrote *Euphues: The Anatomy of Wit*, and when Harvey and his friend Spenser were experimenting with English verses written in quantitative metres. It was a time, then, of 'silly humanity': the innocent pursuit of harmless literary pastimes. Harvey explains: 'that was the simplicitie of the age, that loved frendship, more then gold, & esteemed every thing fine, that was neat, & holesome: all was pure, that was seasoned with a litle salt; & all trimme, that was besprinkled with a fewe flowers'. It was a veritable Golden Age of what Harvey elsewhere in this text calls 'English Humanity' (sig. Y4r). However, Harvey had good reason to look back with mixed feelings on the 'old world' he had left behind him over ten years ago. It had never been quite as 'silly' as he liked to think. For example, Lyly had turned on Harvey as early as 1580; and the circumstances in which the two men fell out offer a telling illustration of the way in which courtship, or, more precisely, courtiership, might impinge on the amicable and learned *societas litteratorum* that lay at the heart of the traditional model of Ciceronian humanism. Harvey had written what he himself calls a 'bolde satyricall Libell' on an unnamed 'Italianate Englishman', which was then printed in *Three Letters* in 1580 (p. 625). Lyly, who, as a friend of Harvey's, may well have known the identity of the gentleman in question, told his new master,

Edward de Vere, Earl of Oxford, that his lordship was the intended victim. But although Lyly may well have been correct in his 'application' of the libel, Oxford had no wish to admit that he might bear any similarity to the absurd figure satirised in Harvey's poem. Lyly was reprimanded; and he bore a grudge against Harvey ever afterwards (Stern, 1979, pp. 65–6). In *Pap with an Hatchet*, he writes: 'this tenne yeres have I lookt to lambacke him' (p. 400). It was, of course, badly done of Lyly to inform on his friend in order to ingratiate himself with his master; but such betrayals were seen by satirists as part and parcel of the courtier's trade. As the freshly reformed Euphues demands of the unregenerate courtier Philautus in *The Anatomy of Wit*: 'Art not thou one of those . . . which sekest to win credite with thy superiors by flatterye . . . & undermine thy equals by frawde' (p. 308). But nor was Harvey exactly 'innocent'. The 'boldness' of Harvey's libel is 'courtly' as well; it is a part of Harvey's intention about this time to abandon the cloistered world of the bookish scholar and to practise the more active and remunerative kind of 'bowld Courtly speaking' (*Marg.*, p. 145).[1] In fact, Harvey's attempts to secure himself a place in courtly circles was short-lived; it did not survive his libel by many months. Nevertheless, Harvey's career is an extremely interesting and revealing example of the conflicts between scholarship and courtiership that beset the Elizabethan humanist or humanitian.

The Cambridge scholar

Harvey may be the first English writer to call himself a humanitian, but we should not be too quick to see this as self-praise. The epithet 'silly' seems to add a touch of irony to this self-description; and we have already seen how Harvey would, a few years later, compare 'superficial humanists' very un-favourably to 'exquisite artists, & curious universal schollers' (*Marg.*, p. 161). In fact, Harvey seems to have been reluctant to be considered as a writer who was especially devoted to humanity. This is not to say that Harvey declined to worship at the altar of *humanitas* when it suited him, but really he was more interested in 'philosophy' in the wide sense. More than any other writer of his generation he deserves to be called a polyhistor. He was not merely 'interested' in the whole spectrum of the humane arts as they were understood by the Elizabethans, he also bought books on these arts, read them, filled their margins with notes, and, by the end of the century, seems to have been in a position to write on most of them as well. In 1598, Harvey wrote a letter to Robert Cecil, trying to secure his assistance in his candidacy for the mastership of his old college, Trinity Hall, Cambridge;

and as evidence of his appointability, he declared that he had already penned a considerable portfolio of useful works of literature and learning:

> Traicts & Discourses, sum in Latin, sum in Inglish, sum in verse according to the circumstance of the occasion, but much more in prose; sum in Humanitie, Historie, Pollicy, Lawe, & the sowle of the whole Boddie of Law, Reason; sum in Mathematiques, in Cosmographie, in the Art of Navigation, in the Art of Warr, in the tru Chymique . . . & other effectual practicable knowlage.[2]

We see that 'Humanitie' heads the list, but it is quickly overtaken by a host of more 'practicable' arts and sciences. This letter comes from late in Harvey's career; but as a younger man he shows much the same attitude towards humanity, as we can see from another letter Harvey wrote to a prospective patron a quarter of a century earlier in 1573.

Like his kinsman Sir Thomas Smith, Harvey was born into a commoner family in the small Essex town of Walden, now Saffron Walden. Like Smith he was a clever boy and an ambitious young man, and did well at Cambridge. However, unlike Smith, Harvey had to face a university in which more and more students and fellows were gentlemen born and bred. The gentry had taken note of the warnings issued by Ascham and other educationalists that their sons might have to give place to the sons of commoners unless they were skilled in the arts; and, naturally, Oxford and Cambridge had begun to develop a rather more amateur collegiality than had been the case in the days of Smith and Ascham. There was rather more hunting and heavy drinking, for example, than there had been in the years when the right pronunciation of scholarly Greek had threatened to shake the foundations of university life at Cambridge. Undergraduates took their hounds to lectures, got their tutors drunk, and generally enjoyed a good deal of high-spirited and sometimes violent revelry without much regard for the college fellows.[3] Ascham would have said that the university had been invaded by courtly delinquents; and Harvey himself complains in *Three Letters* (p. 622) of the lack of respect students showed to their academic superiors:

> Many *Pupils*, Jackemates, and Hayle fellowes wel met, with their *Tutors*, and by your leave, some too, because forsooth they be Gentlemen, or great heires, or a little neater and gayer than their fellowes, (shall I say it for shame? beleeve me, tis too true) their very own Tutors.

Things were much the same at Oxford, as Lyly had already reported in *Euphues* in 1578.[4] But Harvey speaks here from personal experience of humiliation at the hands of certain university 'gentlemen' at Pembroke Hall.

In the spring of 1573, Harvey, then a young fellow of Pembroke Hall in Cambridge, was obstructed in what should have been a routine advancement to the degree of Master of Arts by certain enemies of his in the college. Reduced to a condition of anxious exasperation, Harvey eventually wrote a letter to the Master of Pembroke Hall, Dr Robert Young, then resident in London, in which he gives his side of the events leading up to the confrontation between himself and his ill-wishers. We never learn why Harvey and his enemies fell out. Harvey refers once or twice to an old grudge, but does not go into detail. But what was probably at the bottom of the conflict was Harvey's unenviable status as an 'upstart'. Harvey was a commoner who wished to be a gentleman. He could not claim gentry by birth, but he could claim it by letters if he was advanced to the MA. Then he could style himself 'Master' – the form of address used for gentlemen – by virtue of his degree (*magister artium*). Perhaps this was what lay behind the particular insistence with which his enemies pursued their attempt to block his elevation to the higher degree. They wanted to 'keep him in his place'.

The leader of the pack was a certain Thomas Neville. He was a gentleman born, though, according to Harvey's report, not gentle, but harsh and unyielding in temperament: 'M. Nevil is flinti, and is M. Nevil stil; I must needes abide the brunt of his displeasure; what is a gentleman but his pleasure?' (*Letter-book*, p. 15). Harvey was painfully aware that Neville was his social superior, and that it was this brute fact which allowed him to do as he pleased with respect to the clever commoner. Neville seems to have brought this home to Harvey by his haughty insistence on the petty deferences which a bachelor was supposed to show a master (p. 5):

> For mi self, whitch in deed am an inch beneath him, as he ons made his vaunt; he can not deni it, he hath confest so mutch to me himself, that I passing bi him, and moving mi cap, and speking unto him, he hath lookd awri an other wai, nether afording me a word, nor a cap; purposing, as I take it, to make of his inch a good long el, and to show a lusti contempt of so silli a frend.

This vicious campaign of snubbing and abuse must have left Harvey in no doubt as to the vacuity of the principle of 'gentility'. Neville (at least in Harvey's account) seems to have been a typical gentleman-bully.

This leads us to Neville's first reason for trying to prevent Harvey's taking his MA: 'He laid against me mi commun behaviur, that I was not familiar like a fellow, and that I did disdain everi mans cumpani' (p. 4). By 'commun behaviur', Neville is not referring to any vulgar demeanour on Harvey's part, but means that Harvey does not 'common', or 'mix', with the other fellows. And the phrase 'familiar like a fellow' is also worth remarking on. I would suggest that Neville has a much more convivial and less obviously academic idea of the word 'fellow' than Harvey. A particular charge he lays against Harvey is that he would not take a part in the usual Yuletide merry-making. Harvey reports this accusation as follows: 'I wuld needs in al hast be a studdiing in Christmas, when other were a plaiing, and was then whottist at mi book when the rest were hardist at their cards' (p. 14). Harvey was not 'hearty' enough for Neville and his crew; and he seems to have been aware of this himself when he denies the charge of aloofness: 'I was wunt to be as familiar, and as sociable and as gud a fellow too, as ani' (p. 4). A 'good-fellow' was a somewhat boisterously convivial companion.[5] Harvey tried to be jolly at 'commonty fires' – convivial evening gatherings around the hearth:

> Marri so, that at usual and convenient times, as after dinner and supper, at commenti fiers, yea and at other times too, if the lest occasion were offrid, I continuid as long as ani, and was as fellowli as the best. What thai cale sociable I know not: this I am suer, I never avoidid cumpani: I have been merri in cumpani: I have bene ful hardly drawn out of cumpani.

Of course, the point is that Harvey really did not know what Neville and the other gentlemen called 'sociable'. Despite his pathetic eagerness to be seen as a merry companion, Harvey was no roisterer. As far as the record shows, young Harvey was more at ease in more private and personal relationships, rather than the 'public' ones which governed the ties which clearly bound together Neville and his companions. The 'fellowly' life at Elizabethan Oxford and Cambridge could be rather rough, and we may be sure that Harvey came in for a good deal of 'ragging' at the hands of his socially superior but academically less talented colleagues.

This leads us to the second charge laid against Harvey by Neville: intellectual arrogance. Neville claimed that Harvey 'misliked those which bi commun consent and agrement of al have been veri wel thout of for there lerning' (p. 6). This applied not only to Harvey's judgements on the prominent English scholars of the day, but also to the philosopher whose works still provided the very foundation of traditional scholarship and learning: Aristotle. Neville asserted that Harvey was a 'great and continual patron of paradoxis and a main defender of straung opinions, and that communly against Aristotle too' (p. 10). Furthermore, said Neville, such an addiction to paradox – the challenging of established opinion – might be very dangerous if Harvey were to proceed to the study of divinity. Neville's objections here are not merely based on an ignorant conservatism (although that is their main foundation). He rightly judged his adversary to be a lover of novelty. Ironically enough, however, in matters of religion, Harvey was as moderate and uncontroversial as any established churchman could have wished him to be.

Harvey brushes aside Neville's charge by explaining that his treatment of all of these paradoxes – 'as he termid them' – is quite in line with the thinking of the best modern scholars, such as Melanchthon or Ramus. Moreover, he has always spoken well of Aristotle: 'as highly as I wel culd'. But Harvey was clearly impatient with the criticisms laid against his searching mind by more pedestrian talents, and launches into the sort of tirade which lesser intellects such as Neville clearly found inconvenient (p. 11):

> Unles we wil onli admit of that to be done whitch wc our selvs onli have dun, in philosophical disputations to give popular and plausible theams, de nobilitate, de amore, de gloria, de liberalitate, and a few the like, more fit for schollars declamations to discurs uppon then semli for masters problems to dispute uppon: and more gudli and famus for the show then ether convenient for the time, or meet for the place, or profitable for the persons. Sutch matters have bene thurrouly canvassid long ago: and everi on that can do ani thing is able to write hole volumes of them, and make glorius shows with them. I cannot tel, but me thinks it were more fruteful for us and commodius for our auditors to handle sum sad and witti controversi. But I never found ani fault with them for duelling in there own stale quaestions. I wuld it miht have pleasd them as litle to envi me for mi nu fresh paradoxis.

Philosophy, says the young Harvey, is no longer a question of 'masters problems to dispute uppon', but 'schollars declamations to discurs uppon'. Philosophical disputations – the staple form of intellectual debate at Tudor Oxford and Cambridge – have been replaced by rhetorical declamations on a set theme such as nobility, love, glory or liberality, like those which constituted the chief exercises of the higher forms at the grammar school.[6] In other words, they belong more to *humanitas* as taught at school, rather than to *philosophia* as it should be taught at university.

Furthermore, these 'popular and plausible theams' which are 'gudli and famus for the show' are clearly similar to ancient panegyric or epideictic oratory. They are 'show pieces' (*epideiksis*: 'display'). Harvey insists on their facile ostentation: 'everi one that can do ani thing is able to write hole volumes of them, and make glorius shows with them'. Here is another connection with *humanitas*. We have seen that in Cicero's *De oratore* the sort of oratory best suited to display one's knowledge of the *artes humanae* was precisely the one which Cicero chooses not to discuss: epideictic. But the connection between general moral-philosophical themes and *humanitas* is most clearly anticipated by Antonius's comments on the relative ease in speaking on legal matters as opposed to the abstract philosophical themes like love and glory. He says to the younger and less experienced Catulus: 'It is but game to that man which hath some wit, & training-up, and hath also experience of ordinarie letters & more polished humanitie' (2.72). A very similar sentiment lies behind Harvey's dismissive remarks on 'popular and plausible theams': anyone who has been to a grammar school and acquired a basic knowledge of humanity can turn out volumes of brilliantly showy orations on themes like nobility or love.[7]

Harvey always regarded humanity as simple and elementary; and we have seen that this is a common attitude in the Elizabethan age. But Harvey also resembled Cicero's Crassus in that he felt that not only grammar but all the other humane arts were easy to pick up as well. His commonplace book is full of observations on the speed with which the various disiciplines can be learnt. 'Ower litle Hubert', as Harvey approvingly observes of a promising Walden boy, was 'hable to discourse reddily in Law, in Divinity, in all kyndes of historyes, in Arithmetique, Geometry, the Sphaere, in a manner universally in all Lerning'. His accomplishments are put down to mental facility: 'A good witt, apt & quick: speedy dispatch of on thing atonce with often repetition, & practis, upon every light occasion' (*Marg.*, pp. 90–1). But can we really take the following remarks seriously: 'Any Art, or science, liberal, or mechanical may summarily be lernid for ordinary talke, in *three dayes*; for use, practis, & profession, in *six*; any language, to understande, in *six*: to speake, & write, in *twelve*' (p. 91).[8] Such greedy remarks do not reflect well on Harvey's own scholarship; so it is only fair to point out that the margins of his book reveal that he did read some of them very carefully indeed. But they may well reveal his true opinions as the degree of learning required in a polyhistorical or gorgiastic 'discourser'. Perhaps three days really is enough to pick up what you need for 'ordinary talke' (*sermo communis*).

These private observations should be set against the more cautiously encyclopaedic element of Harvey's *Ciceronianus* (1577). This is a highly polished version of the lecture Harvey delivered in Cambridge at the commencement of Easter Term in 1576. Harvey was a Ramist; and he makes much of his conversion to true Ciceronianism after reading Ramus's own *Ciceronianus* (1556). He learnt, for example, 'that all the learning of the Liberall and Humane Artes is bownd together in a single bonde of Feloship' (p. 74 [MP]). It seems odd that Harvey should have had to go to Ramus for this familiar piece of Ciceronian wisdom; and he admits that it is something he 'miht have lernid of Tullie long befor'.[9] However, Ramus's teachings on rhetoric inclined strongly towards the practical rather than the idealistic side of Crassian universalism. His most important innovation was to insist that rhetoric was concerned only with 'elocution': the choice of apt words and phrase. The selection and ordering of material ('invention' and 'disposition', respectively) belonged to logic. Ramist rhetoric, then, is chiefly an art of figurative ornament; and we have seen how Crassus's ideal of polymathic learning serves similarly ornamental purposes in practical oratory. However, Harvey still regards Cicero himself as a kind of encyclopaedic resource of such material. Read his works, he says, and you improve 'not onely as Grammariens & Orators, but also as Dialectiques, Philosophers Ethique and Politique, Historians, and even, Natural Philosophers, Jurisconsults, & Cosmographers' (p. 100). Harvey is thinking here of Cicero's philosophical works, but he means them to be plundered in much the same way as Crassus recommends the reading of scholarly writers:

> Nor shal you meerli declare these thinges, with vain & empti pompe, in the scholeroom, or in the shadi walkes of this Academie; but wherever men are come togither; & in your dayli conversations [*sermones*]; at home, and abrode; at holi-day, & in your busy affaires; with commun folk, & cowrtli, and with al maner of men indeed.

Though Harvey was an accomplished lecturer, he was really less concerned with formal orations than with *sermo*. He wants his students to be able to discourse fluently on any topic in any company; and his polymathic sights are therefore set at a fairly low level (all you need to know is already in Cicero). Even here, perhaps, we can detect an element of condescension towards *humanitas* and the *artes humanae*. And we are fortunate enough to have a conversational discourse written by Harvey by which we may judge his own practise in the light of such suspicions.

The scholar in civil conversation

Harvey's contribution to *Three Letters* included a 'Pleasant and Pithy Familiar Discourse of the Earthquake in April Last'. Harvey relates to Spenser how he was playing cards in a company of gentlemen and gentlewomen in Essex, doubtless near his home in Saffron Walden, when the famous earthquake of 6 April 1580 shook the house to their considerable alarm. Harvey, as a man of learning, was asked to give his opinion on the causes of earthquakes; and so he did. First, he spoke to the two gentlewomen of the company, whom he calls Inquisitiva and Incredula; and then he gives a very different account of his thoughts on earthquakes to the gentlemen. (In fact, he returns to the matter yet again in another set of remarks, this time meant for the ear of his learned correspondent.) In each case, Harvey uses a different stylistic register to deliver his views. With the gentlewomen, he is arch and frivolous, even flirtatious; but with the gentlemen, he is serious yet informal in his display of erudition. Harvey's 'Discourse of the Earthquake' is a very revealing document in the history of Elizabethan humanism. It displays Harvey's adherence to the Ciceronian ideal that an eloquent man should be able to discourse on any matter that comes to hand: 'All thinges whatsoever which may fall unto the discussion of Men, he must treat well & aptlie, that will laye claim to this Vertue, or he must forgoe the title of an Eloquent Man' (De orat., 2.5).[10] The cause of earthquakes is such a topic. Its natural causes require the attention of the philosopher, and the divine will be concerned with any supernatural causes that might give rise to conjecture; but ordinary and unlearned people are interested as well. Such a topic, then, offers the scholar ample opportunity to shine as a humanitian; and Harvey certainly rises to the occasion. But the piece also reveals how difficult it could be to manage the relationship between the scholarly and courtly sides of Elizabethan humanism.

When the gentleman of the house asks Harvey to give his opinion, he at first says only a few words on causes of earthquakes: 'But the Termes of Arte, and verye Natures of thinges themselves so utterly unknowen, as they are to most heere, it were a peece of woorke to laye open the Reason to every ones Capacitie' (p. 614). Inquisitiva correctly perceives that it is she and Incredula who are meant by that last remark, and so she teasingly demands that Harvey should divulge a piece of his 'deepe Universitie Cunning'. Harvey plays up to the part with good humour by impersonating a grave pedant: 'with a good will, quoth I: and then forsooth, very solemnly pawsing a whyle, most gravely, and doctorally proceeded'. The scene recalls the point in the second book of the De oratore, where Antonius is prevailed upon to give his opinions on eloquence for the benefit of the younger and less experienced speakers in the company. Here he imitates the professional teacher of rhetoric: 'Hark ye, I saie, heark ye! for ye shal heare a man that hath bene to the schole, and hath bene polished by the handes of a master, and by the studie of Greke letters' (2.28). Now this would pass very well as a caricature of the Renaissance humanist in his grammatical aspect, especially in the proud advertisement of Greek; but Harvey imitates a philosopher rather than a rhetor. Moreover, when Harvey puts on his little performance, it is to amuse not young men but young women. This makes all the difference between Ciceronian *humanitas* and the courtly humanism of the Elizabethan Age.

Antonius makes his noble companions laugh with his impersonation of the huckstering banter of the professional *magister*: 'I shall teach you, my deare Pupilles, what I have never learned, and namelie, my great and compendious Oratoricall Methode' (2.29). However, Antonius does indeed go on to explain at great length his views on oratory. Harvey, however, only plays the fool with the gentlewomen, and keeps his erudition for the 'learned Gentlemen' (p. 615). In his comic guise of the grave doctor, Harvey proposes explanations which may have some truth in them, but are expressed in a series of grotesquely humorous similes: an earthquake is compared to the effects of flatulence, or a bad head-cold, or vomiting after too much drinking. Finally, he declares his own private opinion: earthquakes are caused by the subterranean conflicts of 'Woormes, and Moules, and Cunnyes, and such other valiauntly highminded Creatures, the Sonnes and daughters of Mars, and Bellona'. At this point, Inquisitiva cuts him short and asks him to give them no more of his 'great doctorly learning'. Her ironic remark is telling. Harvey has not been drawing on his learning as an advanced scholar at all, but rather on his acquaintance with humanity. His story of the wars between the moles and voles is an allusion to the well-known mock-epic poem *Batrachomyomachia* ('The Battle of the Frogs and Mice': 5th cent. BC). The poem was sometimes thought to have been written in a merry hour by great Homer, but it seems to be Aesopian in origin and is the sort of thing boys started with when learning Greek. It is, however, doubtful whether Inquisitiva would pick up this allusion, as it is extremely unlikely that she had been to grammar school. It is the fantastic and light-hearted character of the theme that must have recommended it to Harvey as appropriate for the entertainment of what he considers intellectually incapacious female minds; but Inquisitiva is still commonsensibly aware that Harvey has spun her and Incredula a yarn rather than taught them anything.

The account given to the men is a much more learned piece. It is evident that Harvey has a reputation for erudition which goes beyond that of his fellow gentlemen in the company. It is they who ask him to give his opinion, after all. But even so, Harvey does not try to impose his learning on the others. There is only one passage of any length quoted in Latin: six lines from Ovid's *Metamorphoses* (15.299–304). But this is what they have all read in grammar school: 'humanity'. It is the kind of text that Stanyhurst's humanitian would be familiar with. But Harvey does not make any claim to more profound learning either. In fact, he pretends not to remember exactly the sources of two Latin tags which find their way into his works. On the other hand, he drops into conversation a sufficient quantity of technical terms, such as *natura naturans* or operations *in genere* and *in specie*, to let us know that he has some knowledge of formal scholastic learning. It is a clever piece of work, especially since Harvey actually tells us very little at all about the topic in hand. He quickly rehearses the main points relating to the 'natural' causes of earthquakes, but does not dwell on them because they are so easy to understand. You do not even have to read 'Aristotle in the seconde Booke of his *Meteors*' (p. 616), since you can pick up what you need in Ovid. This is child's play, then, which is why Harvey elaborates on these themes in his discourse to the gentlewomen. But he is not much more interested in the 'supernatural' causes which relate earthquakes and other phenomenal prodigies and the divine will. Harvey does not rule out such relationships, but declares they are 'incomprehensible mysteries' (p. 617). He knows that people nevertheless do try to decipher God's inscrutable designs, but rejects these attempts as unscholarly – and vulgar. Harvey will not venture an opinion on what the present earthquake might 'mean', because he has no wish to be associated with the productions of the popular press. In his remarks to Spenser, Harvey predicts the imminent appearance of 'some odde freshe paulting threehalfepennie Pamphlet for newes: or some Balductum Tragicall Ballet in Ryme, and without Reason, setting out the right myserable, and most wofull estate of the wicked, and damnable worlde at these perillous dayes' (p. 619). The learned doctor is naturally reluctant to be associated with such trash.[11]

The conversation which takes place between Harvey and the other gentle-men in the provincial town-house is a fair reflection of the one in Crassus's Tusculan villa. This was perhaps Harvey's intention. *Ciceronianus* begins with an allusion to Harvey's recent vacation at his father's house in Walden as a 'Tusculane, and, as it were, suburbane Schole [*gymnasium suburbanum*] of Rhetorique, and Philosophy' (p. 44 [MP]). The phrase is clearly meant to recall the *suburbanum gymnasium* of Cicero's *De oratore* (1.98). In any case, the occasion of the conversation in the 'Discourse of the Earthquake' seems very appropriate to leisurely, witty, convivial *humanitas*. But the presence of women in the company complicates matters. Harvey seems to introduce Inquisitiva and Incredula merely in order to flirt with them. He begins his report by explaining to Spenser that he had gone to the gentleman's house 'of purpose' to dally with '*A coople of shrewde wittie new marryed Gentlewomen*' (p. 613). Harvey italicises this phrase with a sort of leer and a wink to his young friend at court, as if to let Spenser know that there are attractive female companions in Essex, too.

Harvey is 'courting it' with these women. For example, he emphasises the somatic theory of earthquakes so that he can make allusions to the women's own 'prettie bodyes' as they lie dreaming in bed (p. 615). Inquisitiva's repsonse is telling:

> You are very merily disposed, God be praysed, quoth Mistresse Inquisitiva, I am glad to see you so pleasurable. No doubt, but you are marvellous privie to our dreames. But I pray you now in a little good earnest, doo you Schollers thinke, that its is the very reason in deede, which you spake of even now?

Inquisitiva is well aware of the tendency of Harvey's comments. She knows that Harvey's allusions to her dreams are meant to imply that he has knowledge of her sexual activities (we recall that she is 'new marryed'). But she really does want to know what the answer is 'in a little good earnest'.

Harvey, however, refuses to take her seriously, and ends his ridiculous tale of the war of the worms with another slightly *risqué* remark on the happy occasions when scholars and gentlewomen discuss learned topics (p. 616):

[. . .] when by the favourable, and gratious aspect of some blessed Planet, and specially our Mercury, or your Venus, it is our good Fortune, to lighte on such good friendes, as you, and some other good Gentlewoomen be, that take pleasure, and comfort in such things. Wherat Mistresse Inquisitiva, laughing right out, and beginning to demaunde I know not what, (me thought, shee made, as if it shoulde have been some goodly plausible Jest, wherat shee is, and takes her selfe prettily good:) Well, well, Master H. quoth the Gentleman of the house, now you have playde your part so cunningly with the Gentlewoomen, [. . .] I pray you in earnest, let us men learne some thing of you too.

The part that Harvey is so cunningly playing with the women is a flirtatiously courtly one. His remarks on the good fortune scholars sometimes have to 'lighte on' women, and the 'pleasure, and comfort' they take from such encounters, are plainly bawdy, despite his disingenuous confusion at the way in which Inquisitiva, much amused by his wit, commends him for his 'plausible Jest'. But whatever learning he has to impart to others, as opposed to merely displaying it for the purposes of amusement and titillation, is for men only.

It is tempting to see the influence of Castiglione in the courtly flirtatiousness of Harvey's conversation with the women. Count Lodowick, after all, advises the courtier that he may profitably use his acquaintance with 'those studyes, which they call Humanitie' to procure 'pleasaunt interteinments with women which ordinarylye love such matters' (*Courtier*, p. 80). However, there is no indication that Inquisitiva and Incredula love humanity. They do not take much notice of the ludicrous but learned tale of the worms and moles which Harvey bases on the *Batrachomyomachia*; and during supper their minds run instead on the grotesquely physical comparisons he calls up between the tremor and the 'drinking, and Neesing [sneezing] of the Earth' (p. 618). Their sense of humour is not really 'courtly' after all, but 'rustic'. Despite a good deal of fervent fantasy, Harvey was never able to imagine courtly gentlewomen with the ease of a Lyly. This is not necessarily a bad thing. Harvey's apparently autobiographical manuscript tale 'A Nobleman's Suit unto a Country Maid' depicts his sister Mercy as a witty and resourceful young woman whose 'country' ways are more than a match for her suitor's 'courtly' behaviour, including attempted rape (Wilson, 2001). But other manuscript works from his letter-book suggest that he tended to regard country women as discursively coarse and inept. The Miller's mistress mixes an impossibly inkhorn prose with scatological skeltonics ('At the most you

gett but a sluttish worde, / In your sluvins teeth a sloovenly torde': p. 95).
Her attempt to write in a fine style reveals her to be incorrigibly rustic.
Greater restraint is shown by Mistress Katherine, in the prologue to the
'garden communication or dialogue in Cambridge' (p. 96) which Harvey
wrote in the summer of 1580 as a possible *mise en scène* to introduce a
collection of his manuscript poetry and prose. This is the report of another
conversation between Harvey and a mixed company of gentlemen and
gentlewomen. The talk soon turns to love; but Mistress Katharine, 'a proper
wise gentlewoman and prettily lernid', good-humouredly interrupts the
theme: 'I beseech you reserve your king of looves for the courte or the
cuntry; it is no university peece of lerning' (p. 96). She asks the gentlemen
there to 'enter into sum witty schoolpoynte, that were not aboove my sonne
Antonyes, and my capacitye'. Katharine's learning does not extend to
much, then, but she would rather hear a 'schoolpoynte' than Ovid's 'Res
est solliciti plena timoris Amor ["love is passing full of feare"]' (*Epistulae*
1.12; trans. Turberville, 1567, sig. B1r). On the other hand, the mistress
addressed by the positively medieval student-poet of 'The Scholar's Love',
though presumably a Cambridge woman, is represented as the typically
lecherous, treacherous flirt of the misogynistic fabliau.[12] In the end, Harvey
seems simply to have lacked the delicacy required to make his women speak
with a courtly accent.

The scholar in courtly conversation

Harvey's inability to imagine courtiership is what prevented him from
mastering the skills required in a courtier, even though he knew what these
were from reading Castiglione and other courtesy manuals of the period.
However, despite his eager conviction that any art could be learnt in a
few days, courtesy, especially the courtesy of the court, had to be acquired
more as a habit than as a technique. Harvey should have understood from
his failure to ingratiate himself with the fellows of Pembroke Hall that
his own attempt as convivial *humanitas* could be regarded as clumsy and
artificial; but he seems to have been blind to his own defects, preferring to
blame his sometimes disastrous social life on the malice of enemies (which
was indeed part of the reason). It was the same with Harvey's attempts to
pass himself off as a courtier, as we can see from his behaviour at Audley
End, near Cambridge, in 1578. Elizabeth was on 'progress': a summer tour
of the shires. The queen was a learned woman who relished academic
disputations, and Harvey was chosen to head the trio of university scholars
opposing the theses that 'Clemency in a Prince is More Laudable than

Severity' and that 'The Stars do not Impose Necessity on Human Affairs'. Unfortunately, the texts do not survive; but the first would have given Harvey an opportunity to make some controversial remarks on *humanitas*. Harvey's side won; and he was presented to the queen after dinner that afternoon, when Elizabeth accepted a sheaf of Harvey's poetry called *Gabrielis Harveii* Χαιρε, *vel gratulatio Valdinensis* ('Gabriel Harvey's welcome, or: Greetings from Saffron Walden'). Even more significantly, she let Harvey kiss her hand, and said that he looked like an Italian. Harvey was exultant. He dashed off poems on the kiss ('De osculo') and his Italian looks ('De vultu Itali'); and these were included in the printed volume of the *Gratulationes*, a copy of which Harvey presented to Elizabeth at Hadham Hall later in her progress on 15 September 1578. It was a momentous episode in the young scholar's life, and Harvey wished to preserve it for posterity. Unfortunately, his poetry came back to haunt him nearly twenty years later, when Thomas Nashe ridiculed Harvey's escapades at Audley End in *Have With You to Saffron Walden* (1596). But let us first look at Harvey's own awkwardly rapturous account.

The pieces which make up the *Gratulationes Valdinenses* are examples of the rhetorical verse which served for poetry on ceremonial occasions such as a royal welcome. Each one takes a theme and varies it by the ingenious application of tropes and schemes until the poet decides he has done enough. They are technical exercises of the kind which crowd the prefaces of every scholarly book of the period: *encomiasticon, encomion, epaenticon, apobaterion, protrepticon*, and so on (see Binns, 1990, pp. 60–80). However, one or two poems do indulge in poetic fantasy, and 'De osculo' is one of them. It is a strange and almost phantasmagorical piece, in which time stands still whilst Harvey watches the queen leave the dining-hall, dreaming that he may be presented to her so that he may give her his poems. The poem is inhabited by deities, amongst whom, of course, Elizabeth is supreme. But mortals also flit in and out, such as the Earls of Leicester and Sussex. And a surprising degree of attention is focused on a certain 'Snaggus'. Apparently, the queen exchanged a word or two with him as she entered the dining-hall, and Harvey was enviously transfixed (sig. C1r):[13]

> *Butt now, Snagg allone, midst all stood gatherid withall,*
> *Him most felicitous, meethouht; him allone did I*
> *Wonder at, silentli, and the mans most fortunat stars praise.* [MP]

The inclusion of such lines was surely unwise. It is not so much that the name 'Snaggus' sounds and looks rather comical in Latin ('Iamque mihi Snaggus'). Nor is it that Harvey's lines are unremarkable; though Nashe says that they are the 'bungerliest vearses . . . that ever were scande' (*Have*

With You, p. 78). It is rather that Harvey fixes his aim too low. Here is Nashe's translation of another slightly misrepresented line: '*Imo, vidi ipse loquentem cum Snaggo*, I saw her conferring with no worse a man than Master Snagge'.[14] The phrase which Nashe adds here – 'no worse a man' – exactly catches Harvey's anxiousness about his own worth, which, for all his deliberate audacity, always holds him back even in his fantasy.[15] His dream is haunted by Snagge's *imago*, which is only exorcised when Harvey takes Snagge's place: 'I was another Snagge [*Snaggus ego alter eram*]' (sig. C2v). Yet Snagge, Harvey's alter ego, as it were, remains a mere shadow, a vaguely articulated aspiration of courtierly success.

This haziness is all the more surprising because Harvey thought he was an expert on courtiership. In his *elegia* to Sidney, who was also present at Audley End, Harvey includes versifications of the list of qualities expected of a courtier and a waiting-gentlewoman to his translation of *The Courtier*. These are of some interest, as Harvey makes very little of the scholarly accomplishments needed in the courtier, but emphasises the vernacular tradition: 'Lett him know ower letters, weav pleasauntlie owr vers; / Lett his Witt bee salt, but alsoe care it bee Urbane' (sig. L1r). Harvey hopes that his 'Cowrtli Muse [*Aulica Musa*]' will be strengthened by Sidney's presence and so allow him to 'turn out cowrtli posies [*Aulica tornare poemata*]'. Then, Harvey continues, he will be able to sing in the 'Castilionaean Quire [*Castilionaeo choro*]'. But the expertise he displays in this poem is little more than a digest, indeed, little more than the digest of a digest.[16] Harvey boasts to Sidney that he has compressed whole treatises into a few lines: 'as is mi way [*more meo*]'. But did he expect such a vaunt to be taken seriously? His poem on the court-lady is even more difficult. Little is made of her intellectual accomplishments, but much is said about the way she should look and how she should hold her fan. And once again, Harvey cannot resist a slightly racy allusion to women's sexual parts or activities. He concedes that he has little experience of women at all: 'Fewe secrets of the Rooms, I kno, wher Ladies live [*Pauca gynacei mysteria calleo*]' (sig. L3v). But he has read all the right books from Ovid to Boccaccio to Gascoigne; and also, he adds lubriciously: 'Ther bee prettye things, withal, in Physique bokes [*in Physicis dramata pulchra libris*]'. Presumably he means pictures or descriptions of female bodies in medical texts. The poem (and the volume) ends with a question: What do these court-ladies think of all this? The answer: 'Eche is silent [*Quaeque tacet*]' (sig. L4r). Harvey means that he has found out their little secrets and they are embarrassed to say anything; but we might like to see the women as rather appalled by Harvey's impertinence.

This is how Nashe saw Harvey's attempts to ingratiate himself with the ladies of the court: inept and coarse. We do not know whether Nashe's report in *Have With You* is true or not; what matters is his ability to construct such a plausible travesty of courtly humanism. Nashe gleefully depicts Harvey as a lecherous boorish pedant (pp. 75–6):[17]

> In selfe same order was hee at his pretie toyes and amorous glaunces and purposes with the Damsells, & putting baudy riddles unto them. In fine, some Disputations there were, and he made an Oration before the Maids of honour . . . beginning thus:
>
> > Nux, mulier, asinus simili sunt lege ligata,
> > Haec tria nil recte faciunt, si verbera desunt.
>
> > A nut, a woman, and an asse are like,
> > These three doo nothing right, except you strike. . . .
>
> The proces of that Oration was of the same woofe and thrid with the beginning: demurely and maidenly scoffing, and blushingly wantoning & making love to those soft skind soules & sweete Nymphes of Helicon, betwixt a kinde of carelesse rude ruffianisme and curious finicall complement; both which hee exprest by his countenance than anie good jests that hee uttered.

This is an amusingly hostile account: the scholar acts like a boor when he tries to be courtly. But it also neatly captures the way in which humane learning might be turned to the courtly trifle: a bawdy riddle in Latin proposed to the pretty amorets in the court. And Nashe smartly turns Harvey's relations with the Muses – the 'sweete Nymphs of Helicon' – into another example of gross discourtesy in courtship.

Nashe is also careful to note Harvey's inability to talk properly to the gentlemen of the court. He maliciously relates how 'Doctour Hum' – one of his innumerable abusive names for Harvey – 'thrust himselfe into the thickest rankes of the Noblemen and Gallants, and whatsoever they were arguing of, he would not misse to catch hold of, or strike in at the one end, and take the theame out of their mouths, or it should goe hard' (p. 75). Nashe imaginatively recreates Harvey in terms of a debased Ciceronian humanism. We know that the eloquent man should be able to discourse on 'All thynges whatsomever whych may fall unto the discussion of Menne' (*De orat.*, 2.5). But Nashe makes Harvey an aggressive interruptor – exactly what Cicero warns against in his remarks on *sermo* in the *De officiis* (1.134–6). Did he but know it, Nashe has intuitively grasped one of Harvey's maxims at the time: 'All is now, in bowld Courtly speaking' (*Marg.*, pp. 144–5). Nashe is an untrustworthy and malicious reporter, but he describes exactly the sort of thing that Harvey was telling himself to do in the late 1570s. Nashe tells us that Harvey's impertinence was unbounded. He cheerfully addressed his superiors as his equals: 'Haile fellowe well met with those that looke highest' (p. 77). Of course, this is exactly what Harvey complains of in his earthquake letter to Spenser: 'Many *Pupils,* Jackemates, and Hayle fellowes wel met, with their *Tutors*' (*Three Letters,* p. 622).

The scholar as ruffian

Nashe ends his account of the courtly phase of Harvey's career of failure with a few comments on the aftermath of *Three Letters.* Again, we see how Harvey seems to have simply lacked the finesse required to make himself seem amusing but discreet and useful to his superiors. Harvey's impatience with the traditional authorities at Cambridge has already been noted; he thought himself above such things. Unfortunately, he went too far in his criticisms of the university and its fellows, especially Dr Andrew Perne. Perne was the vice-chancellor – a dangerous target for Harvey to aim at. Indeed, Harvey would later claim that he never intended his letter to be published. But the evidence of the letter-book suggests that he had a hand in the preparation of *Three Letters,* and Harvey had a life-long addiction to witty summary judgements of people who stood in his way or otherwise displeased him. In any case, Harvey's lack of discretion in his comments on Spenser's 'olde Controllers new behaviour' (*Three Letters,* pp. 611–12) were misconstrued as referring to the Controller of the Household, Sir James Croft, rather than to Perne; and Harvey was called to account by the senior statesman to explain himself. In *Four Letters Confuted* (Nashe, 1592), Harvey says that his explanations were 'not onely received courteously, but accepted favourablie, and commended honourablye' (p. 33).

Harvey would have us think that he came out rather well from the scandal; but we may be more inclined to think that it had a good deal to do with his losing credit with the influential patron – most probably the Earl of Leicester – who had sponsored him at Audley End. Nashe tells the story in *Have With You* as follows (p. 79):

> He that most patronized him, prying more searchingly into him, and finding that he was more meete to make sport with than anie way deeply to be employd, with faire words shooke him of, & told him he was fitter for the Universitie than for the Court, or his turne, and so bad God prosper his studies, & sent for another Secretarie to Oxford.

Leicester must have known of Harvey's real intellectual qualities, since he cannot have been unaware that Harvey had been acting as a sort of research assistant for his nephew, Sir Philip Sidney (Grafton and Jardine,

1986).[18] But he cannot have been blind to Harvey's fatal love of libel: Harvey was too much of a political liability.

In other words, Harvey's description of himself as a 'silly humanitian of the old world' in *Pierce's Supererogation* is not entirely to be trusted. Harvey's polymathic learning and extensive training in the arts of composition failed him when he tried to be courtly. There was always too much 'bowld Courtly speaking'. He was perhaps temperamentally incapable of genuine courtesy with women, always tending towards what Nashe aptly describes as 'care-lesse rude ruffianisme and curious finicall complement'. He tries to mix sexual swagger with condescending erudition. But he was a 'ruffian' with other men as well. Harvey was certainly the victim of other men's malice, but much of it he seems to have brought upon himself by his own lack of *humanitas*. His vicious and pusillanimous attack on the newly deceased Robert Greene in *Four Letters* has rightly been described as 'worm's work' (Lewis, 1954, p. 354). The same point was made by Henry Chettle in his *Kind Heart's Dream* (1593). Several ghosts appear to the author, including that of Robert Greene, who has a message for 'Pierce Penniless', in other words, for Thomas Nashe. The ghost does not mention *Four Letters* by name, but that must be what he is referring to when he remarks that Envy has dis-turbed his rest and spat on his grave, as Harvey's attacks provoked a good deal of scandal in London literary circles. The ghost observes: '*Adversus mortuos bellum suspicere, inhumanum est*. There is no glory gained by breaking a deade mans skull' (sig. E1r). The inhumanity of Harvey's attack is empha-sised a few lines later: 'every halfe-eyd humanitian may account it, *Instar belluarum immannissimarum saevire in cadaver* [To savage a corpse is the mark of the cruellest beasts of prey]' (sig. E1v). Greene was no Pompey, but his ghost is right to remind us of the Valerian tradition of *humanitas* as clemency. Harvey could have held his tongue, but the urge to triumph was too strong. This 'half-eyd humanitian' is a far cry from Harvey's self-image as a 'silly humanitian of the old world'. Chettle's is an ugly, purblind creature: he is thinking of the owl, perhaps, but more as a bird of ill omen than of wisdom.

These two retrospectives on Harvey the humanitian provide us with a useful point of departure for the second half of this book. They both date from the 1590s, when the vogue for literary and dramatic satire cast a pall on the more idealistic aspect of Elizabethan humanism, perhaps even extin-guishing it. But first we deal with three texts which were all written in the late 1570s, the period to which Harvey's remarks on 'silly' humanism refer. Lyly, Spenser and Sidney were all closely connected with Harvey at this time, and it is possible to trace his shadowy influence on all of them. However, all three writers seem to resist the claims of the kind of *humanitas* which Harvey so passionately advocated (when it pleased him). They are rather lukewarm in their devotion to encyclopaedic or even neoclassical scholarship, and each proposes – though just as half-heartedly – an alternative emphasis in the literary culture of their time.

Notes

1. Ascham makes it clear that courtly 'boldnesse' is to be avoided in a young man, since it really means 'to dare do any mischief, to contemne stoutly any goodnesse, to be busie in every matter, to be skilfull in every thyng, to acknowledge no ignorance at all' (*Schoolmaster*, p. 207).

2. Cit. Stern, 1979, p. 125.

3. For a vivid picture of undergraduate life in Elizabethan Oxford, see McConica, 1986, pp. 645–732.

4. Euphues complains of the disorder at his own alma mater under the veil of the 'University of Athens' in a carelessly controversial passage in *Euphues* (pp. 283–6).

5. We might think here of the festive prankishness Shakespeare's Puck in *A Midsummer Night's Dream*, who is also known as 'that shrewde and knavish sprite / Call'd Robin goodfellow' (2.1.388–9). Hoby uses the term to describe courtiers who indulge in obscenity: 'they practise this beastlinesse for none other cause, but to bee counted good felowes' (*Courtier*, p. 143). This sort of sociability, then, is far removed from *humanitas*.

6. See the chapters on themes and orations in Baldwin, 1944, 2.288–354.

7. Elyot says exactly the same thing in *The Governor* (see above, ch. 4, n.9).

8. Or again: 'Any serviceable poynt, ether civil, courtly, or militar, is very soone learnid, by Art, & practis' (p. 89). If you are a 'sensible man', it would not take long to learn how to handle a horse, a sword, a gun: 'all three in one weeke, by good direction'. Harvey had clearly never learnt to ride a horse.

9. Cf. Cicero, *Pro Arch.*, § 2, *De orat.*, 3.21. Harvey's *Ciceronianus* is peppered with allusions to the *De oratore*.

10. Cf. Moryson: 'as an Orator and poet must have some skill in all Sciences, so the Humanist must have some knowledge of *all things which fall into practice and discourse*' (3.1.2, p. 11: italics added).

11. Abraham Fleming's *Bright Burning Beacon* (1580) is such a work, 'containing a generall doctrine of sundry signs, especially Earthquakes' and a 'commemoration of the late earthquake the 6 of April 1580' (title page). Fleming lists

several other authors who had already written on the topic by the time his own book was entered for publication on 27 June.

12. This tedious skeltonic rhapsody, composed in 1573, was the 'very first peece of Inglish Ryme that ever the autor committed to wrytinge' (*Letter-book*, p. 101). As Harvey was no partisan of rhyme, it is probably meant to be very bad, but this is a risky strategy.

13. The Latin reads: 'Iamque mihi Snaggus, cunctis a stantibus unus, / Esse videbatur faelicior: illum ego solum / Intueor, taciteque hominis bona sydera laudo'. I have attempted to render these lines into Harveian hexameters.

14. The Latin reads: 'vidi, vidi ipse loquentem / Cum Snaggo' (sig. D4v).

15. McKerrow suggests that Snaggus may be Thomas Snagge (1536–92), who was attorney-general for Ireland 1577–80 (1966, iv. 340). If so, Snaggus is a man with whom Harvey might well wish to compare himself; and it is worth noting that Harvey as well as Spenser had interests in Ireland at this period (Jardine, 1993).

16. Harvey seems to have consulted the summaries of the qualities required in courtiers and waiting-gentlewomen provided by Hoby at the end of his translation of *The Courtier*.

17. This is substantially the picture of Harvey in the satirical Cambridge play *Pedantius* (ms. 1581). See Moore Smith, 1905, pp. xxxiii–l.

18. At about the same time, Harvey was also writing to Arthur Capel on political and historical texts (*Letter-book*, pp. 167–8). Capel had been a particular friend at Cambridge. In another letter, Harvey asks Capel to remember him as 'the selfe same man that you fownd him by the fierside in his pore chamber the night before your departure from Cambridge, when you knowe what secrets and privityes he revealid unto you' (p. 182). It was at Capel's home in Hadham Hall that Harvey not only presented Elizabeth with the printed volume of his *Gratulationes* but also wrote the libellous 'Speculum Tuscanismo'.

PART TWO

Texts

CHAPTER SIX

Pregnant Wit: John Lyly's
Euphues: The Anatomy of Wit

John Lyly is in many ways the Elizabethan humanist *par excellence*. He was well read in classical literature; he was a polite author in his own right; and his work everywhere reveals the attitudes of the *homo humanus*. But he did not immediately discover the truly humane character of his muse; and Lyly's literary career begins with a piece in which his *humanitas* struggles to assert itself against the dead hand of godly moralism. But that is what makes *Euphues: The Anatomy of Wit* (1578) all the more interesting as a document in the history of the development of literary humanism in the later sixteenth century. Here we have a very good illustration of the tensions between the various strands of Elizabethan humanism and other elements in the literary culture of the period. For one thing, Lyly's humanism is what Harvey would call 'superficial'. Although Lyly completed the conservative Arts course at Oxford in 1575, and therefore must have had at least some exposure to the mathematical sciences as well as the arts of discourse, there is almost no evidence that the disciplines of the quadrivium made much impact on his mind. In fact, Lyly's own remarks on his education at Oxford seem to suggest that he received very little benefit at all from the six years he spent there.[1] On the other hand, he was clearly a lively student of the principal elements of humanity: poetry and rhetoric; and he followed the advice of Cicero's Crassus in using what he knew of philosophy – largely the moral philosophy of Plutarch and the natural philosophy of Pliny – in order to provide interesting decorative material with which to adorn his extremely stylish prose. However, he was very much aware that his particular talent for writing in a superabundantly ornamental kind of English could be counted against him. In the dedication to *Euphues*, he says: 'It is . . . methinketh a greater show of a pregnant wit, then perfect wisedome, in a thing of sufficient excellencie, to use superfluous eloquence' (p. 181).

Lyly knew he was indeed a 'pregnant wit', that is, a writer whose mind was 'teeming' with words and phrases and all the other literary bits and pieces that he had collected from other authors and stored in his mind. Harvey knew this, too, and would later recall how young Lyly used to boast about his 'euphuing of Similes' in *Pierce's Supererogation* (sig. I4v). Harvey here refers to the time he was friends with Lyly, when the latter was busy writing *Euphues* and perfecting, so it would seem, that element of his style which would come to be the salient feature of 'euphuism': similes drawn from works on natural history such as Pliny's great encyclopaedia – or simply invented. Harvey mutters: 'I could name the party, that in comparison of his owne naturall Inventions, tearmed Pliny a barraine woombe'. However, Lyly's reservations about his own pregnancy of wit may be traced not to Harvey, but to Ascham's comments on verbal excess in *The Schoolmaster*. Indeed, the main source of Lyly's artistic vexations in *Euphues* lies in his uneasy relationship with the authority of the great mid-Tudor humanist; and it is with this relationship we begin this chapter.

Lyly's Euphues and Ascham's *Euphuēs*

It is well known that Lyly's Euphues takes his name from the list of qualities required in a student drawn up up by Ascham in his *Schoolmaster*. The first of these 'Trewe notes of a good witte' reads as follows (p. 194):

I. *Euphuēs*.

Is he, that is apte by goodnes of witte, and appliable by readines of will, to learning, having all other qualities of the minde and partes of the bodie, that must an other day serve learning, not trobled, mangled, and halfed, but sounde, whole, full, & hable to do their office: as a tong, not stamering, or over hardlie drawing forth wordes, but plaine, and redie to deliver the meaning of the minde: a voice, not softe, weake, piping, womannishe, but audible, stronge, and manlike: a countenance, not werishe and crabbed, but faire and cumlie: a personage, not wretched and deformed, but taule and goodlie: for surelie, a cumlie countenance, with a goodlie stature, geveth credit to learning, and authoritie to the person: otherwise commonlie, either, open contempte, or privie disfavour doth hurte, or hinder, both person and learning.

This description might have seemed to Lyly's first readers a rather odd description of the *euphuēs*, since the Greek word *euphuïa* was regularly used in school handbooks of rhetoric as a synonym for the Latin *ingenium*, which we would call 'natural talent', and which the Elizabethans usually translated as 'wit'. Yet Ascham concentrates less on the 'qualities of the minde' and much more on the 'partes of the bodie'.

This is because Ascham's description is based on the passage in the *De oratore* where Crassus delineates the 'giftes of Nature' required in the perfect orator: 'a slipper tong, a sonable voice, goode lunges, & vigorousnes, and a certaine shapelines of his whole face and bodie' (1.114). Here we have what we would call mental as well as, and opposed to, physical qualities; but to the Romans, especially those trained in Greek rhetorical traditions, there was no such sharp opposition. The Greek word for 'nature' is *phusis*, which is the origin of our word *physical*; but for the Greeks and Romans, the mind was 'physical' as well: the mental part of the natural body. Hence, the word *euphuēs* – which means 'naturally well developed' (*eu-phu-ēs*) – is an apt one to cover the full range of mental and physical qualities required by Ascham in his student.[2]

On the other hand, Ascham's account gives us not only the perfect but also the imperfect specimen. This antithesis seems to spring naturally from his source, but it may also be informed by Ascham's sensitivity to the inhumanity of a post-lapsarian world marked by verbal abuse: 'open contempte'. This rather unexpected final emphasis on the scorn faced by the physically imperfect – Ascham was himself small and weakly – provides an interesting though perhaps unconscious link with a less common sense of the word *euphuïa*: 'scurrility'. In any case, the shadow of the 'quick wit' whom Ascham so much distrusted falls on his description of the *euphuēs*. For Ascham, there were two kinds of students: 'quick wits' and – he cannot bring himself to call them 'slow' – 'hard wits'.[3] These are the ones he prefers; they do not learn quickly, but what they learn they remember. It is very different with quick wits, however (p. 188):

> Quicke wittes commonlie, be apte to take, vnapte to keepe: soone hote and desirous of this and that: as colde and sone wery of the same againe: more quicke to enter spedelie, than hable to pearse farre: even like over sharpe tooles, whose edges be verie soone turned.

Ascham gives a strongly disapproving moral inflection to his description of naturally quick wits. They have that excess of 'boldness' which he regarded as a symptom of inhumanity: 'bolde, with any person: busie, in every matter; sothing, soch as be present: nipping any that is absent'. This is particularly true of young wits: 'In yougthe, they be readie scoffers, privie mockers, and ever over light and mery'. Ascham had been a teacher for many years when he wrote these lines; and we may be sure that personal observation of the way clever boys treated their 'hard-witted' fellows informs his emphasis on the quick wit's disposition to mockery and mirth.

But when we turn to Lyly's Euphues, we see that the youthful writer – he was in his mid-twenties – has reversed what Ascham intended in a very remarkable way. This is how *Euphues* begins – with already fully developed euphuistic trimmings (p. 184):

> There dwelt in Athens a young gentleman of great patrimonie, & of so comely a personage, that it was doubted whether he were more bound to Nature for the liniaments of his person, or to fortune for the encrease of his possessions. But Nature impatient of comparisons, and as it were disdaining a companion, or copartner in hir working, added to this comlinesse of his body suche a sharpe capacitie of minde, that not onely she proved Fortune counterfaite, but was halfe of that opinion that she hir selfe was onely currant. This young gallant, of more wit then wealth, and yet of more wealth than wisdome, seeing himselfe inferiour to none in pleasant conceipts, thought himselfe superiour to al in honest conditions, insomuch that he deemed himselfe so apt to all things, that he gave himselfe almost to nothing, but practising of those things commonly which are incident to these sharp wits, fine phrases, smoth quipping, merry taunting, using jesting without meane, & abusing mirth without measure.

The verbal debt to Ascham must be obvious. Even Lyly's rechristening of the 'quick wit' as the 'sharp wit' is authorised by Ascham's simile of 'over sharpe tooles'.[4] But equally obvious, and more puzzling, is Lyly's naming this character after Ascham's perfect student. Lyly must have known that his readers would be surprised by this transformation – indeed, degradation – of Ascham's *euphuēs*, since *The Schoolmaster* was virtually required reading by educated men of his generation. We return to Lyly's likely purpose in making so radical an alteration to his source at the end of this chapter; but let us close this section by returning to Lyly's anxieties about his own 'pregnant wit'.

Ascham's 'quick wits' are so called because they are 'quicke to enter spedelie' into their studies; but it is not only such celerity that gives them their title. The word 'quick' can also mean 'pregnant' (as in the archaic phrase 'quick with child'). It is therefore associated with that 'fulness' which Ascham deplored in literary style, and dimly connected with the excess of animal spirits which so easily led men from humanity to brutishness. Not surprisingly, then, Ascham uses the word 'quick' in his remarks on the need for certain writers to practise epitome on their own style. Such excess is a particular fault of 'quicke inventors, and faire readie speakers', whose heads are 'over full of matter' (p. 263). He mentions Smith's old adversary in the Greek controversy in this context: 'The Bishop of Winchester Stephen Gardiner had a quicke head, and a readie tong, and was yet not the best writer in England' (p. 264). Lyly must have read these lines with a certain amount of misgiving. If Harvey may be trusted, Lyly, privately amongst his friends, exulted in the fertility of his 'naturall Inventions'; but he seems to have invested so heavily in Ascham's moralised prescriptions in *The School-master* that he could hardly declare his delight in his own inventiveness in public. Rather, he apologises – but not always with a good grace. *Euphues* is an imperfect work, and its defects may be traced to this conflict with the authority of Ascham and the literary culture he represented. Let us now look at Lyly's own position within this culture in more detail.

The prodigal scholar

Lyly came from a family of distinguished scholars. His grandfather, William Lilly, was one of the most eminent 'professors of humanity' of the Tudor period. A graduate of Magdalen College, Oxford, he was the first High Master of St Paul's School, and the co-author (with Erasmus) of 'Lilly's Grammar', the book which was used in almost every Elizabethan school to teach boys Latin. Lyly's uncle, George Lilly, was a formidable scholar, too, and another Magdalen graduate. George Lilly spent much of his time in Italy, as secretary to the young and learned Cardinal Pole. Consequently, his works are less well known; but it is interesting to note that he appended a eulogy of the foremost English scholars and their lives and works to Paulus Jovius's *Descriptio Britanniae, Scotiae, Hiberniae, et Orcadum* ('A Description of Britain, Scotland, Ireland, and the Orkneys': 1548). Here were scholars – indeed, 'humanists' in the modern sense – whose excellent example John Lyly might have been expected to follow; and he did indeed go up to Magdalen himself in 1569.[5]

But it seems that Lyly was not at all like Ascham's *euphuēs*. Antony à Wood tells us in his *Athenae Oxonienses* ('The Learned Men of Oxford': 1691) that Lyly was 'esteemed in the University a noted Wit' (cit. Bond, ed., 1902, 1.7). However, he was also 'averse to the crabbed studies of Logic and Philosophy', choosing rather to tread the 'pleasant paths of Poetry'. How much we can trust Wood's words is hard to tell, but the gossipy historian of Oxonian worthies is only saying what Lyly himself more frankly admits in a letter to his kinsman, William Cecil, Lord Burghley, in May 1574, towards the end of his first year of the MA. Burghley, whom Lyly addresses in this letter as his *patronus*, was the single most important person in Lyly's career as a client; and here Lyly is asking him to use his influence with the queen – he was Lord Treasurer – to have his young cousin installed as a fellow of Magdalen, apparently against the wishes of the other dons. The Latin letter which Lyly wrote to Burghley on this occasion survives. Lyly gratefully alludes to Burghley's 'Humanitie and helpfulnes to all lovers of letters [*humanitas et in litterarum studiosos pietas*]' (Bond, 1902, 1.13 [MP]).[6] But more important is Lyly's admission that he is essentially immature: 'a rash youth and recklesse'. He explains: 'Advancing age hath not rypened my reason, nor have my maners been made whole by holiness of life, nor yet am I laden with learning in artes & sciences'. This is the sort of feckless young man, as Lyly well knows, to whom places in university colleges or elsewhere in the established order are not easily given; he might almost be describing one of Ascham's 'quick wits' – and it is interesting to note that Ascham's widow had dedicated *The Schoolmaster* to Burghley's protection. Most damning, one would think, must have been Lyly's frank admission that he is not 'laden with learning'. What had he been doing for the past five years?

On the other hand, Lyly also knows that he might be able to use his talents as a wit in order to pass off as a sort of merry lark what is actually an abuse. Lyly flatteringly refers to Burghley as a 'most noble Hero, who sleepeth not, that our realm may rest, who well defendeth the weal publique, and all our fortunes'. But then he asks Burghley to modify this heroic role as the defender of the commonweal in order to take advantage of his power and influence on the behalf of his irresponsible young kinsman. Lyly suggests that Burghley should act rather like a bully: 'your Highnes might stoope to the extraction [*extorqueo*] of certayne letters, if my Latin may be let slip, of Mandation, from her Most Serene Majestie, that I may steal in amongst the society of the Magdalenians by surprise [*obrepere*], these letters laid before them, I led by your Highness as my guide'. Lyly contrives to present the imposition on the fellows of his college as a parody of the Siege of Troy, and yet at the same time seems to be more interested in a lapse in his Latinity than in the overthrowing of collegial good order he proposes. However, Lyly puts his wit aside at the end of the letter, when he promises to reform his ways, declaring that henceforth he should not be found wanting in 'diligence in the acquisition of learning' either. What teacher or parent or patron has not heard such a promise? Certainly nothing came of the attempt, and Lyly took his MA the following summer, a year earlier than would normally be expected, and left Oxford behind him.

Lyly's movements over the next year or two are obscure; but in 1578 we find him in London, at the Savoy, in the company of Gabriel Harvey, and no doubt other literary-minded young men. Lyly seems to have brought with him the reputation of a wit, at least, according to Harvey's testimony. As we have seen, Lyly and Harvey fell out shortly after the publication of *Euphues*; and though it had been Lyly's own fault, he was still looking to get his own back on Harvey when he was asked by the bishops to respond to the anti-presbyterian satirist 'Martin Marprelate'. The result was his pamphlet *Pap with an Hatchet* (1589). Here Lyly makes a few casually insulting allusions to Harvey as a 'mad lad and such a one as cares as little for writing without wit as Martin doth for writing without honesty' (p. 400). And Harvey returns the same jibe in the 'Advertisement for Pap-Hatchet' which he published four years later in *Pierce's Supererogation* (sig. R4r):

> He hath not played the Vicemaster of Poules and the Fool master of the Theatre for naughte: himself a mad lad, as ever twangd, never troubled with any substance of witt, or circumstance of honesty, sometime the fiddle-sticke of Oxford, now the very bable of London.

This passage is a darker version of one that occurs earlier in the 'Advertisment' (sig. K1v):

> They were much deceived in him, at Oxford, and in the Savoy, when Master Absolon lived; that tooke him onely for a dapper & deft companion, or a pert-conceited youth, that had gathered-togither a few prettie sentences, and could handsomly helpe young Euphues to an old Simile: & never thought him any such mighty doer at the sharpe.

These remarks confirm that Lyly already was known as a wit at Oxford and in his early days in London. Indeed, it was this reputation which must have persuaded the bishops to commission his services on their behalf in the Marprelate scandal as a duellistic 'doer at the sharpe'. But when Lyly wrote *Euphues*, he seems to have wished to escape from such a reputation (at least partly).[7]

Since Richard Helgerson's study *The Elizabethan Prodigals* (1976), we have become used to locating *Euphues* within the tradition of 'literary prodigalism'. This was a strategy used by several writers of the period to represent themselves as repentant prodigals who wished to prove their reformation by being given some responsible and remunerative employment. The original prodigal was George Gascoigne, who died in 1577, the year before Lyly wrote *Euphues*; and it can be demonstrated that Lyly quite consciously positioned himself as Gascoigne's successor in this respect. *Euphues* is peppered with authorial asides which reveal Lyly's interest in assuming the role of a reformed prodigal; and we have already seen him use the same tactic with Burghley. It is in this context that Lyly makes his comments on 'pregnant wit' as opposed to 'perfect wisedome' in the dedication to the work. The opposition is intended tactfully to imply that Lyly knows the difference between wit and wisdom, and is inclined towards the latter, however much he may seem naturally predisposed towards the former (for there could be no disguising the ornamental abundance of his style). The problem was that there was no real substance to such a hint. Lyly was no wiser now than he had been when he left Oxford; and this meant that he had to fall back on a traditional 'anti-humanist' position with which he surely had little real sympathy.

Humanity and divinity

Despite his protestations to Burghley, Lyly did not apply himself to learning in the years that followed. Wood's account of Lyly's career at Oxford, and his aversion to 'the crabbed studies of Logic and Philosophy', though not exactly trustworthy, is nonetheless very plausible. Lyly certainly shows no interest in logic. The only time he deploys the formal Aristotelian syllogism is in a ribald travesty to do with the gallows in *Pap with an Hatchet* (1589).[8] Moreover, the euphuistic simile, with its insistence on 'arguments from analogy', is an affront to the formal logic of his day. Nor can we say much for Lyly's attention to philosophy. He liked the 'natural philosophy' of Pliny's *Historia naturalis* ('Natural History') because it afforded him a treasury of arcane titbits which he could use in his similes; and he may have prized Plutarch's moral-philosophical pieces in the *Moralia* ('Moral Essays') for their anecdotal character. In fact, the only kind of 'philosophy' he seems much to have studied was magic. For example, in *Euphues and his England*, he shows first-hand knowledge of Johannes Wier's *De praestigiis daemonum* ('The Conjuration of Demons': 1569; see Roberts, 1979). However, 'divinity', and its associated literature, offered him an alternative kind of knowledge to which he might show some kind of nominal allegiance, as if he were dissatisfied with the secular character of what he had learnt at university and since.

We have already seen that 'humanity', as 'secular knowledge', was apt to be placed in a subordinate and sometimes antagonistic position to 'divinity'. Lyly takes advantage of this habit of mind to continue Euphues's transition from youthful wit to mature wisdom, and, by implication, his own reformation in the direction of civil responsibility. In fact, he goes one step beyond what he probably had in mind for himself, since Euphues ends up in isolation 'in the countrey' (p. 321). However, even this is part of the logic of the opposition between humanity and divinity. The two terms are used in their usual complementary relation by Lyly when he first has occasion to castigate Euphues for his self-conceit. He lists the discursive vices of those who pride themselves on their 'sharpe capacitie', beginning with the Aschamian observation that 'if one bee harde in conceiving, they pronounce him a dowlte' (p. 195). The list ends: 'if there be reasoning of divinitie, they cry, *Quae supra nos nihil ad nos*, if of humanitie, *Sententias loquitur carnifex*'. The point here is that sharp wits do not like to discuss any learned topic with due seriousness ('What is above us is not for us to talk about' and 'The hangman speaks sententiously'). But what matters to us is that it indicates that Lyly observes the usual division of learning between divinity and humanity. Euphues, of course, inclines towards the latter. His speech is peppered with allusions to classical authors; and in his first extended oration he actually uses the word 'humanity'.

Euphues has left Athens and come to Naples, where he meets a wise old man called Eubulus, who tries to persuade him to live a little more soberly. Euphues treats this advice with scorn; and he is particularly incensed by Eubulus's tactfully veiled comments on the need to rein in his natural exuberance, since this seems to him to be a criticism of his very being (his name, as we have seen, signifies 'naturally well developed'). Euphues spends most of his reply in defence of natural talent: 'Nature was had in such estimation and admiration among the Heathen people, that she was reputed for the onely Goddesse in Heaven' (p. 192). This is a remark ill-calculated to please the divine, and it comes after the claim – which is perhaps worse – that there 'yet was never any Impe so wicked & barbarous, any Turke so vile and brutish, any beast so dull and senceless' that would not praise Nature. Here the usual terms used to describe the antitype of *humanitas*, such as 'barbarous' and 'brutish', mingle with words which have a moral emphasis, such as 'wicked', and the inclusion of the 'Turke' suggests a specifically Christian viewpoint. Yet the whole passage, together with support from the ancient philosophers Cicero and Aristotle, could be taken as suspiciously 'heathen'. Euphues himself, however, only argues that to deny these arguments one would have to be a liar or 'an enemye to humanitie', by which he probably means a person who is simply antagonistic to humane learning.

Euphues does not change his mind until much later in the book, after he has cheated his friend Philautus by wooing and apparently winning the latter's fiancee, Lucilla, only to be jilted by her in turn for a fool called Curio. Now Euphues wishes he had never left his native city and its university (p. 241):

> I will to Athens ther to tosse my bookes, no more in Naples to lyve with faire lookes . . . Philosophie, Physicke, Divinitie, shal be my studie. O the hidden secrets of Nature, the expresse image of morall virtues, the equall ballaunce of Justice, the medicines to heale all diseases, how they beginne to delyght me. The *Axiomaes* of Aristotle, the *Maxims* of Justinian, the *Aphorisms* of Galen, have sodaynelye made such a breache into my minde that I seeme onely to desire them which did onely earst detest them.

In other words, Euphues now sets his sights on the superior degrees associated with the professions. It would seem, then, that he has already completed the

Athenian equivalent of his MA, although traces of the quadrivium are hard to find in his speech.[9] However, Euphues does not, in fact, go on to study anything but philosophy.

Nor do we learn much of what he discovered. The 'Ephebus', a tract on education, is supposed to have been written soon after his return to Athens, and is in any case a translation of Plutarch, rather than Euphues's own work (although he never tells us so). It is only after he has delivered this oration that he truly settles down to his own private study (p. 286):

> Euphues having ended his discourse, & finished those preceptes which he thought necessary for the instructing of youthe, gave his minde to the continuall studye of Philosophie, insomuch as he became publyque Reader in the Universitie, with such commendacion as never any before him, in the which he continued for the space of tenne yeares, onely searching out the secrets of Nature & the hidden misteries of Philosophy, & having collected into three volumes his lectures, thought for the profite of young schollers to sette them forth in print, which if hee had done, I would also in this his *Anatomy* have inserted, but hee alteringe his determination, fell into this discourse with himselfe.

It is hard not to see here a reflection of Lyly's own interests in Pliny's *Historia naturalis* and in the more speculative sciences. However, this is all we hear. In other words, Euphues's ten years of philosophy are passed over in as many lines. Lyly teases us with the dismal prospect of three volumes of Euphues's lecture notes, but withholds them because he wishes to remain true to Euphues's wishes. 'I was determined to write notes of Philosophy,' Euphues tells the gentlemen scholars of Athens in the preface to his 'Atheos', a dialogue in which he converts an atheist to faith, but he has changed his mind because this would have been to 'feede [them] fat wyth follye' (p. 289).

Lyly thus neatly sidesteps the problem of demonstrating to Burghley – or to anyone else for that matter – his studious application to the kind of learning which Oxford had to offer but which he had declined to accept. Thus he saves himself from writing any 'discourses' which might reveal his genuine ignorance of any other philosophical authors than the chatty Plutarch or the encyclopaedic Pliny. True, Euphues does sprinkle his writings with references to philosophers such as Plato and Pythagoras; but the period was rich in handy collections of wise saws, drawn up under headings and attributed, often erroneously, to one or other of the ancient sages.

The case is settled by Euphues's sudden conversion at this point to godliness (pp. 286–7):

> Why Euphues art thou so addicted to the studye of the Heathen that thou hast forgotten thy God in Heaven? shal thy witte be rather employed to the

attaining of humayne wisedome then devine knowledge? Is Aristotle more deare to thee with his bookes, then Christ with his bloude? What comfort canst thou finde in Philosophy for thy guiltie conscience, what hope of the resurrection, what gladde tidinges of the Gospell?

Here Euphues finally banishes any doubts we might have had about the 'heathen' affinities of his earlier attchment to 'humanity'; and he also confirms his godliness by means of a positive valediction to the humane arts: 'Farewell therefore the fine and filed phrases of Cicero, the pleasaunt *Eligies* of Ovid, the depth and profound knowledge of Aristotle. Farewell Rhetoricke, farewell Philosophie, farewell all learninge which is not sprenge from the bowels of the holy Bible' (p. 287).

From such a declaration we might expect Euphues to go on to become a divine; but he does not. Instead, he remains 'a scholler in Athens' (p. 306). Perhaps he studies divinity; but that is by no means clear. He also seems to be living 'in the countrey' (p. 321). This may mean no more than 'not at court', since he makes this remark to Livia, a gentlewoman at the imperial court of Naples; in this case, Athens might still be meant. This Athens is marked not by learning alone, but also by piety. Euphues tells Livia: 'We thinke it as great mirth to sing Psalmes, as you melody to chaunt Sonnets'. Lyly seems to have in mind Ascham's picture in *The Schoolmaster* of St John's College, Cambridge, after the accession of Elizabeth and the restitution of the reformed faith, which he sees as a grove in which flourish '*Religio* for sinceritie, *literae* for order and advauncement' (p. 282). It is from such a viewpoint, in any case, that Euphues writes the series of letters to various friends and acquaintances which forms the final section of *Euphues*. His writings now mingle humanity and divinity in roughly equal quantities; but he still relies on the humane arts rather than Scripture for his materials – for Euphues can only know as much as Lyly did.[10] The divinity, however, shows through not in terms of the learning associated with the term, but in a rather uncompromising moral stance which Euphues confuses with godliness. It would not be too much to say that Euphues has become, in the loose sense of that term, a 'Puritan'. And we end this chapter by examining Euphues's descent into *severitas*.

Humanity and severity

Remarking on the literary culture in which Lyly produced *Euphues*, particularly on the desirability of seeming a serious-minded young man rather than a mere wit, C.S. Lewis observes: 'Moral severity was modish as well as prudent' (1954, p. 314). On the whole, Lyly generally inclines towards *humanitas* rather than *severitas*; but his muse struggles with his Aschamian material in *Euphues*. It is not that Ascham's treatise is itself inhumane; it was written, after all, partly to denounce the common idea that boys had to be regularly beaten in order to make them obedient students. Rather, Lyly seems to have been influenced by the way Gascoigne developed *The School-master* in one of the several works he wrote intended to prove his own moral reformation: *The Glass of Government* (1575). This is a 'tragical comedy', and the tragic part of the play deals with two prodigal sons who are modelled quite explicitly on Ascham's quick wits. Gnomaticus, the schoolteacher hired to prepare them for university, comments: 'the quickest wits prove not alwayes best, for as they are readie to conceive, so do they quickly forget, & therewithall, the finenesse of their capacitie doth carie oftentimes to delight in vanities' (p. 38). There are also two younger brothers, hard wits who learn their lessons well with their schoolmaster and later at university, and are eventually preferred to positions of responsiblity: one becomes a minister in Geneva, the other secretary to the palsgrave. The elder sons, however, become entangled with harlots and other low types, leave university, and come to bad ends. One takes to fornication and is whipped until he cannot stand; the other commits robbery and is executed on the palsgrave's orders: 'yea even in sight of his Brother' (p. 86). When the margrave of the boys' home city, Antwerp, hears this, and how the younger brother's pleas were unable to save the elder, he murmurs with grim satisfaction: 'It is a happy common wealth where Justice may be ministred with severitie, and where no mediacions or sutes may wrest the sentence of the Law'.

Gascoigne's Margrave – he is actually called Severus to make the point clear – represents a particularly harsh inflection of the prodigal son story which was favoured by many Tudor writers.[11] For example, Gascoigne's play seems to owe much to the anonymous morality play *Nice Wanton* (c. 1550, pr. 1560). Dalilah and Ismael skip school and die badly: one of the pox and the other hanged in chains. The moral is announced in the first two lines of the play: 'The prudent Prince Salomon, doth say, / He that spareth the rod, the child doth hate' (sig. A1v). Dalilah and Ismael should have had wisdom beaten into them, then. As we have seen, it was partly in order to challenge the old proverb 'Spare the rod and spoil the child' that Ascham wrote his *Schoolmaster*. In the conversation on the virtues of beating that gave rise to Ascham's book, Solomonic authority is invoked by Sir William Petre, 'as one somewhat severe of nature' (p. 176). But Ascham deplores the use of violence in schools, and although Lyly has nothing to say on this particular matter, he responds much more warmly to the humane aspects of Ascham's *Schoolmaster* than Gascoigne. He allows the quick wit to be saved from the sentence of death or extreme corporal punishment which the severe treatment of the prodigal story seems to insist on. On the other hand, since, for the reasons suggested above, Euphues is pushed towards the character of a godly moralist in the second part of *Euphues: The Anatomy of Wit*, he tends in this latter phase of his incarnation to deal with others more severely than he himself was dealt by in the first part of the book. Indeed, it is not clear to modern readers that the reformed Euphues is really any better than the unreformed one.

The younger Euphues is certainly vicious enough, however. In his conversations with other young people, he displays a certain degree of courtly *humanitas*: he is witty and urbane, and his playful and flirtatious use of learning would have recommended him to Castiglione. On the other hand, he can be extremely rude. This is most shockingly evident in the first episode of the story, in which the wise old man of Naples, Eubulus, advises Euphues to keep his wits about him and live a little more moderately. Euphues deliberately misunderstands Eubulus and accuses him of trying to impose on others a 'severitie of lyfe' (p. 194) which nobody could achieve. But this is mere hyperbole. Although he claims to have no love for 'sophistrye' (p. 190), Euphues amuses himself by taking Eubulus's oration to pieces as a means of displaying his own sharp capacity, but in doing so allows his genuinely learned wit to slip into taunting, as when he declares that Eubulus has a 'waxinge and melting brayne' (p. 191), or that in his youth must have been a 'very vicious and ungodly man' (p. 192). He leaves Eubulus with 'teares trickling downe his cheekes' (p. 195).

Eubulus, however, is eminently 'humane'. He is a learned man whose mind has been formed by his education. His speech is a model of formal rhetoric, whereas Euphues's response is not much more than a series of clever taunts. But Eubulus is also kindly and well-spoken, and his modest eloquence – though it seems laughably 'aged & overworn' to Euphues (p. 193) – would have recommended him to both Cicero and Ascham. And once Euphues has reformed, he wants to let it be known that he models himself on the old man he once vilified. Eubulus's last words to Euphues are repeated more-or-less verbatim by the reformed Euphues to the young readers for whom his 'Ephebus' is written. Eubulus, for example, states: 'Bee merrye but with modestie, be sober but not to sulloume' (p. 189). Euphues repeats the advice: 'bee merrye but with modestie, bee sober but not too sullen' (p. 286). Unfortunately, though he remembers Eubulus's precepts very exactly, he has never much heeded them. The first part of these complementary maxims clearly derives from Ascham's 'over light and mery' (*Schoolmaster*, p. 188) and Lyly's 'mirth without measure' (p. 184). The second looks like an obvious development from the first; yet it too can be traced back to Ascham, and it provides the clue to the elder Euphues's sullenness.

Ascham provides a sketch of the progress of the quick wit from youth to age (p. 189):

> In yougthe ... they be, readie scoffers, privie mockers, and ever over light and mery. In aige, sone testie, very waspishe, and alwaies over miserable: and yet few of them come to any great aige, by reason of their misordered life when they were yong: but a greate deal fewer of them cum to shewe any great countenance, or beare any great authoritie abrode in the world, but either live obscurelie, men know not how, or dye obscurelie, men marke not whan.

Gascoigne cuts off his quick wits in their prime; but Lyly takes the gentler alternative in Ascham's splendidly gloomy prospect. Euphues becomes a relentlessly dyspeptic correspondent. For example, Philautus is given a lashing for his behaviour at court: 'It is nowe in everye mans mouth, that thou, yea, thou Philautus, art so voyde of curtesie, that thou hast almost forgotten common sence and humanitie, havinge neither care of religion (a thing to common in a courtier) neither regard of honestie or any vertuous behaviour' (p. 307). The hectoring tone of these words betrays that Euphues really wants to assert his moral authority by criticising his old friend. The same tone mars his other letters; only the one to Botonio 'to take his exile patiently' is merely pompous but without obvious rancour. On the other hand, Euphues's letter to Eubulus displays an intolerably smug severity.

Here we learn that the old man had a daughter, but that she is now dead. One might expect the reformed Euphues's letter to be consolatory. In fact, it is just as shocking as the young Euphues's earlier scoffs and insults (p. 310):

> Thou weepest for the deathe of thy daughter, & I laugh at the folly of the father; for greater vanitie is there in the minde of the mourner, then bitternesse in the deathe of the deceased, but she was amyable, but yet sinful, but she was young & might have lyved, but she was mortall and must have dyed. I but hir youth made thee often merry, I but thine age should once make thee wise, I but hir greene yeres wer unfit for death, I but thy hoary haires shoulde dispise lyfe.

Lyly impatiently exhorts Eubulus to be patient, but he lacks true humanity. The letter looks like a school exercise in the 'epistle consolatory'. To make matters worse, Euphues actually quotes Eubulus's own words at him. The memorable list of precepts which the old man delivered to the young one at the start of the story begins: 'Descende into thine owne conscience' (p. 189). Now it is Euphues's turn: 'Descende ... into thine owne conscience' (p. 311). It seems almost like a taunt; and it is difficult to see how Lyly could have made the reformed Eupheus any more despicable than he is at this point in his development. Certainly, there is a hard sanctimoniousness in Euphues's philosophical or even 'godly' laughter at Eubulus's grief which is difficult to reconcile with *humanitas*.

Matters do get worse, however. In the first edition of *Euphues*, the letter of consolation was written to Lucilla's father, Ferardo; but Lyly had forgotten that Ferardo had died of grief when Lucilla announced her intention to marry Curio, so he changed the correspondent to Eubulus. So the dead daughter was really Lucilla, and in the following letter, addressed to Philautus, we find out what happened to her. According to Philautus's report as rehearsed by Euphues, she turned courtesan and came to a bad end (p. 312):

> She was stricken sodaynely beeinge troubled with no sickenesse: It may be; for it is commonly seene, that a sinfull lyfe is rewarded with a soddayne deathe, and a sweete beginning with a sowre ende. Thou addest moreover that she being in great credite with the states, died in great beggarie in the streetes, certes it is an olde saying that who so lyveth in the courte shall dye in the strawe, she hoped there by delyghtes to gayne money, and by hir deserts purchased misery.

Lucilla has clearly converted all the lands left to her by Ferardo into money and spent it, turning to the profession of a courtesan in order to provide for herself for a while, until, finally rejected by the court's appetite for the delights she was able to offer, she dies in poverty in the streets. In other words, Lucilla is a female prodigal.

Philautus remembers her loveliness, but Euphues dismisses the appeal: 'Thou sayest that for beautie she was the Helen of Greece, and I durst sweare that for beastlines she might be the Monster of Italy' (p. 312). Beauty and beastliness: much lies in the eye of the beholder. Euphues recounts with disgust the regret at the fair Lucilla's passing which seems to be shared by Philautus and his fellow courtiers, using this regret to bully and hector Philautus:

> If thou meane to keepe me as a friende shake of those vaine toyes and dalyaunces wyth women, beleeve me Philautus I speake it wyth salt tears trickling downe my cheekes, the lyfe thou livest in court is no less abhorred then the wicked death of Lucilla detested, & more art thou scorned for thy folly, than she hated for her filthinesse.

These are ugly words, and it is hard to believe that Lyly wants us to approve of them. Euphues's rhetoric of scorn and hate excludes Lucilla from the order of humanity by degrading her to a beast or a monster, and he threatens Philautus with the same exclusion if he continues to court it with ladies. But we cannot help feeling that it is Euphues who is here inhumane in apparently refusing to believe that Philautus might feel pity for Lucilla. Euphues seems to think that Philautus and the others are vexed merely because they have lost a tasty morsel ('snatched out of the jawes of so many young gentlemen'). He forgets that Philautus once loved Lucilla.

The severity with which Lucilla is treated here is made all the more remarkable, indeed puzzling, by the close and revealing parallel in the fate of Dalilah in *Nice Wanton*. Dalilah becomes a prostitute and eventually dies of a 'pockes, taken at the stewes' (sig. B4v). But she does not die in the streets. Terribly disabled and disfigured by disease, and stricken by a guilty conscience, she meets her godly brother Barnabas, who, although he does not recognise her at first, takes her in and looks after her. He is glad to report that she fully repented her sins and died in the hope of redemption through God's mercy. Severity, then, is tempered by mercy. Even Gascoigne's courtesan Lamia escapes with a mere ducking.

But it is very tempting to see an allusion in Euphues's account of Lucilla's death to Robert Henryson's well-known *Testament of Cresseid* (first printed in 1532). Henryson takes up the story told by Chaucer in *Troilus and Criseyde* and offers his own version of what happened to Criseyde. Chaucer tells us how Criseyde abandoned Troilus and took up with Diomede instead, leaving her there at the end of his poem. But Henryson relates how Diomeid soon grew tired of Cresseid and cast her away: 'Than desolait scho walkit up and doun, / And sum men sayis into the court commoun' (lines 76–7). Henryson is courteously reluctant to acknowledge that she became a courtesan; but he repeats the charge and tells how, shamed, Cresseid returned in disguise to her father's house. Here she rather unwisely blamed Venus and Cupid for betraying her, and a council of the gods decides that she shall be punished with leprosy. Reduced to beggary and misery, she eventually meets again with Troylus, who though he fails to recognise her, is somehow stirred by memories of 'fair Cresseid, sumtyme his awen darling' (line 504). He throws a golden chain in her lap and rides off in confusion; and when Cresseid learns who it was, she faints, and after lamenting her own faithlessness, soon dies. When Troylus hears of her sorry fate, and 'how scho endit in sic povertie', he is grievously moved: 'For greit sorrow his hart to brist was boun: / Siching full sadlie said: 'I can no moir – / Scho was untrew and wo is me thairfoir' (lines 598, 600–3).

I have told Henryson's tale at some length because it serves to show up what Cresseid calls Troylus's 'greit humanitie' (line 534) in comparison to Euphues's pusillanimity. Even Barnabas, who is equally sanctimonious as Euphues, passes over Dalilah's sins and gives her hope of salvation though Christ. But Euphues is hard and unforgiving and entirely untouched by *humanitas*. We recall how Valerius Maximus praised Caesar's *humanitas* in his treatment of the remains of his dead rival Pompey. The death of an enemy brings out true magnanimity in those who possess the quality. Lucilla's death only reveals Euphues's incorrigible meanspiritedness. This is not a happy place to end this chapter, especially since Lyly would almost immediately abandon this rather hard-hearted pose, and, much later, in a play called *Love's Metamorphosis* (c. 1590, pr. 1601) would present an entirely sympathetic portrait of a woman who surrenders her unmarried maidenhead to Neptune.[12] But Elizabethan humanism was an arena of many and various conflicts, and the author of *Euphues* was perhaps too young and inexperienced to resolve them. In the next chapter, we witness a similar struggle, though better handled, in another work written in the late 1570s, and one, incidentally, which Lyly must have known about whilst it was in the process of composition: Spenser's *Shepherd's Calendar*.

Notes

1. He complains that Oxford 'gave me boanes to gnaw' in a letter included in the second edition of *Euphues* (1579; rpt. Bond, 1.324–6).

2. Harvey rightly translates Euphues as 'good nature' in his reproving remarks to Lyly in *Pierce's Supererogation* (sig. I4r).

3. Ascham supports his liking for staffishness with a half-remembered allusion to the *De oratore* (1.1).

4. It is amusing to note that Lyly also reverses Ascham's attempt to erase Cicero's admiration for the 'quick wit'. Crassus approves of 'quick motions of the wyt [*ingenii celeres motus*]' in a speaker (*De orat.*, 1.113), which he also describes as 'sharpe [*acutus*]'. Ascham plays this down because he is suspicious of celerity of mind, but Lyly, who is privately of a different opinion, quietly reinstates it.

5. Details of the Lilly family may be studied in Hunter, 1962, pp. 17–30.

6. I have tried to translate Lyly's Latin into euphuistic English – which is much harder than it looks.

7. Lyly's attitude towards self-reformation is equivocal (see Pincombe, 1995).

8. 'Double V.' (alias John Lyly) meets a young university wit busily syllogising Martin's sentences, 'everie conclusion beeing this, *Ergo*, Martin is to bee hangd' (p. 399).

9. Nonetheless, Euphues says elsewhere that the speaker should decorate his orations with terms taken from philosophy, law, logic, arithmetic, geometry, astrology, music, poetry, and physic (p. 272).

10. But cf. Mueller, 1984, pp. 418–23, for the 'Scripturalist Euphues'.

11. For a somewhat less severe Severus, see the emperor of that name delineated by Sir Thomas Elyot in his *Image of Governance* (1541).

12. In the original version of the myth that Lyly uses in this play, the woman, according to Erasmus, is an allegorical representation of the prostitute (Pincombe, 1996, pp. 154–6).

CHAPTER SEVEN

Pastoral Rudeness: Edmund Spenser's
The Shepherd's Calendar

The Shepherd's Calendar (1579) is an extraordinary volume of poetry by any standards. It is not merely that the quality of the poetry represents such an advance on most of what had previously been written in the pastoral genre in England; what is really astonishing, even at the distance of four hundred years and more, is the way in which the volume so blatantly advertises its contents as new and superior. An Elizabethan readership, accustomed to apologetic forewords which deprecated rather than extolled the author's poetic effusions, must have been greatly surprised by the claims made for 'this our new Poete' (p. 416) in the prefatory letter written by E.K. to Gabriel Harvey.[1] The poet is not named as Spenser, but 'Immeritô'. This name might be translated as 'Undeserving', which would indicate to the public that, whatever his friend E.K. might think, the new poet himself took a more traditionally unemphatic view of his own worth. Another translation, however, might be 'Blameless'; and this seems to open up an even wider gap between the poet and his admirer. Immeritô seems to hint that he knows that some readers – and Elizabethan readers were quick to carp – may accuse him of secret complicity in E.K.'s 'puff'. Indeed, many critics are persuaded that E.K.'s letter and the notes he wrote to accompany each of the twelve poems are really the work of Edmund Spenser himself.[2] For the purposes of this chapter, though, let us assume what seems most obvious: that E.K. really is a separate 'voice' in the volume (whether he was a real person or an extremely lifelike hoax concocted by Spenser). In any case, the real puzzle lies in a second and much more likely candidate for Spenserian ventriloquism: Colin Clout. E.K. informs us that under that name 'this Poete secretly shadoweth himselfe' (p. 422). Yet Colin does not simply 'represent' Spenser the man in *The Shepherd's Calendar*; rather, he is a projection of Spenser as 'The New Poet'. The poet is 'new' because he is, as

E.K. puts it, 'uncouthe', or 'unknown'. But he is also 'uncouth' in the modern sense: 'rude and unrefined'. In choosing to introduce himself to the public as a pastoral poet, Spenser is following an ancient and learned – or 'humanist' – tradition; but he is also anxiously preoccupied (almost obsessed) with what E.K. calls the 'pastorall rudenesse' (p. 416) of his verses. In this chapter, we try to understand why Spenser may have thought he was unworthy both of praise and blame in writing as he did by placing *The Shepherd's Calendar* in the context of one of the great debates fostered by academic humanism in the later sixteenth century: the relative merits of ancient and vernacular prosody. I argue that Spenser, though he was deeply committed to the vernacular tradition, and had a proper understanding of his own achievements in this kind of verse, was nonetheless worried that his poetry would be dismissed as 'barbarous' by humanist critics. But let us start by looking more closely at E.K.'s remarks in this respect.

Rudeness: pastoral and rustical

E.K.'s remarks on 'pastorall rudenesse' occur in a passage in which he aims to advertise the qualities of the New Poet. He rejoices to think that Immeritô will soon be famous (p. 416):

> No lesse I thinke, deserveth his wittinesse in devising, his pithinesse in uttering, his complaints of love so lovely, his discourses of pleasure so pleasantly, his pastorall rudenesse, his morall wisenesse, his dewe observing of Decorum everye where, in personages, in seasons, in matter, in speach, and generally in al seemely simplycitie of handeling his matter and framing his words.

These are all words of praise, so 'pastorall rudenesse' is presumably a positive quality in terms of Spenser's endeavour in *The Shepherd's Calendar*. But the phrase is paradoxical: rudeness was the vice of roughness and ignorance which humanism sought to eradicate and replace with *eruditio* (literally 'the removal of rudeness'). Somehow, then, the epithet 'pastorall' qualifies and perhaps even reverses the sense of 'rudenesse'.

But E.K. shows that he is aware of the usual connotations of the word 'rudeness' a few lines later, when he explains that Immeritô may have used so many old words in *The Shepherd's Calendar*, either because he was unconsciously reproducing the poetic diction of the 'most excellent Authors and most famous Poetes' in the old vernacular tradition, or 'of set purpose and choyse, as thinking them fittest for such rusticall rudenesse of shepheards, eyther for that theyr rough sounde would make his rymes more ragged and rustical, or else because such olde and obsolete wordes are most used of country folke' (pp. 416–17). This is a complex and perhaps slightly confused explanation, but it is not hard to unravel. E.K. defends the use of archaisms in this kind of poetry on the grounds of decorum: country folk really do speak that way. But this takes second place to the real reason: these old words sound 'rough' to E.K.'s civilised ear. That is why they sound so appropriately in the mouths of the shepherds, whose every activity is indelibly marked by their 'rusticall rudenesse' (or 'roughness of manner'). Country folk should speak that way, whether they do or not in actual fact.

E.K.'s mind is thus fruitfully divided on the matter of the 'rudeness' of Immeritô's poetic diction. Indeed, the various ways in which he seeks to defend it reveals the basic problem besetting the theory of stylistic decorum which was so fundamental to academic humanism. The most important thing was to obey the rules of art: literary shepherds may not speak like real shepherds, but they nonetheless used a diction whose decorums had to be observed consistently. On the other hand, there was a persistent if somewhat dimly perceived conviction that these poetic conventions should to a certain extent reflect the speech which real shepherds used: 'naturall rudenesse' (p. 417). The local rules of art should not be arbitrary, but informed by the basic mimetic principle that art imitates nature. However, though such ideas were fairly commonplace, the detail with which E.K. expounds this theory is really very unusual, as a brief survey of Spenser's predecessors in the composition of formal eclogues may indicate.

Most important is the interpretation of the Greek name given to the genre. The word 'pastoral' is Latin in origin. It means 'pertaining to herding'; this includes the shepherd's life, but it could also refer to the life of cowherds, or, more significantly, goatherds. The Greek word for the genre, however, was generally misunderstood in Elizabethan times. Those who spelt the word *eclogue* understood that this kind of poem was a 'conversation'. That is how Abraham Fleming interprets the word in his prefatory material to his translation of *The Bucolics of Publius Virgilius Maro* (1575): 'For what youngling in the Grecian language is ignoraunte, that this word, *Ekloga* properlye doth signifye . . . *Colloquutionem*, a talking togeather' (sig. B2v). But more usually, the word was spelt *eglogue*, and it was derived from the Greek word *aigos*: 'goat'. E.K. is very insistent on this point (p. 419):

> They were first of the Greekes the inventours of them called Aeglogai as it were *aegon* or *aegonomon logoi*. that is Goteheards tales . . . [W]ho seeth not the grossenesse of such as by colour of learning would make us beleeve they are more rightly termed Eclogai, as they would say, extraordinary discourses of unnecessarie matter, which difinition albe in substaunce and meaning it agree with the nature of the thing, yet no whit answereth with the *analysis* and interpretation of the word: For they be not termed Eclogues but Aeglogues.

It is almost as if E.K. were deliberately contradicting Fleming here, or accusing scholars who take Fleming's view of deliberately trying to impose a false idea 'by colour of learning' on the less well read, perhaps the grammar-school boys for whom Fleming wrote his translation. Other scholars, however, such as E.K. himself, easily see through the 'grossenesse' of such an imposition.

But E.K.'s oddly aggressive stance here is unusual. Earlier writers took a view which tended, consciously or unconsciously, to blend elements of the 'eclogue' and the 'eglogue'. Alexander Barclay was the first English poet to write eclogues. He produced five pieces in the early years of the reign of Henry VIII, which were finally published as a set in 1579, the same year in which *The Shepherd's Calendar* appeared. Barclay says he follows the Greek poet Theocritus, who was the first 'to write / Certayne Egloges or speeches pastorall, / Inducing Shepherdes, men homely and rurall[,] / Which in playne language, according to their name, / Had sundry talking' (Prologue, lines 20–4). Theocritus put his verses in the mouths of goatherds rather than shepherds, but that is all one to Barclay. For him, 'eglogues' are characterised by 'playne language, according to their name', the sort of language used by the 'homely and rurall' men who herd animals for a living. But something of the 'eclogue' still hangs about the phrase 'sundry talking', which suggests the inconsequentiality of 'extraordinary discourses of unnecessarie matter' which irks E.K.

The same combination of elements may be found in George Turberville's translation of *The Eglogues of the Poet B. Mantuan Carmelitan* (1567). Mantuan was a student when he wrote his ten Latin eclogues in the 1460s, which is why he called them his *Adolescentia* ('Juvenilia'). They were widely imitated throughout sixteenth-century Europe (by Barclay, for example), and they were put on the syllabus of most Elizabethan grammar schools because they were deemed to be morally instructive. But Mantuan could have little to say on the question of the sort of 'rudeness' with which we are mainly concerned. His shepherds spoke in Latin, after all. At one point, one shepherd says to another: 'Rusticus es, "crates" enim pro "gratibus" inquis' (8.159), or: 'Thou art a clowne, for that thou saist dhankee zur in stead of thank you sir'.[3] But Mantuan's Latin is by its very nature *eruditus*. Turberville, on the other hand, deliberately chooses a 'low' style. In his address 'To the Reader', he explains that this is because he desires to observe 'that which we terme *Decorum* in eche respect'; and he continues: 'For as the conference betwixt Shephierds is familiar stuffe & homely: so have I shapt my stile and tempred it with suche common and ordinarie phrase of speach as Countreymen do use in their affaires' (sig. A3v). Here, then, 'rudeness' is defended on neoclassical rules of decorum.

But in the dedication of the book to his uncle, Turberville is more apologetic, conceding that his eclogues might seem at first glance 'overrude and barbarous', since they deal only of 'Countrey affaires'. He nonetheless hopes that 'Mantuans Shephierds will use the matter with such dyscretion, and so set their rusticke Pipes in tune, as you will rather commend their melodie, than myslike their audacity'. Here Turberville presents his eclogues as if they themselves were shepherds, intruding their rude and rustical presences on 'Maister Hugh Bamfield Esquier'. It is a harmless conceit, but it illuminates the deep vein of social conformity that pervades Elizabethan literary criticism: How should a civil gentleman find anything of interest in country chit-chat? What may be defensible in terms of humanist aesthetics may still be offensive to a wider reading public: 'overrude and barbarous'.

We can see in Turberville a concern to distinguish between different degrees of rudeness in speech: 'rudeness' may be acceptable, but 'over-rudeness' clearly is not. When E.K. came to write his critical essay a dozen years later, he seems to differentiate between kinds of rudeness as well. He is not entirely consistent, but by 'rusticall rudenesse' he means the real 'natural' language used by shepherds and country-folk generally. However, 'pastorall rudenesse' is also artifical. It may use old or dialect words, but these are woven into a highly refined and sophisticated poetic structure. To make the difference plain, we might take the first two or three lines of Colin's spech in 'January' and compare them with the stage dialect used by the shepherd Corin in the anonymous play *Clyomon and Clamydes* (c. 1576, pr. 1599). Colin sighs (lines 13–16):

> Ye Gods of love, that pitie lovers payne,
> (If any gods the paine of lovers pitie:)
> Looke from above, where you in joyes remaine,
> And bowe your eares unto my dolefull dittie.

This is a very different 'dialect' from the one revealed in the first lines spoken by Corin (lines 1289–92): [4]

> Gos bones turne in that sheep there and you be good fellowes[.] Jesu how
> cham beraide,
> Chave a cur here, an a were my vellow, cha must him conswade,
> And yet an cha should kisse, looke you[,] of the arse, cha must run my
> selfe, an chil,
> And cha should entreat him with my cap in my hand ha wad stand still.

This is 'Mummerzet': a generalised caricature of the rural dialects of the south of England. It is not simply invented; some older people in Somerset still say 'vellow' for 'fellow'. On the other hand, it is still as conventional as the language spoken by the shepherds of *The Shepherd's Calendar*. But it is calculated to sound absurd to educated ears, which is certainly not the case with Spenser's shepherds.[5]

E.K. must have known that Spenser's decision to use dialect words and archaisms so plentifully as he does would cause controversy. Philip Sidney, writing very shortly after the publication of the *Calendar*, complained of exactly those qualities which E.K. seeks to praise as 'pastoral rudeness': 'The *Sheapheards Kalender* hath much Poetrie in his Eglogues: indeede worthy the reading, if I be not deceived. That same framing of his stile to an old rustick language I dare not alowe, sith neyther Theocritus in Greeke, Virgill in Latine, nor Sanazar in Italian did affect it' (*Apol.*, p. 196). Sidney's view on the *Calendar* is divided: he likes its poetry, but cannot accept its poetic diction because no classical or neoclassical poet has written eclogues this way. Sidney is not quite right here: Virgil did not write in a rustic dialect; and nor, therefore, did the neo-Latin tradition, which included the eclogues of the Italian poet Jacopo Sannazaro. However, Theocritus wrote in a literary style based on the Doric dialect of Greek, which would have seemed an 'old rustick language' to its original readers. Sidney probably knew this, since it was a humanist commonplace. But he cannot bear the thought of serious poetry being written in a style too strongly redolent of the speech of ignorant peasants. And he was not alone in the period. Spenser's poetry did much to give a certain currency to 'old rusticke language' in pastoral, but the style always had as many enemies as friends. In the late 1570s, of course, it was a bold innovation, and one can understand Spenser's acquiescence in the inclusion of E.K.'s essay in his début volume, despite its lack of conformity with his own poetics at many points. Critics tend to regard E.K. as a foolish pedant, and some of his notes really are obtuse and confusing. But his defence of 'pastoral rudeness' is subtle and convincing, and Spenser may well have been glad of it, since E.K.'s insistence on different kinds of rudeness supports and explains a preoccupation which marks much of Spenser's poetry: the difference between 'shepherds' and 'clowns' as figures of the poet.

Shepherds and clowns

The Shepherd's Calendar marks Spenser's literary début, but it was not his first published work. In 1569, as a 17-year-old schoolboy, he contributed several pieces to Jan van der Noodt's *Theatre for Voluptuous Worldlings*. Two of these pieces provide the young poet with images which he will bear with him for the rest of his literary career. The first is taken from a sequence of six poems called by Spenser 'Epigrams', a translation of the French poet Clément

Marot's rendering of a visionary poem originally written by Petrarch. In the fourth, the poet describes a spring in a wood, where 'many Muses, and the Nymphes withall' sing sweetly in tune to the waters (p. 606). This is a description of what we might call a *mouseion*: a place sacred to the Muses (Greek: *mousa*). Spenser tells us, however, that this place is approached by neither 'The homely Shepherde, nor the ruder cloune'. It is as if their presence would be sacrilegious; and the *mouseion* is indeed a fragile paradise, since it suddenly and inexplicably disappears into the gaping earth at the end of the poem, leaving the poet puzzled and depressed. The second poem comes from Spenser's translation of another visionary poem: Joachim Du Bellay's 'Songe' ('Dream'). Here the poet sees another spring around which 'An hundred Nymphes sate side by side about' (p. 608). There are no Muses present, but I think we may discern a fundamental similarity to the literary *mouseion* here, since the spring is no doubt meant to be one of the many sources sacred to the Muses, such as Hippocrene on Mount Helicon. This vision also comes to a sudden and violent end: 'When from nie hills a naked rout of faunes / With hideous cry assembled on the place, / Which with their feete uncleane the water fouled'.

These two poems must have been particularly interesting to the young Spenser. The first depicts a world of poetry which has to be kept away from those who are too rude to appreciate it. Marot calls these 'pasteurs' and 'bouviers': 'shepherds' and 'cowherds'. These two terms are more-or-less equivalent: 'peasants'. Spenser introduces a distinction of degree between the 'homely Shepherde' and the 'ruder cloune'. Shepherds are 'clowns', that is, 'country-folk'; but Spenser suggests that shepherds are not as rude as other people who live in the country. Even the word 'homely' may suggest an honest yeoman-like quality. In the second poem, the unstated but implicit threat to the *mouseion* posed by the uncultured is recast as a direct assault, with the peasant degraded yet further down the scale of *humanitas* as the semi-human faun: half man, half goat. The point here is that the fauns are the enemies of the Muses: *misomousoi*, as Sidney puts it in the *Apology* (p. 187). That is why they are only half human: all enemies of the Muses are also enemies of *humanitas*, since they are the same, as Cicero explains in the *Disputationes Tusculanae*, where he talks of familiarity with the Muses: 'id est cum humanitate et cum doctrina ["that is, with humanity and learning"]' (5.66).[6]

Spenser's distinction between the shepherd and the clown is crucial to his later development as a pastoral poet. Whereas Petrarch keeps both shepherd and cowherd away from his *mouseion*, Spenser only excludes the 'ruder cloune', whilst allowing the 'homely Shepherde' to have some kind of access to the Muses. But the excluded and suppressed character 'returns', as it were, as the angry and brutal faun, who invades and destroys the *mouseion*. The scene is already set for later original poetry by Spenser, as, for example, *The Tears of the Muses* (1591). The central figure in this procession of the Muses, mourning for the neglect of poetry in England, is Euterpe, the Muse associated with pastoral. She relates how their pleasant places have been despoiled by Ignorance and his 'ragged rout / Of Faunes and Satyres' (lines 267–8). The 'sacred springs' have been defiled by their 'fowle footings trade', and they have thrown down the bowers 'in which the Shepheards swaines / Were wont so oft their Pastoralls to sing'. She concludes: 'So all is turned into wildernesse, / Whilest ignorance the Muses doth oppresse'. There is some debt here to Du Bellay's *Musagnoeomachie* ('Battle between the Muses and Ignorance': 1550); but Spenser adds the shepherds and the fauns. They are part of his poetic scheme: both are emanations of the 'peasant', one towards and one away from *humanitas*. But it is a scheme which is constantly under threat of collapse, as we shall see.

This picture, no doubt, has complex psychological origins. Spenser came from the lower and more obscure reaches of the Tudor gentry. His father was a gentleman by birth, but he worked for his keep as a free journeyman of the Merchant Taylor's Company, living in East Smithfield, near the Tower of London. Later on, Spenser would lay claim to more distant but more exalted origins. In *Prothalamium* (1596), he reveals that he takes his name from a 'house of auncient fame' (line 131). And it would appear that he really was in some way related to the Spencers of Althorp in Northamptonshire. But the facts of his early life (as far as we know them) must have impressed a sense of humility on the young Spenser. He was a 'poor scholar' at the Merchant Taylors School, and a 'sizar' at Pembroke Hall, Cambridge, a student who paid his way by performing menial tasks for richer boys. It seems likely that Spenser would have genuinely identified his own lowly status with that of Colin Clout as it is described in the first line of the 'January' eclogue: 'A Shepeheards boye (no better doe him call)'.

On the other hand, Spenser must have realised from a very early age that he was only a 'poor scholar' in the crassly pecuniary sense. How many other boys of seventeen years would be capable of translating Marot and Du Bellay? Moreover, the schoolboy Spenser translates Du Bellay into blank verse, which was still a very uncommon metre at the time (it was so strange that it even lacked a name until 1589). This is the work of a young but independent and experimental poetic intelligence. We need to remember that Spenser is writing these lines a year before the topic of unrhymed English verse was put squarely on the critical agenda by Ascham's *Schoolmaster* in 1570. One can certainly see why Spenser might have wished to divide the mere peasant or commoner into two distinct degrees of rudeness.

Moreover, Spenser's early interest in neoclassical prosody also provided him with an interesting perspective on the fauns and satyrs who invade the pastoral landscape. We have seen that 'eglogues' were thought to have been what E.K. calls 'Goteheards tales'. Fauns and satyrs are half goat; and the word 'Goth' was pronounced so similarly to the word 'goat' four hundred years ago that Touchstone can make a learned play on words to the rustic Audrey in Shakespeare's *As You Like It* (c. 1600, pr. 1623): 'I am heere with thee, and thy Goats, as the most capricious Poet honest Ovid was among the Gothes' (3.3.1571–2). The 'Goth/goat' pun occurred to earlier writers, too, particularly in the debate over prosody. Here is Thomas Blennerhasset in *The Second Part of the Mirror for Magistrates* (1578): 'It is great marvaile that these ripewitted Gentlemen of England have not left of their Gotish kinde of ryming, (for the rude Gothes brought that kind of writing fyrst), & imitated the learned Latines & greekes' (p. 450). Rhyming is 'Gotish' because it is how the Goths wrote their verses; but also, I suspect, because it is 'goatish'. It is only 'half humane', just as the faun or satyr is only 'half human'. Blennerhasset's phrasing suggests that he had in mind the passage from *The Schoolmaster* where Ascham wishes that English poets would 'acknowledge and understand rightfully our rude beggerly ryming, brought first into Italie by Gothes and Hunnes, whan all good verses and all good learning to, were destroyed by them' (p. 289). Now that humanist scholarship has recovered the true principles of metrical composition, however, according to Ascham, the English have no excuse to use rhyming when they could be writing 'good verses' in neoclassical metres: 'surelie, to follow rather the Gothes in Ryming, than the Greekes in trew versifiyng, were even to eate ackornes with swyne, when we may freely eate wheate bread emonges men'. Ascham is thinking of pigs, but Blennerhasset sees the punning associations with goats, and so, perhaps, did Spenser; and in the next section I wish to examine how Spenser's divided loyalties towards the vernacular tradition and the formal neoclassicism embraced by his friend Harvey impinge upon the pastoral landscapes of *The Shepherd's Calendar*.

Pan and Apollo: the 'June' eclogue

Quantitative experiments in English versification enjoyed a surprising vogue in the later sixteenth century. They led nowhere, so we have come to regard them as eccentric and deviant; but that is not how they appeared to the educated Elizabethan. There seems to have been a particular vogue around the period when Spenser wrote his *Shepherd's Calendar*. In a letter to Harvey written in October 1579, Spenser reports that certain courtiers have taken to writing quantitative poetry, particularly Philip Sidney and his close friend Sir Edward Dyer, with whom Spenser can boast 'some use of familiarity' (*Three Letters*, p. 634). Spenser is a partisan of the new prosody as well: 'I am, of late, more in love with my Englishe Versifying, than with Ryming: whyche I should have done long since, if I would then have followed your councell. *Sed te solum iam tum suspicabar cum Aschamo sapere: nunc Aulam video egregios alere Poëtas Anglicos* [But then you were the only one whom I perceived to share Ascham's knowledge, whereas now I see the court is nurse to excellent English poets]'. This is a somewhat backhanded compliment (perhaps that is why it is written in Latin). Spenser admits that Harvey was right all along, but he waited until the project was endorsed by the authority of courtier-poets before he would take part in it himself. Perhaps Spenser is teasing Harvey here, since Harvey prided himself on what he took to be his own leading role in 'our new famous enterprise for the Exchanging of Barbarous and Balductum Rymes with Artificial Verses' (p. 623). However, Spenser rather mischievously reveals that the courtier-poets are not following Harvey's rules but those, now lost, of the noted neo-Latin poet Thomas Drant. Harvey is annoyed, takes him to task for certain mistakes in scansion, and dismisses any appeal to Spenser's 'gorbellyed Maisters Rules' (p. 640). Harvey's *urbanitas* slips for a jealous moment. Spenser must have known that his friend was passionately devoted to the new prosody, but he himself was unable to summon up the like enthusiasm. Spenser's own experiments with unrhymed (though not exactly quantitative) verse go back to the late 1560s; but, apart from an unremarkable ditty called 'Iambicum Trimetrum', Spenser published nothing in the quantitative line. Compared with Sidney, who wrote quite a number of poems in ancient metres, Spenser's interest seems to have been minimal, whatever he says in his letter to Harvey.

The point is worth making because Spenser's relative lack of concern with the new prosody needs to be put within the larger context of his attitude towards the English vernacular tradition. He had already begun work on *The Fairy Queen* – much to his learned friend's annoyance. In *Three Letters*, Harvey worries lest 'the *Faerye Queene* be fairer in [Spenser's] eie than the *Nine Muses*, and Hobgoblin runne away with the Garland of Apollo' (p. 628). By 'the *Nine Muses*', Harvey probably means Spenser's *Tears of the Muses*. This was not published until 1591, but it may have been written much earlier, and indeed, seems to spring from the same disillusion with English literary culture which emerges from 'October' in *The Shepherd's Calendar*. Harvey may have liked 'the *Nine Muses*' (if it is Spenser's *Tears*) because the poem bears strong similarities with his own series of elegies for his kinsman Sir Thomas Smith: *Lachrymae Musarum*; but there are wider issues at stake. This poem represents the learned tradition of neoclassical humanism, whereas *The Fairy Queen* must have seemed all too much like the romantic tales of medieval chivalry which the learned kind of humanism professed to despise. We have already seen Ascham's withering comments on the *Morte d'Arthur*, but Harvey is more concerned with the folk and fairy elements in Spenser's new poem, as if they marked a regression to old wives' tales. He imagines Spenser as sitting in the laureate's throne, with Apollo, Leader of the Muses, about to place the laurel garland on his brows – when suddenly Hobgoblin snatches it from his hands and scampers away with it. Hobgoblin – half man, half goat – should be seen as one of the henchmen of the Ignorance who despoils the *mouseion* in *The Tears of the Muses*, since the shepherds are evicted by 'fowle Goblins and Shriekowles' (line 283). Harvey was no doubt privy to Spenser's literary inclinations at this time, and he clearly felt that Spenser was moving away from the career which he would have him follow.

I think we may still perceive the traces of this muted conflict between Spenser and Harvey in *The Shepherd's Calendar*. When he wrote as a human-ist, Spenser found it easy enough to defer to Harvey. *Three Letters* includes a Latin poem which Spenser wrote on the eve, as he thought, of a journey abroad in the train of the Earl of Leicester. In it, he implores Harvey to remember him and to send him news and poetry whilst he is away. The poem is saturated with the hyperbolic compliments customary in such verse, but its first lines are still worth noting: 'Sic malus egregium, sic non inimicus Amicum: / Sicque novus veterem iubet ipse Poëta Poëtam [A poore Poët, newe yet not unfriendlie, giveth salute unto a peereless Poët, olde-excellent and friendlie' (p. 637). Spenser even goes so far as to call Harvey his 'Apollo'. But in the context of his public début as a vernacular poet in the native tradition, the roles are reversed. There is no doubt that Colin Clout is the supreme artist, and that Hobbinol, who represents Harvey, is only one of Colin's many lesser-talented admirers amongst the shepherd community. Moreover, Colin does not worship Apollo, but Pan. In 'January', Colin prays to Pan as the 'shepheards God' (line 17); nor does his allegiance ever waver, as he is still addressing his prayers to Pan as 'the God of shepheards all' in 'December' (line 7). Pan, of course, is a close relation to Harvey's Hobgoblin, since he is physically identical to fauns and satyrs: he is half man, half goat. His horns may even point to a kinship with the devil and other infernal figures such as the goblins 'Borne in the bosome of the black Abysse' who vandalise the *mouseion* in *The Tears of the Muses* (line 260). However, Spenser does not follow this line of association to its logical conclusion. Christian writers could trace the process of dehumanisation one step further than the writers of pagan antiquity, since they could extend it beyond mere beastliness to devilishness. But Spenser stops short at 'rude-ness', as we may see from the 'January' eclogue.

In 'January', Colin complains of his unrequited love for a certain Rosalind, whom E.K. calls a 'countrie lasse' (Argument), but whom Colin says he met when foolish curiosity took him to 'the neighbour towne' (line 50). But wherever she may come from or live now, her residence in the town seems to have made her scornful of the country. She despises Colin's 'rurall musick' and 'Shepheards devise she hateth as the snake, / And laughes the songes, that Colin Clout doth make' (lines 64–6). Rosalind, then, has taken on the worst aspects of *urbanitas*. It is one thing to look down on the country pleasures she no longer takes delight in, but quite another to behave so roughly towards them as Colin seems to tell us. This aggressive attitude is quite typical, however, of the more exclusive kind of scholarly humanism, as we have seen with Ascham and also with Harvey; and I wish to argue that Rosalind serves as a focus for Spenser's own anxieties about his relationship to this neoclassical tradition of *humanitas*. She is, as it were, the muse of that tradition. Colin desperately wishes to please her, but she rejects him and eventually settles instead for a certain Menalcas. But this narrative is a mask for the real situation in which Spenser found himself in the late 1570s. It was he who had rejected the neoclassical humanism of Ascham and Harvey; and he projects his guilt and anxiety at having made this break on Colin Clout. This is why Colin must destroy his pipe at the end of 'January' (lines 67–72):

> Wherefore my pype, albee rude Pan thou please,
> Yet for thou pleasest not, where most I would:
> And thou unlucky Muse, that wontst to ease
> My musing mynd, yet canst not, when thou should:
> Both pype and Muse, shall sore the while abye.
> So broke his oaten pype, and downe dyd lye.

Rosalind is not Colin's own 'Muse'. He may seek to please Rosalind, but she does not inspire him in the same way that, say, Petrarch was inspired by Laura. In fact, Colin's 'personal muse' is a fleeting and elusive figure in *The Shepherd's Calendar*. She is nameless and invisible, as if suppressed by the superior authority of the canonical Muses, whom we meet on several occasions. But it would not be too fanciful, I think, to imagine her as one of the nymphs who traditionally attended the deity whom Colin here calls 'rude Pan'.

Apollo's rival was not Hobgoblin, but Pan. One of the great commonplaces of Renaissance humanism was the musical contest between these two gods, as related by Ovid in the eleventh book of his *Metamorphoses*: Pan was piping to his nymphs one day, when he boasted that 'Apollos musick was not like too his' (11.155; trans. Golding, p. 222). Apollo is vexed, and a competition is arranged with Mount Tmolus as judge, who finds in his favour. However, the competition is also witnessed by the foolish King Midas, a worshipper of Pan, who challenges Tmolus's decision. Apollo is furious and gives him the Ass's Ears as a sign of his beastly lack of *humanitas*. This is the myth that lies at the heart of Spenser's 'June'.

Colin, disappointed in love, has left the pastoral world behind and haunts the hills, where, as Hobbinol reminds him, live 'elvish ghosts' and 'gastly owles' (line 24). These hills are glossed by E.K. as 'the North countrye' (p. 443). Apparently, Spenser advised E.K. on this point; but E.K. makes heavy weather of the fact that the south, to which Colin has returned, is also 'full of hylles'. We may suspect some mischief here; and in any case, what really matters is that these hills are the place where the enemies of humanity dwell. The ghosts and owls Hobbinol mentions recall the goblins and shriek-owls who lay waste the *mouseion* in *The Tears of the Muses*, together with the fauns and satyrs, who, we recall, descend 'from nie hills' for the same purpose in Spenser's translation of Du Bellay's 'Songe'. Hobbinol tries to persuade him to stay with him for good in his happy valley. There are no such horrors in the dale, he says (lines 25–32):

> But frendly Faeries, met with many Graces,
> And lightfote Nymphes can chace the lingring night,
> With Heydeguyes, and trimly trodden traces,
> Whilst systers nyne, which dwell on Parnasse hight,
> Doe make them musick, for their more delight:
> And Pan himselfe to kisse their christall faces,
> Will pype and daunce, when Phoebe shineth bright:
> Such pierlesse pleasures have we in these places.

Hobbinol's image of these moonlight dances is very attractive, not least because it presents a union between the worlds of Pan and Apollo. The latter is not present in person, but the literary culture he stands for is represented by the Muses, who were often regarded as Apollo's disciples. But the Muses play alongside Pan; and mingling with the graces and nymphs of classical tradition are English fairies. Neoclassical and native vernacular traditions work together here, and it is interesting that Spenser should put these words in the mouth of Hobbinol, whose counterpart in life tried hard to persuade Spenser not to let the latter contaminate the former. It is as if he is trying to reform Harvey along his own eclectic lines.

Hobbinol goes yet further when he recalls a moment which he hopes will flatter Colin into staying longer (lines 57–64):

> I sawe Calliope wyth Muses moe,
> Soone as thy oaten pype began to sound,
> Theyr yvory Luyts and Tamburins forgoe.
> And from the fountaine, where they sat around,
> Renne after hastely thy silver sound.
> But when they came, where thou thy skill didst showe,
> They drewe abacke, as halfe with shame confound,
> Shepheard to see, them in theyr art outgoe.

Hobbinol here undoes the work he did with his first image. The Muses are moved by the beauty of Colin's music to abandon their own *mouseion* (signified by the fountain) and seek him out. But when they see it is a mere shepherd who has thus captivated them, they are confused, angry, and ashamed. There is even a slight sexual *frisson* here, as if a great lady should have allowed herself to be seduced by a peasant.

Colin is certainly unhappy with the thought and quickly evades the implications of Hobbinol's account of the attraction his pipe may exercise over the Muses:

> Of Muses Hobbinol, I conne no skill:
> For they bene daughters of the hyghest Jove,
> And holden scorne of homely shepheards quill.
> For sith I heard, that Pan with Phoebus strove,
> Which him to much rebuke and Daunger drove:
> I never lyst presume to Parnasse hyll,
> But pyping lowe in shade of lowly grove,
> I play to please my selfe, all be it ill.

Colin now reminds Hobbinol of the musical contest between Apollo and Pan, which signifies the permanent opposition between what we call 'high' and 'low' in art and culture. In the context of the late 1570s, Apollo and the Muses represent the high art of neoclassical humanism and especially quantitative versification, whereas Pan and the fairies (including the Fairy Queen) represent the low art of the vernacular tradition and rhyme. Colin is aware of the 'Daunger' if a worshipper of Pan should intrude himself, like Midas, into the company of Apollo and the Muses, worst still to compete with them.[7] After all: 'I wote my rymes bene rough, and rudely drest' (line 77). Therefore he does not seek their company; and so Spenser may tactfully detach himself from the academicism of Harvey's aesthetics.

Pan and Eliza: the 'April' eclogue

The competition between Pan and Apollo was always biased in favour of the latter; but not everyone took Apollo's part. When John Lyly came to dramatise the scene in his play *Midas* (wr. 1589, pr. 1592), Pan is presented as Apollo's equal. The Olympian and Parnassian Apollo derisively inquires: 'What God is Pan, but the god of beastes, of woods, and hilles?' (4.1.23–4). Pan replies: 'So I am Apollo! and that of Hilles so high, as I can prie into the jugling of the highest Gods. Of woods! So I am Apollo! of woods so thicke, that thou with thy beames canst not pierce them'. Lyly uses the scene in order to present a conflict between the values of the court and the country, with what seems strong support for the latter (Pincombe, 1996, pp. 122–6). Pan exclaims: 'Beleeve me Apollo, our groves are pleasanter than your heavens, our Milk-maides than your Goddesses, our rude ditties to a pipe than your sonnets to a lute'. But Spenser, writing ten years earlier, and still in the shadow of Harvey and the learned tradition, could not be so assertive. Nonetheless, he can still make a claim for what E.K. calls 'pastorall rudenesse'.

In 'April', Hobbinol tearfully explains to Thenot that Colin has broken his pipe because Rosalind does not love him or his music. Thenot asks Hobbinol to sing one of Colin's ditties, and he agrees readily to recite Colin's 'laye / Of fayre Eliza, Queene of shepheardes all' (lines 33–4). Interestingly, this lay begins with an invocation of the canonical sources of inspiration whom Colin shuns in 'June'. He calls on the Nine Muses, and also on the nymphs, who, as water-deities, have an affinity with 'the learned well' of the neoclassical tradition (line 42). Perhaps Colin feels he must run the risk of their acquaintance because he is writing about Eliza. The only other time he calls on them is in 'November', where he invokes the aid of Melpomene, Muse of Tragedy, to help him lament the death of Dido, who mysteriously yet irresistibly suggests an allusion to Elizabeth (the classical Dido's other name was Elissa or Elisa). Moreover, Colin anticipates Hobbinol's image of the enraptured Muses in 'June' when he relates how they run to sing and play for Eliza: 'I see Calliope speede her to the place, / where my Goddesse shines: / And after her the other Muses trace, / with their Violines' (lines 100–3). No wonder Colin was discomfited by Hobbinol's flattering revision of this scene, in which he places the humble shepherd in the place of his 'Goddesse'.

But Pan is also in the picture. Colin explains that Eliza really is a goddess: 'shee is Syrinx daughter without spotte, / Which Pan the shepheards God of her begot' (lines 50–1). E.K.'s long gloss on these lines explains that 'Syrin[x] is the name of a Nymphe of Arcadie, whom, when Pan being in love pursued, she flying from him, of the Gods was turned into a reede' (p. 434). This is part of the extensive parallelism which exists between Pan and Apollo (which is why they quarrel). Apollo loved and pursued the nymph Daphne, whom, at her request, the gods transformed into a laurel tree before Apollo could catch her, so that ever afterwards the laurel has acted as a symbol of the tradition of poetry associated with Apollo. Similarly, Pan made pipes out of the reeds, and the reed-pipe is the symbol of the tradition of pastoral poetry. E.K. does not need to tell us that Pan wished to rape Syrinx – and wisely, since he is keen to inform us that Pan is none other than 'the most famous and victorious King, her highnesse Father, late of worthy memorye K. Henry the eyght'. This seems slightly tactless, since it calls to mind that Syrinx was Anne Boleyn, whom Henry pursued, captured and later destroyed. But E.K.'s final comment may explain why he wanted to draw attention to the relationship between Elizabeth and Henry.

E.K. notes that Pan is sometimes used to signify 'Christ himselfe, who is the verye Pan and god of Shepheardes'. Christ, of course, is 'The Good Shepherd'; and churchmen are frequently referred to as shepherds or pastors in Renaissance literature. This is certainly the case in *The Shepherd's Calendar*. Several poems deal directly with matters of church government, with a particular emphasis on the extent to which the Church of England had carried out the reforms it had set itself since the 1530s. Indeed, Spenser refers unmistakably to certain individuals; and he also uses small forms such as the beast-fable which were traditionally associated with satire. Here it is tempting to interpret 'pastorall rudenesse' in satirical terms. Pan, after all, is very like a satyr, and the words 'satyr' and 'satire', though etymologically unrelated, were productively confused in the Renaissance. The rustic satyr used 'rude speech' to display the vices of his victims, whereas 'fine speech' was associated with courtly flattery. It would be difficult to imagine good shepherds like Colin and the others praying to such a deity. However, it seems very likely that Spenser might have intended Pan to call up allusions to Christ and Henry VIII, as E.K. indicates. Spenser's personal commitment to the Protestant Reformation was deep but complex; however, like most of his contemporaries, he was ready to accept that Henry's break with Rome, though he himself remained an English if not a Roman Catholic, gave him a special place in setting England in the right direction towards true Christianity, as opposed to Roman Catholicism, which was increasingly demonised in the latter half of Elizabeth's reign. In this reading, Colin represents a specific aspect of Spenser's own self-identification as an 'English Protestant Poet'.

Such an interpretation offers up many interesting perspectives on *The Shepherd's Calendar*. For example, it may suggest that Rosalind is the dark sister of Eliza. E.K. tells us that this name (also spelt 'Rosalinde' and 'Rosalende') is an anagram, 'which being wel ordered, will bewray the very name of hys love and mistresse' (p. 423). With a little ingenuity, the name can be made to yield various allusions to Elizabeth.[8] It can be argued that Spenser was worried, as many were in the late 1570s, that Elizabeth might marry a Catholic prince of France, the Duke of Alençon, with possibly disastrous consequences for the reformed religion in England. We may perhaps see an allusion to the prospect even in 'April', where we learn that 'the Chevisaunce, / Shall match with the fayre flowre Delice' (lines 43–4) – the fleur-de-lys of France. This possibility is much more clearly represented, however, in Rosalind's rejection of Colin and her apparent acceptance of his rival Menalcas. This reading of Rosalind is quite attractive, but it does not fully elucidate the problematical relation between her and Colin, which, after all, provides *The Shepherd's Calendar* with whatever scanty narrative it may have.

Let us return to the crucial passage in 'January' where we learn of Colin's unrequited love for Rosalind. She despises his 'rurall musicke' and 'Shepheards devise'; but 'rude Pan' is pleased. The emphasis is not on Colin's person, but on his poetry; and this is surely how we must understand their relationship. The Protestant element is important. Pan may well be located within the culture of plain-speaking that was intrinsic to Protestant literary culture in Tudor England. We might see Rosalind's disdain for Colin's songs as evidence of Elizabeth's temptations to succumb to the blandishments of the Catholic Alençon and his smooth-talking agent Jean Simier; but the context of the passage in 'January' seems to argue otherwise. Rosalind is first mentioned as the recipient of the 'clownish giftes' which Hobbinol showers on Colin: 'His kiddes, his cracknelles, and his early fruit' (lines 57–8). Colin simply passes them on to Rosalind. We know that Hobbinol represents Harvey; and it seems likely that here we have an allusion to what Harvey gave Spenser: love, certainly, but also literary and poetic instruction in *humanitas*.[9] The pleasant valley in which Hobbinol is situated in 'June' may perhaps be deciphered as Cambridge, the 'schole of humanitye & learning', as Harvey's kinsman Smith calls it in the *De linguae Graecae pronuntiatione* (p. 100). Of course, Cambridge is notoriously flat; but we are dealing here with poetic topology not physical topography. Sheep, after all, graze on uplands, not lowlands. But Spenser may be thinking here of Cambridge as a *campus*, literally a 'field', and figuratively a 'university'. Cambridge was a 'pasture' in which young scholars were looked after by 'pastors'. One way of reading these lines, then, is that Spenser wished to mark a break with the youthful study of the *artes humanae* in his passage to more adult employment as a secretary to Harvey's defender in the quarrels with Neville: John Young, Bishop of Rochester.

Spenser was still Young's secretary when he wrote *The Shepherd's Calendar* in 1579; and the relationship is shadowed in the poem in 'April', where Hobbinol describes Colin as 'the Southerne shepheardes boye' (line 21). But Young is a *pastor* in terms of divinity rather than humanity; and in 'September' he appears as Roffy (from the Latin form of his episcopal title: *Roffiensis*). Diggon Davie reports to Hobbinol how Roffy slew a wolf that had learnt how to impersonate his voice and so delude the shepherd's trusty dog Lowder. E.K. tells us: 'This tale of Roffy seemeth to coloure some particular Action of his' (p. 455). We never learn what this might have been; but the tale serves to underline the post-lapsarian world in which Colin now lives, as opposed to the idyllic world to which Hobbinol tries to beckon him in 'June'. This world is now lost; and even Hobbinol complains of exhaustion: 'I am so stiffe, and so stanck'. It is, indeed, the season of the Fall: 'the Westerne wind bloweth sore, / . . . / Beating the withered leafe from the tree' (lines 47, 49–51). The world of 'September' is one of social and religious corruption. Diggon bitterly attacks the Roman Catholic rites of exorcism, in which an alleged power over the devil is acquired at the cost of salvation: 'Marrie that great Pan bought with deare borrow, / To quite it from the blacke bowre of sorrowe' (lines 97–8). Pan here is unquestionably Christ; and Diggon's angry reports of abuses in the world are part of the tradition of Protestant complaint. Indeed, Hobbinol warns him to use more indirection: 'thou speakest to plaine' (line 136). On the other hand, Colin reveals in 'June' that he knows that Rosalind despises him because his 'rymes bene rough, and rudely drest' (line 77). They please 'rude Pan' ('January', line 67); and here Spenser alludes to the Protestant aspect of his own perception of himself as the 'New Poet'. But in 'June', we are told that '[t]he God of shepheards' is a certain 'Tityrus' (line 81). According to E.K., Tityrus is Chaucer; but Virgil is on the whole more likely to lie behind this figure. As E.K. himself notes, Virgil was believed to have inserted himself into his own *Eclogues* 'under the name of Tityrus' (p. 422). And in 'June', the Virgilian connection is made very plain when Colin tells us Rosalind has been won by Menalcas – a speaker in Virgil's *Eclogues*. Moreover, Menalcas, unlike all the other shepherds named in the poem, has a name which belongs to the learned Graeco-Roman tradition, rather than the Anglo-French tradition of the *bergerie* to which Colin and the others belong.[10] This is where Rosalind, despite her English name, really belongs as well. Virgil's *Eclogues*, as we have seen, were the foundation of the grammatical and literary humanism; they were what you learnt in the first year of studying *humanitas* at school. By choosing Menalcas rather than Colin, she establishes her true place in the *campus* which Spenser, with some reluctance, was leaving behind him with *The Shepherd's Calendar*. In the last lines of the poem, Colin says farewell to the world and those he has loved best: 'Adieu good Hobbinol, that was so true, / Tell Rosalind, her Colin bids her adieu' ('December', lines 156–7).

Notes

1. It was usual for a volume of poetry to come armed with commendatory verses by the poet's friends, but not a critical essay. Moreover, these verses are generally so hyperbolical in their praise of the poet that they appear to be playful compliments rather than serious attempts to persuade the reader of the superiority of what they are about to peruse.

2. The most ambitious essay along these lines is Schleiner, 1990, where E.K. is deciphered as mainly Spenser with a tincture of Harvey. For a recent contribution to the debate, see McCarthy, 2000.

3. My translation; not surprisingly, Turberville does not attempt to render this line into English.

4. A 'translation' might read: 'God's bones, be a good chap and turn in that sheep there. Good Lord! How muddy I am! I have a cur here who I have to consuade [*sic*] to do my bidding as if he were my fellow-man, as if I should have to kiss his arse, you see, I have to do all the running myself, thank you very much, and if I should beg him cap in hand to run after the sheep, he'ld just sit there'.

5. Only once does Spenser slip into this very heavily marked dialect. The 'September' eclogue begins with a curiously phrased greeting by Hobbinol to Diggon Davie: 'Diggon Davie, I bidde her god day: / Or Diggon her is, or I missaye'. Davie replies: 'Her was her, while it was daye light, / But now her is a most wretched wight'. People still use the pronoun 'her' to mean 'he' in this way in the West Country; but E.K.'s note reads: 'The Dialecte and phrase of speache in this Dialogue seemeth somewhat to differ from the comen. The cause whereof is supposed to be, by occasion of the party herein meant, who being very freend to the Author hereof, had bene long in forraine countryes' (p. 455). Perhaps; but the point here is that this dialect is dropped completely after the first four lines of the eclogue, when Hobbinol and Davie return to the normal pastoral speech used by all the other shepherds. A few words of 'Mummerzet' are introduced at the beginning of the eclogue to establish the 'foreignness' of Diggon Davie's speech and experience; but Spenser does not make him speak this way throughout the poem because it would have made him too 'rustical' in the comic sense.

6. Dolman writes: 'familaritie, not wyth the muses onely, but eyther with any part of honestie, or learninge' (sig. 2C1v).

7. Midas was made to look ridiculous, but he was not in 'Daunger'. This element comes from the similar tale of a musical contest between Apollo and the satyr Marsyas, who was flayed for his presumption (Ovid, *Met.*, 6.382 ff.)

8. For the basic positions, see Greenlaw, 1943, 1.651–5.

9. Harvey also supplied books to young Arthur Capel in the late 1570s, lending him Osorius, Castiglione, Sturm, and English works such as *The Schoolmaster* and *A Mirror for Magistrates* (*Letter-book*, pp. 167–8).

10. For the late-medieval *bergerie* tradition, see Cooper, 1977, pp. 50–70.

CHAPTER EIGHT

The Companion of the Camps:
Sir Philip Sidney's
An Apology for Poetry

Sidney's *Apology for Poetry* is probably the most famous and widely read critical essay of the Elizabethan Age. It was published in 1595, a decade after Sidney's early death in 1586, and about fifteen years after Sidney seems to have completed the manuscript. But its existence became known to the general reading public a few years before it was published, when it was praised by Sir John Harington in his own 'Brief Apology for Poetry' (1591). We may assume that this mention created considerable interest in Sidney's essay, since it was published twice in 1595, by different publishers, and under different titles. William Ponsonby simply called it 'The Defence of Poesie. By Sir Phillip Sidney, Knight'. But Henry Olney was more generous in his advertisement of the work and its author: 'An Apologie for Poetrie. Written by the right noble, vertuous, and learned, Sir Phillip Sidney, Knight. Odi profanum vulgus, et arceo.' The Latin motto is a well-known tag ('I scorn and shun the uninitiated crowd') taken from the opening line of the third book of Horace's *Carmina* ('Odes': 23 BC) Olney knows that by publishing an essay written for circulation amongst Sidney's friends and associates, he risks the charge of grievous misappropriation; and he answers this charge with a quite remarkable allegory: 'Those great ones who in themselves have interr'd this blessed innocent wil with Aesculapius condemne me as a detractor from their Deities: those who Prophet-like have but heard presage of his coming wil (if they wil doe wel) not onely defend but praise mee as the first publique bewrayer of Poesies Messias' (cit. Smith, 1904, 1.149). Olney's baroque conceit brings two literary cultures into conflict. To the 'great ones' who have access to the magic circle of elite manuscript poetry, he may seem a grave-robber; but to the 'publique' Olney represents himself as sort of evangelist, bringing Sidney's Word to the people, from whom it had been jealously guarded by the quasi-priestly caste of manuscript-readers. Indeed, Olney must have known that Sidney himself would have disapproved of his publication of the essay, since he has harsh words to say of 'Prose-printers' (p. 202). For Sidney, print poses a sinister threat both to prose and poetry; and at the end of this chapter we see how he depicts the impact of print-culture on poetry as an assault on the *mouseion* and a rape of the Muses. Sidney, on the other hand, associates himself with the martial and chivalric orders, devoted to cherishing womankind and especially damsels in distress. But let us begin by tracing the origins of this lurid vision in Sidney's view of the place of poetry in relation to the traditional complementarity of humanity and divinity.

Poetry, humanity, divinity

Sidney's attitude towards the relationship between literature and learning was complex. He was an exceptionally erudite young man. He had read very widely in the *studia humanitatis*; and he was on friendly terms with experts in various arts and sciences all over Europe. This latter point is well worth the making. Students of English literature tend to think of Sidney as a courtier-poet; but he was also a curious enquirer, at one time or another, in studies such as botany, physic, philosophy, chemistry, and astronomy and mathematics (Shepherd, 1965, p. 10). Small wonder, then, that Gabriel Harvey should have had Sidney in mind as the antidote to the 'superficial humanist'. Harvey himself had witnessed Sidney's wide-ranging intellectual curiosity at first hand, when he had read the Roman historian Livy with (and for) Sidney in the late 1570s. Moreover, he would have very much approved of Sidney's particular interest in political historiography: it was to equip him with knowledge which he might put to use when called to active service. Sidney was the kind of man that Harvey aspired to be.

Yet, for all this, Sidney's scientific interests never got much beyond a fairly idle curiosity. 'The Institution of a Gentleman' was more important to him than a thoroughly extensive education in the quadrivium and natural philosophy.[1] Nor do his interests in the sciences leave much of a mark in his writings. In other words, what Ascham calls 'hie and hard sciences' (*Schoolmaster*, p. 189) and Harvey 'profound or cunning art' (*Marg.*, p. 161) had very little impact on Sidney's own literary *oeuvre*. He does not write like a 'metaphysical'. We look in vain (should we wish to do so) for the sort of arcane allusions to alchemy and astronomy and so on that we find in the poetry of John Donne.

Indeed, the learned sciences tend to be largely dismissed in the *Apology*. To some extent, this is what one would expect from an apology: in order to promote poetry as far as possible, Sidney finds it useful to play down the dignity of her 'rivals'. According to Sidney: 'the ending end of all earthly learning being vertuous action, those skilles that most serve to bring forth that have a most just title to bee Princes over all the rest' (p. 161). In this respect, poetry has two main rivals: 'Therefore compare we the Poet with the Historian, and with the Morall Phylosopher, and, if we hee goe beyond them both, no other humaine skill can match him' (p. 163). Here, then, we are in the old expansive and eclectic realm of the *studia humanitatis*: humanity as opposed to divinity ('as for the Divine, with all reverence it is ever to be excepted'). But the moral philosopher with his 'sullen gravity' (p. 161) and the historian 'loden with old Mouse-eaten records' (p. 162) are not given serious treatment; Sidney does not even build them up in order to tear them down again. But he spends many pages in proving that 'of all Sciences (I speak still of humane, and according to the humaine conceits) is our Poet the Monarch' (p. 172). The other disciplines are mere 'serving Sciences' (p. 161).

Naturally, there is a good deal of special pleading in this argument, but Sidney does his best to put it on a theoretical footing. Poetry is superior to all the other arts because it does not rely on the natural world in quite the way that they do: 'There is no Arte delivered to mankinde that hath not the workes of Nature for his principall object, without which they could not consist, and on which they depend, as they become Actors and Players, as it were, of what Nature will have set foorth' (p. 155). He then goes on to explain how this 'rule' applies to the astronomer, the geometrician, the arithmetician, the musician, the moral and the natural philosopher, the lawyer, the historian, the grammarian, the rhetorician, the logician, the physician, and, finally, the 'Metaphysick'. Having disposed of the professions and the liberal arts to his own satisfaction, he concludes (p. 156):

> Onely the Poet, disdayning to be tied to any such subjection, lifted up with the vigor of his owne invention, dooth growe in effect another nature, in making things either better then Nature bringeth forth, or, quite a newe, formes such as never were in Nature, as the *Heroes, Demigods, Cyclops, Chimeras, Furies*, and such like; so as hee goeth hand in hand with Nature, not inclosed within the narrow warrant of her guifts, but freely ranging onely within the Zodiack of his owne wit.

Here, then, poetry holds an even more exalted position than that of mere sovereignty amongst the humane arts. In fact, it is not really limited to humanity at all, since the poet is the only artist who can truly imitate divine

146

creation. Sidney knows his claims will meet with objections, but he is ready for them (p. 157):

> Neyther let it be deemed too sawcie a comparison to ballance the highest poynt of mans wit with the efficacie of Nature: but rather give right honor to the heavenly Maker of that maker, who, having made man to his owne likenes, set him beyond and over all the workes of that second nature, which in nothing hee sheweth so much as in Poetrie, when with the force of a divine breath he bringeth things forth far surpassing her [i.e. Nature's] dooings, with no small argument to the incredulous of that first accursed fall of Adam: sith our erected wit maketh us know what perfection is, and yet our infected will keepeth us from reaching unto it.

The poet, then, is man in his 'superhuman' aspect: poetic creativity is what proves his 'likenes' to his own creator. Indeed, it is not certain exactly whose 'divine breath' produces the creations: is it the poet's – or is it God's? Sidney would probably have said both: poetry provides a direct link between the mind of man and the mind of God. In any case, Sidney clearly views the poet as more than a mere 'prince' or 'monarch'; he is really an heroic demigod.

So it is, then, that the learned sciences which Harvey valued so dearly meant relatively little in Sidney's theory of poetry. Practitioners of these sciences are only to be regarded in so far as they elucidate the natural order: 'So doth the Astronomer looke upon the starres, and, by that he seeth, setteth downe what order nature hath taken therein' (pp. 155–6). But the poet need not be an expert in astronomy because he is not tied to the natural order: 'freely ranging onely within the Zodiack of his owne wit'. Harvey might well have been disappointed that Spenser was not well versed in his 'Canones, Tables, and Instrumentis of Astronomi' (*Marg.*, p. 162 [MP]), but it is difficult to see what Spenser as a poet was supposed to do with the sort of technical expertise that Harvey and his brothers seem to have possessed. Such calculations might come in useful when writing an astronomical 'signature' to a poem: a conventionally allegorical description of the heavens which reveals to the learned reader the date on which the piece was written or completed. But even Chaucer, whom Harvey praises for his astronomical learning, and who actually wrote a treatise on the astrolabe, is occasionally careless in his employment of such erudition in his poetry.[2] Harvey was wrong to require that poets to should be deeply learned in the arts; but his is only an extreme version of a not uncommon attitude towards poetry and prose in the Renaissance. Sidney, however, regards the deliberate display of learning as vulgar, as we see in the following section.

Courtiers and professors

Towards the end of his essay, where he gives the reader a famously unflattering account of the current state of English poetry, Sidney digresses briefly in the direction of prose. After listing the stylistic poverty of English, Sidney continues: 'But I would this fault were only peculier to Versifiers, and had not as large possession among Prose-printers, and (which is to be mervailed) among many Schollers, and (which is to be pitied) among some Preachers' (p. 202). Here it is not at all certain that Sidney means prose written in English, since he rails at those who try to imitate Cicero and Demosthenes by relying on 'Nizolian Paper-bookes of their figures and phrases' – collections of useful bits and pieces arranged under headings as in (and no doubt mainly drawn from) Nizolius's *Thesaurus Ciceronianus* (1535). Such methods could be used in English composition as well, however, and we may allow ourselves to see a more general attack on grammar-school humanism as applied to any language. Then he moves to one very specifically Elizabethan manifestation of this 'superficial humanism': euphuism.

Sidney probably had Lyly in his sights when he wrote the next passage, since Lyly was not only a more popular stylist than Sidney himself, but also the servant of Lord Oxford, with whom Sidney had famously quarrelled on the tennis court in 1579. Sidney notes (pp. 202–3):[3]

> Now for similitudes, in certaine printed discourses, I thinke all Herbarists, all stories of Beasts, Foules, and Fishes are rifled up, that they come in multitudes to waite upon any of our conceits; which certainly is as absurd a surfet to the eares as is possible: for the force of a similitude not being to proove anything to a contrary Disputer but onely to explane to a willing hearer, when that is done, the rest is a most tedious pratling, rather overswaying the memory from the purpose whereto they were applyed then any whit informing the judgement, already eyther satisfied, or by similitudes not to be satisfied.

Sidney perhaps takes euphuism a little too seriously as 'oratory', but his metaphor is revealing. The conceit looks like another scholar come to court, except this time it is a court of law, with 'the judgement' there to hear the case, and the memory to record its process. But the conceit has brought with him so many similitudes that he defeats his own purpose, since each successive witness by these 'Beasts, Foules, and Fishes' takes us further away from the conceit's original point, confusing the memory and exasperating the judgement. It is as if the conceit's own words are lost in the distracting babble of the menagerie of weird creatures who follow in his train.

Following and set in opposition to this confused scene is Sidney's approving remark on Antonius and Crassus and their dissimulation of their art: 'because with a playne sensiblenes they might win credit of popular eares; which credit is the neerest step to perswasion; which perswasion is the chiefe marke of Oratory' (p. 203). But here the tables have been turned: whereas in the former case, the magistrates are overwhelmed by the 'multitudes' of similitudes which attend upon the conceit, here the patricians are addressing, and apparently mastering, a crowd of people. On the other hand, it is really the euphuists and other 'learned' prose-printers who have won credit of 'popular eares'. Sidney's own works were not intended for general publication, but only for circulation amongst his friends and associates, to persuade them, not the vulgar crowd. Maybe he expected copies to find their way to other writers, who might take note of his criticisms and amend their ways if need be; and there is evidence to suggest that Lyly had read Sidney's remarks on tragicomedy in a manuscript of the *Apology* before he came to write his own first plays in the early 1580s (Pincombe, 1996, p. 35). But we can also see a tendency on Sidney's part to retreat to the security of his own circle in the face of the wave of euphuism that was currently sweeping all before it in the metropolis, and, if we may believe Thomas Nashe, the universities as well.[4] After his remarks on Antonius and Crassus, Sidney offers a brilliant sketch of the courtly prose-writer (p. 203):

> [. . .] I have found in divers smally learned Courtiers a more sounde stile then in some professors of learning: of which I can gesse no other cause, but that the Courtier, following that which by practise hee findeth fittest to nature, therein (though he know it not) doth according to Art, though not by Art: where the other, using Art to shew Art, and not to hide Art (as in these cases he should doe), flyeth from nature, and indeede abuseth Art.

This is a complicated passage, but at least one of its underlying assumptions is already familiar to us: the artful dissimulation of art. The 'professor of learning' takes pains to draw attention to the rhetorical craftsmanship of his prose, but it would be much craftier to hide it (really, to reveal it more cleverly). The courtier, of course, knows better, especially if he has read his Castiglione. It is the old story of the grammatical humanist at court: Gabriel Harvey at Audley End.

But there is more than this to Sidney's words. His courtier has a better prose style than the professor of learning because he obeys his instincts rather than any rules: 'following that which by practise hee findeth fittest to nature'. Sidney means that the art of rhetoric is based in the order of nature; and he has already said as much when he claims that poetry is not: 'the Rethorician and Logitian, considering what in Nature will soonest

prove and perswade, thereon give artificial rules' (p. 156). The consideration, then, comes before the rules, which are only a formulation of an art
which can be still be grasped by direct observation and experiment ('practise'). It follows, then, that the art is itself natural, since it can be worked out
from first principles even by people who have not learnt it as a school
discipline: 'according to Art, though not by Art'. The courtier who follows
his natural instinct for what sounds right and seems to work may well have
a better style than the humanist who has learnt all the tropes and schemes
by heart. Indeed, Sidney wants to say that too much learning actually gets
in the way of the true art of rhetoric by making men concentrate on the
technicalities rather than the technique, and on the technique rather than
the foundations of the art in the natural intuition of its *ratio*, or basic
rationale.

Sidney is thinking in terms of prose here, but his remarks can also be
applied to poetry. However, it is important to note that Sidney is not
fashioning a courtly poetic in the *Apology*, unlike Puttenham, whose intention is to lead the poet 'from the carte to the schoole, and from thence to
the Court' (*Art*, p. 183). Indeed, one suspects that Sidney would have regarded these 'new poets' as upstart intruders. Really, the figure with whom
Sidney identifies in the *Apology* is not the courtier but the knight. Sidney was
a keen martialist (he died of an infected wound received during a skirmish
near Zutphen, in The Netherlands). Not surprisingly, then, heroic is counted
as 'the best and most accomplished kinde of Poetry' (p. 179). More remarkable, however, is that Sidney's partisanship of heroic poetry extends so far
as to include a kind of writing which was expressly denounced by orthodox
scholarly humanism: medieval chivalric romance. In the next section, we
see how this genre, which by Sidney's time had become associated with
popular taste, could be rescued by its emphasis on martial valour, and how
its very 'artlessness' may well have appealed to the sophisticated gentleman.

Honest King Arthur

Sidney's equestrian status as a knight is given some prominence on the title
pages of the first editions of the *Apology*, although when he wrote the essay
he was still a 'mere gentleman'. Nonetheless, Sidney's equestrian aspirations are everywhere evident in the work, as, for example, in its opening
line in which he recounts how, whilst at the court of the Emperor Maximilian
II in 1574, he set himself 'to learne horsemanship of John Pietro Pugliano,
one that with great commendation had the place of an Esquire in his stable'

(p. 150). Sidney's credentials as a *chevalier* are thus established right at the start of his essay, and we never lose sight of them in the pages that follow. This equestrian and martial emphasis leads him almost inevitably into conflict with learned humanism as promulgated by Ascham in his *Schoolmaster*. There, we recall, the humanist scholar had bitterly complained that medieval 'bookes of Chevalrie', especially '*Morte Arthure*', should have survived as courtly staples (pp. 230–1). But Sidney says: 'I dare undertake, Orlando Furioso, or honest King Arthur, will never displease a Souldier: but the quiddity of *Ens* and *Prima materia* will hardly agree with a Corslet' (p. 188). Such a remark seems calculated merely to provoke humanist orthodoxy, but it is really a seriously determined position on Sidney's part.

We have seen that Sidney places poetry above the other humane arts because it is superior to them in exciting people to 'vertuous action' (p. 161). Philosophers fail in this respect because their professional jargon of 'Definitions, Divisions, and Distinctions' is too obscure (p. 162). But poetry works well because it can provide stirring examples of virtuous action, which can move the mind and heart to noble deeds even when the poem may be technically and artistically incompetent. Sidney uses the example of another chivalric romance: 'Truely, I have knowen men, that even with reading *Amadis de Gaule* (which God knoweth wanteth much of a perfect Poesie) have found their harts mooved to the exercise of courtesie, liberalitie, and especially courage' (p. 173). Sidney admits *Amadis* is imperfect as a poem (that is, as a work of fiction – it is in prose). But art is less important to Sidney than effect: if it moves men to virtue, a poem is doing what it is supposed to do. On these grounds, the 'popular' *Amadis* might well be compared to the 'learned' *Aeneid*. Sidney continues: 'Who readeth Aeneas carrying olde Anchises on his back, that wisheth not it were his fortune to perfourme so excellent an acte?'

Similarly, Sidney's remarks on 'Liricke' show him to be open to the admirable affective properties of the popular ballad as well as more elevated examples of the genre. In Sidney's view, lyric is not merely a matter of sonnets and other short poems, but much more . He says that the lyric poet 'giveth praise, the reward of vertue, to vertuous acts'. Its poetic credentials are thus assured. Lyric is also the nearest poetry gets to the two disiciplines which usually take precedence over humanity: philosophy and divinity. Sidney adds that the lyric poet also 'gives moral precepts, and natural Problems' and 'sometimes rayseth up his voice to the height of the heavens, in singing the laudes of the immortall God'. But Sidney is mainly interested in the less exalted eulogistic function of lyric: the praise of virtuous acts and action (and notice how Sidney insists on the active nature of virtue). He makes the following intentionally provocative statement (p. 178):

> Certainly I must confesse my own barbarousnes: I never heard the olde song of Percy and Duglas that I found not my heart mooved more then with a Trumpet; and yet it is sung but by some blinde Crouder, with no rougher voyce then rude stile; which being so evill apparrelled in the dust and cobwebbes of that uncivill age, what would it worke trymmed in the gorgeous eloquence of Pindar?

This, one feels, is what Spenser wanted to say but lacked the audacity to do so. The 'rude stile' of the old ballad we call *Chevy Chase* would have been no real hindrance to his appreciation of the real poetic *energia* of the piece.

Sidney's 'confession' is made possible by the paradoxical nature of his *Apology*: it praises something which is usually despised. But he means what he says here. Sidney had no great respect for mere antiquity in vernacular poetry. Even Chaucer, he says, had 'great wants' (p. 196). These defects (Sidney refers to the same want of poesy that marks *Amadis*) are 'fitte to be forgiven in so reverent antiquity' – but they are not forgotten. The 'mistie time' in which Chaucer wrote is exactly the same (in Sidney's eyes) as the 'uncivill age' which produced *Chevy Chase*. But although Sidney uses the typical humanist allegory which sees what we call the Middle Ages as a time in which literature and learning were cast aside to languish in dusty cellars and attics full of cobwebs, he can still redeem the ballad as a primitive kind of lyric because it still stirs the heart.

Moreover, the allusion to the 'blinde Crouder' opens up an illuminating perspective on the essential continuity between the prestigious poetry of antiquity and the despised works of the Middle Ages. The word 'crowd' comes from the Welsh *crwth*, which was an instrument like a viol, usually played with the bow, but also plucked with the fingers like a harp. Quite possibly, Sidney thought it was more like a harp than a fiddle, since he was certainly familiar with the blind harpers who wandered the country singing old ballads and romances. Whilst still a boy, in 1566, he paid a shilling to a 'blinde harper who is Sir William Holles man of Nottinghamshier' (cit. Shepherd, 1965, p. 191). This musician seems to have been fortunate enough to have the patronage of the gentry, but Puttenham mentions 'blind harpers or such like taverne minstrels that give a fit of mirth for a groat, & their matters being for the most part stories of old time' (*Art*, p. 87). Puttenham, who, as usual, has his own view on the matter, thinks that these stories – 'old Romances or historicall rimes' – were made for the 'recreation of the common people at Christmasse diners & brideales, and in tavernes & alehouses, and such other places of base resort'. For him, then, the blind harpers carry on an old vernacular tradition which has always been *common*: its very roots lie outside the carefully cultivated gardens of humanity. But Sidney takes a different view altogether. He sees ballads like *Chevy Chase* as flowers which have grown from the same seeds as those which gave rise to ancient epic. Surely we see Greek Homer behind Sidney's allusions to the 'blinde Crouder' rather than Puttenham's alehouse harpers. Homer wrote hymns – 'laudes of the immortall God' – as well as his better known epic poems; and lyric and epic are in any case so closely related in Sidney's minds as to be rather confused (it seems to be the fact that lyric poetry is written in stanzas rather than a sequence of single hexameters that makes the difference). But they are both sung to 'the well tuned Lyre' (p. 178).

Sidney seems to view *Chevy Chase* and the genre of verse it represents as poetry which has not yet reached its level. It has a potential for greatness which has not yet been realised. What is required is not inspiration, but art. The great Greek lyric poet, Pindar, was inspired, but he also knew how to decorate his matter in 'gorgeous eloquence'. This is the crucial difference. It is what adds *humanitas* to the picture. *Chevy Chase* is badly dressed, as it were (perhaps we are meant to see the blind crowder as a ragged figure as well). This is because the Middle Ages lacked art; but it is still the case in Sidney's time: no Pindar has arisen who may throw the mantle of style over the shoulders of the 'Liricke'. Yet even here there is doubt in Sidney's mind about Pindar's 'gorgeous eloquence'. A few lines later, he reports the common complaint 'that Pindar many times prayseth highly victories of small moment, matters rather of sport then vertue' (p. 179). The allusion is to Pindar's various odes written in praise of the victors of various games, such as the ancient Olympics. Sidney argues that the ancient Greeks held that kind of victory in high esteem; but the objection remains: Pindar, though eloquent, trivialised the lyric. The emphasis on superficial beauty seems always to go hand in hand with a dilution of manly *virtù*. But sterner societies may still hold out against this tendency. Sidney cites as an example the 'incomparable Lacedemonians': the Spartans (whose name is still a byword for austerity). For them, Sidney says, the lyric was a poetic shrine to virility, and all men composed lyric poems of the heroic kind: 'the lusty men were to tell what they dyd, the olde men what they had done, and the young men what they would doe' (p. 178). Nor was lyric confined to festivals; they were composed to be sung 'even at home'.

The festive version of this martial poetic institution was still to be seen in parts of Europe: 'In Hungary I have seene it in the manner at all Feasts, and other such meetings, to have songes of their Auncestours valour; which that right Souldier-like Nation thinck the chiefest kindlers of brave courage'. Sidney had been to Hungary in 1573, and had presumably listened to this kind of performance whilst visiting various Hungarian noblemen. He seems to have been genuinely impressed by these songs (which he could not have understood) and by their putative role in strengthening the hearts of the Hungarian soldiers who were so active in the defence of the frontier of

Christendom against the Turk (as Ascham also knew). This last observation is of paramount importance to Sidney's poetics. The Hungarians are a 'right Souldier-like Nation'. This matters far more to Sidney than their claim to the literary cultivation required by *humanitas*.

Sidney's emphasis on virtuous action as the chief end of poetry, indeed, all the arts, is not particularly remarkable; but the further emphasis on martial valour is more unusual. It can be explained by Sidney's own aspirations to lead a military career, but it also allows him to make some really quite unexpected statements about English poetry. We have seen that Sidney has a few words of praise for poems which most humanists would despise because they are relatively popular and artless: 'rude'. But Sidney also presses on into areas where he seems to contradict his own precepts. We can see this in his reply to one of the criticisms of poetry often raised by its detractors: 'They alledge heere-with, that before Poets beganne to be in price our Nation hath set their harts delight upon action, and not upon imagination: rather doing things worthy to bee written, then writing things fitte to be done' (p. 187). Sidney dismisses this argument on historical grounds, but he returns to the theme when he tries to explain why there is so little good poetry in the England of his own day (p. 194):

> That Poesie, thus embraced in all other places, should onely finde in our time a hard welcome in England, I thinke the very earth lamenteth it, and therfore decketh our Soyle with fewer Laurels then it was accustomed. For heeretofore Poets have in England also florished; and, which is to be noted, even in those times when the trumpet of Mars did sounde loudest. And now that an over-faint quietnes should seeme to strew the house for Poets, they are almost in as good reputation as the *Mountibancks* at Venice.

Sidney seems to suggest here that war breeds good poetry, which should be seen as another playful but calculated affront to orthodox humanism and its insistence on the absence of conflict as the foundation of *humanitas* and the *artes humanae*. But he is probably thinking of the example of Henry Howard, Earl of Surrey, the foremost soldier-poet of the Tudor period. Sidney singles out for praise 'the Earle of Surries *Liricks*' as possessing 'many things tasting of a noble birth, and worthy of a noble minde' (p. 196). He refers here to Surrey's shorter poems as they had been published in *Sundry Songs and Sonnets* ('Tottel's Miscellany': 1557). Curiously, Sidney makes no mention of Surrey's translation of two books of the *Aeneid*, obliquely praised by Ascham as a primitive attempt at quantitative verse in *The Schoolmaster* (p. 291). But he is thinking in terms of his connection between lyric and heroic, here, and its basis in the values of the equestrian or aristocratic order. Surrey's lyrics include sonnets which are both martial and amorous in nature; they are 'lusty' in the sense about which Ascham had such grave and well-founded reservations (what we call *machismo*). But Sidney was much more open to this connection.

Immediately following his remarks on the scant regard given to poetry in contemporary England comes the following observation: 'Truly even that, as of the one side it giveth great praise to Poesie, which like Venus (but to better purpose) hath rather be troubled in the net with Mars then enjoy the homelie quiet of Vulcan; so serves it for a peece of a reason why they are lesse gratefull to idle England, which nowe can scarce endure the payne of a pen' (p. 194). This is a *risqué* moment in Sidney's essay. He refers to the notorious episode in Ovid's *Metamorphoses*, which tells 'How Venus with the warlike Mars advoutrie [adultery] did commit' (4.171, p. 86). According to Golding, the moral of this fable was straightforward: 'tyme will bring to lyght. The secret sinnes that folk commit in corners or by night'. But it was also used as a warning against effeminacy. Effeminacy weakened the virile member of the *respublica*, and as such it was a commonplace of prodigal literature. Sidney himself repeats the charge (which he denies) 'howe both in other Nations and in ours, before Poets did soften us, we were full of courage, given to martiall exercises, the pillers of manlyke liberty, and not lulled a sleepe in shady idlenes with Poets pastimes' (pp. 183–4). Poetry was regularly linked to effeminacy in the older sense: addiction to women for sexual reasons. This is what Sidney hints at in the phrase 'lulled a sleepe in shady idlenes'. The allusion is to the well-known icon of Mars sleeping in Venus's lap. The primary significance of this immensely pregnant icon has to do with the power women may exert over man by physically exhausting them through excessive sexual intercourse (Mars is the symbol of virility). But it was also given more directly 'martial' interpretations as well, as, for example, in Robert Wilson's late morality play: *The Cobbler's Prophecy* (1594). The discharged soldier Sateros is dismayed to see Mars dallying in this manner with Venus: 'thy bodie lapt in soft silke which was wont to bee clad in hard steele, and thy head so childishlie laid on a womans lap' (lines 880–1). Mars has become both effeminate and juvenile, then, but, more importantly, he has turned aside from his responsibilities as a warrior. Mars soon throws off his submission to Venus and helps Sateros defend Boeotia, an island state which inevitably recalls England and the necessity to remain vigilant after the Great Armada of 1588.

But in the *Apology*, Sidney is writing as a *chevalier*: he is committed to both war and love, as was the typical hero of chivalric romance, such as Sir Lancelot. He is aware of the unorthodoxy of his position, hence his qualifications: 'but to better purpose' and 'a peece of a reason'. But he can still aver that 'Poetrie is the companion of the Campes' (p. 188). He means that poetry flourishes in periods of virile martial activity; but his phrasing inevitably suggests that poetry is a 'camp-follower'. For all his insistence of the capacity of good poems to stir men to virtuous action, Sidney can never entirely banish the old charge that poetry is essentially meretricious: sweet, alluring, deceptive.

Bastard poets

In his critical survey of contemporary poetry, Sidney complains that English poets lack 'forciblenes, or *Energia* (as the Greekes cal it)' (p. 201). The point may be taken generally, but it occurs in a passage on love poetry in which Sidney remarks that 'many of such writings as come under the banner of unresistable love, if I were a Mistres, would never perswade mee they were in love'. The love poet should be a masterful figure: a general or an orator. Here we have the virile, martial, lordly aspect of Sidney's poetics, then. But the next point Sidney raises takes us into a different world: 'Now, for the outside of it [poetry], which is words, or (as I may tearme it) *Diction*, it is even well worse. So is that honny-flowing Matron Eloquence apparelled, or rather disguised, in a Curtizan-like painted affectation' (pp. 201–2). This is a very revealing image. Bad poets have as it were kidnapped a solidly respectable 'matron' and turned her into a superior prostitute; they are ruffianly pimps. Here we return to Sidney's anxieties about the misappropriation of poetry and prose by the operators of print culture; and a few lines later he complains about 'Prose-printers' and the euphuistic excesses in 'certaine printed discourses'.

Sidney follows the same line of imagery in the remarks which follow his slightly *risqué* comparison to poetry as a Venus caught *in flagrante delicto* with Mars. Poetry thrives in time of war, but not in the present condition of 'idle England' (p. 194). With the allusion to idleness, however, Sidney picks up the thread of the traditional view that poetry induces idleness and leads to moral decay; at which point he turns to print culture once again:

> Upon this necessarily followeth, that base men with servile wits undertake it [i.e. poetry]: who think it inough if they can be rewarded of the Printer. And so as Epaminondas is sayd, with the honor of his vertue, to have made an office, by his exercising it, which was before contemptible, to become highly respected; so these, no more but setting their names to it, by their owne disgracefulnes disgrace the most gracefull Poesie. For now, as if all the Muses were gotte with childe, to bring foorth bastard Poets, without any commission, they doe poste over the banckes of Helicon, tyll they make the readers

more weary then Post-horses; while in the mean tyme, they, *Queis meliore luto finxit praecordia Titan* [whose hearts Prometheus fashioned from a better clay], are better content to suppresse the out-flowing of their wit, then by publishing them to bee accounted Knights of the same order.

If more noble captains were to write poetry, Sidney seems to suggest, then it would win respect once more. Instead, 'idle England' is overrun by poets who counterfeit and parody the chivalric class, whose members consequently disdain to be esteemed 'Knights of the same order'. In fact, these 'knights' are really no more than post-riders; and the conceit here, of course, is based on the notion that true poets soar aloft on the back of the winged horse Pegasus. But these 'base men with servile wits' seem to have kidnapped Pegasus, just as the matron Eloquence is kidnapped by the same poets, one assumes, and turned to degraded and ignoble purposes. Indeed, though Sidney does not explicitly state this, one suspects that the 'base men' have invaded Helicon and raped the Muses, to bring forth a race of 'bastard poets' in their own image.

This allegory of the desecration of the *mouseion* will by now be a familiar one, but it needs to be noted how much more particular Sidney's version is than the more general – indeed, much vaguer – instances we have examined in Spenser's writings. Sidney could not identify himself with these 'base men', whereas Spenser certainly could, and hence the difficulty in interpreting the social basis of his depictions of the scene. But Sidney is free to vilify his rivals not only as of low rank, but also as relatively impoverished, since he seems to imagine that they subsist on the proceeds of selling poetry to printers. Needless to say, this is an ill-informed and malicious fantasy on Sidney's part, and his lurid scenario is not informed by a knowledge of working conditions in the metropolis, but rather by his own prejudices and anxieties. What is most remarkable about his picture of the commercial world of print culture is its boundless energy. Sidney seems to suggest that England in the late 1570s was occupied by swarms of poets writing bad verse for printers, so that the conscientious reader becomes 'weary' in his attempts to keep up with all that is produced. But although there were indeed many thousands of volumes of printed poetry in circulation at the time, there were not so many different texts, but rather so many copies of a relatively small number of the same texts. What worries Sidney, then, is the sheer reproductive capacity of the printing press.

Here we may draw an interesting comparison with Lyly's attitude to the same topic in the address 'To the Gentlemen Readers' in *Euphues*. This begins: 'I was driven into a quandarie Gentlemen, whether I might send this my Pamphlet to the Printer or to the pedler. I thought it to bad for the presse, & to good for the packe' (p. 182). Lyly, then, has at least some respect for the productions of the press, although he also concedes that 'bookes be stale when they be printed, in that they be common'. Lyly is clearly aware of the *cachet* of the manuscript-book, seen only by a privileged few. But he also knows that gentlemen like novelty and that their appetites drive the production of various kind of goods, including clothes and books: 'In my mynde Printers and Taylors are bound, chiefely to pray for Gentlemen, the one hath so many fantasies to print, the other such divers fashions to make, that the pressing yron of the one is never out of the fyre, nor the printing presse of the other any tyme lyeth still'. Lyly is very much at home in this world: he is a gentleman reader, too, and seems to admire the energy of the printers who supply him and his class with 'fantasies'. But where Lyly sees the press as feeding an appetite, Sidney sees it as wearing the reader down with its insistent and importunate claims.

Sidney can never quite rid himself of the idea that poetry is a 'camp-follower', whose charms tend to debilitate rather than fortify the virile martialist. There were plenty of legendary and historical women whose strengths and virtues would have made them more appropriate figures for poetry than the figure of Venus. Plutarch's well-known collection in his essay 'Mulierum virtutes' ('The Strengths and Virtues of Women') would have provided him with all he needed, as would collections based on it, such as Boccaccio's *De claris mulieribus* ('Famous Women': 1362), translated by Henry Parker in the 1530s. He might have gone to the legendary material relating to the Amazons, as he certainly did when composing his romance *Arcadia*. But instead of a 'warrior woman', Sidney chooses a female figure who seems to be little better than a prostitute. His image of the genteel reader exhausted by incessant encounters with the poetry sired by base men on the Muses suggests a genuine anxiety about the ease with which the more exclusive kind of literary *humanitas* might be overtaken by vulgar productions and merged with them indistinguishably. His call to his fellow gentlemen to publish their works, and so take up arms against the army of bastard poets, was already too late, however. The printing press had long since created a literary culture that was quite independent of the aristocracy, a culture which, by the time the *Apology* was printed, had become indissolubly linked to that peculiarly English variation on Renaissance theatre: the professional stage. In the next two chapters, we move on from this relatively early trio of texts, in which the claims of a social elite to literary *humanitas* seem hard to challenge, to two of the most well-known works for the common stage: Marlowe's *Doctor Faustus* and Shakespeare's *Hamlet*. Even here, however, we shall see that Sidney's intuition that literature was somehow best served by the *chevalier* was still working powerfully in the imaginations of these base-born writers.

Notes

1. In a letter to his brother Robert, dated 15 October 1580, Sidney picks out arithmetic and geometry as useful arts (they were needed for the military art of fortification); but he requires only a casual knowledge of astronomy. Music is good, too, but as a practical accomplishment rather than a theoretical interest. The letter may be conveniently read in Duncan-Jones, 1989, pp. 291–4.

2. There are problems, for example, with Venus in *The Parliament of Fowls*, but cf. North, 1988, pp. 326–41.

3. Sidney may have had another Canterbury man in mind: Stephen Gosson (who went to school with one of Lyly's brothers). In 1579, Gosson had dedicated his *School of Abuse* to Sidney, perhaps rather ill-advisedly, since it contained a somewhat unenlightened attack on poetry (or, at least, its abuses). According to Spenser in *Three Letters*, Gosson was 'for hys labour scorned' (p. 635). Spenser's words cannot be taken at face value, since Gosson must have seemed a rival at the time; but it is tempting to see Sidney's *Apology* as somehow prompted by Gosson's pamphlet (see Duncan-Jones and van Dorsten, 1973, pp. 61–2). Moreover, Gosson also wrote in 1579 a set of linked dialogues called *The Ephemerides of Phialo*, which is probably the first imitation of *Euphues: The Anatomy of Wit*. In *Euphues and his England* (1580), Lyly returns the compliment paid him by his countryman in a flattering allusion to the 'pretie discourse of one Phialo' (p. 99). Perhaps Sidney saw Lyly and Gosson as associates.

4. In *Four Letters Confuted* (1592), Nashe admits that when he was at Cambridge in the mid-1580s, he thought *Euphues* was '*Ipse ille*' – 'the very dab' (p. 319).

CHAPTER NINE

Divinity, Adieu:
Christopher Marlowe's
Doctor Faustus

Doctor Faustus is without question one of the great Elizabethan plays. In-deed, had Shakespeare never lived, it would probably be esteemed as the greatest. No other Elizabethan play has been reprinted so frequently (nor, one suspects, appeared on so many school and university courses). But *Doctor Faustus* presents several intractable problems to anyone with a serious interest in the play. For one thing, there are really *two* plays called *Doctor Faustus*: the so-called A Text printed in 1604, and the B Text of 1616. Here we use the A Text, which is usually regarded as the more authoritative. Moreover, although it is conventional to refer to the play as written by Christopher Marlowe, he was in fact responsible (so it seems) for only two-thirds of the material which has survived as the A Text, and less than one-half of the B Text (Bevington and Rasmussen, 1993, p. 70). To simplify: Marlowe wrote the tragic parts at the beginning and the end of the play, and his collaborator wrote the comic parts in the middle.[1] Who this col-laborator was, we do not know, but let us call him 'A' for convenience; in any case, he was clearly not as well educated as his more famous co-author. Marlowe was very much the literary humanist. The son of a poor cobbler, he proved so apt at his grammatical studies at King's School in Canterbury (Lyly's school) that he received a scholarship to study at Corpus Christi College, Cambridge. All of his works show how deeply he was immersed in the *litterae humaniores*. He translated Ovid's *Amores* and the first book of Lucan's *Pharsalia*; he made an extended English version of Musaeus's *Hero and Leander*; and his *Dido, Queen of Carthage* is in parts a very close rendering of the second and fourth books of Virgil's *Aeneid*.[2] But all his other plays bear the mark of a literary education in Roman and to a lesser extent Greek poetry. This is true also of the scenes he contributed to *Doctor Faustus*, but what makes this especially interesting to readers of this book is that the main source for the play – the so-called English Faust Book – is almost entirely devoid of any interest at all in humane letters.[3] It draws on a wide variety of practical and popular sources: technical volumes on sorcery, jest-books, chronicles and travel-books, and so on. But it never glances at *belles lettres*. Nor does A in his adaptation of this material for the comic scenes of *Doctor Faustus*. But Marlowe, of course, cannot help bringing his love for the *litterae humaniores* into the tragic part of the play. Moreover, like Sidney, Marlowe associates poetry with chivalry. However, as we shall see at the close of this chapter, Marlowe, with Mephistophelean relish, also points up the glamorous futility of this association. But let us begin with another aspect of the complex and conflictive context into which *humanitas* is placed in *Doctor Faustus*.

Divinity and magic

The main source for *Doctor Faustus* is a prose book called *The History of the Damnable Life and Deserved Death of Doctor John Faustus*. This is a translation made by a certain P.F. from the anonymous German text called the *Historia von D. Johann Fausten* ('The History of Dr John Faust').[4] This was first pub-lished in Frankfurt in 1587; and the latest research indicates that P.F.'s translation was printed the next year in 1588, with the composition of *Doctor Faustus* following hard on its heels in 1589.[5] P.F. was an inventive translator. He adds here and takes away there; and there are countless occasions where the slight alteration of a detail reveals a purposeful revision at work. One such detail offers a useful point of departure towards Marlowe's own conversion of the material in his turn.

The German *Historia* tells us that Faust's father was a poor farmer, who sent his son to a rich and childless cousin in Wittenberg, where he was put to university to study theology: 'But he turned away from this pious under-taking and abused God's word' (p. 13). P.F. renders this rather bland state-ment more dramatically: 'But Faustus being of a naughty minde & otherwise addicted, applied not his study, but toke himselfe to other exercises' (sig. A2r, p. 92). P.F. wants to put as much emphasis and as soon as he can on Faust's fundamentally 'naughty' or wicked character. This not only helps to bring Faust to life on the page, but it also serves to align his material with the Calvinist othodoxy of the Elizabethan church settlement: Faustus was always one of the 'reprobate', condemned by predestination to end up in hell, so it made sense to stress his viciousness right at the start of the tale.

Here again it is useful to compare the German *Historia* with the *Damnable Life*. The *Historia* states that Faust simply 'did not much care for theology' and started to take up sorcery instead (p. 14). This soon became well known, and his uncle warned him against such studies. But P.F. says: 'he gave himself secretly to study Necromancy and Conjuration, in so much that few or none could perceive his profession' (sig. A2r, p. 92). This small alteration is immensely significant. The German Faust seems quite open about his interest in magic, but P.F.'s is very furtive. The effect of this is to make sorcery seem much more unacceptable, since it must be concealed. It becomes even more 'occult' (Latin: *occultus*, or 'hidden'). This lays the ground for a conception of sorcery and magic generally as a kind of learning which is set apart from all other knowledge, as it is represented in Marlowe's contributions to *Doctor Faustus*, but not in the original Faust Book.

The main reason why *Doctor Faustus* resists an easy assimilation to Elizabethan humanism is because its source has no conception of the division of learning between divinity and humanity on which Renaissance humanism ultimately rests.[6] In the *Historia*, divinity is so strongly represented that all other kinds of learning are displaced or quite literally 'demonised'. For example, Faust must have been to grammar school and learnt Latin in order to proceed to divinity in the first place; but this is not mentioned. Perhaps the author felt that this was simply too obvious to be stated, but this only proves the point: grammar is not regarded as a truly significant discipline. Learning is directed so exclusively towards the apex of the conventional hierarchy – divinity – that all the lower orders are eclipsed. Either they become invisible, like grammar, or the shadow cast upon them renders them suspiciously 'occult'. Faust, of course, is keenly interested in learning which is still regarded as occult even today, and this interest skews the world of learning that he inhabits. We are not surprised to find 'Necromancie, Charmes, South-saying, Witchcraft, Inchantment' castigated as 'infernal Arts' (sig. A2v, pp. 92–3). But the Faust Book comes close to suggesting that mastery of the 'Chaldean, Persian, Hebrew, Arabian, and Greeke tongues' is also tantamount to meddling with 'divelish Arts', since the secrets of sorcery are so often locked up in these learned languages.

This tendency to demonise what would otherwise be considered legitimate arts, such as the study of languages, including the biblical languages Hebrew and Greek, may be seen most clearly in the way in which medicine is implicated in magic by Faust's participation in it. We are told that he was so delighted by his occult studies that 'hee could not abide to bee called Doctor of Divinitie, but waxed a worldly man, and named himselfe an Astrologian, and a Mathematician: & for a shadow sometimes a Phisitian, and did great cures, namely, with hearbs, rootes, waters, drinks, receipts, & clisters'. The word 'shadow' here means what we would call a 'cover': the good work he does as a physician makes people blind to his other and far less respectable activities as an astrologer (which is what the words

'Astrologian' and 'Mathematician' both mean in this place). But the fact that Faust has given himself over to sorcery raises questions about his medical expertise. Are these herbs and roots the same that witches brew in their cauldrons? Are other unmentioned and perhaps unmentionable ingredients also used in his remedies? There is something deviant and troubling about Faust as a medical doctor, partly because his motives are impure, and partly because the route by which he has presumably reached his mastery of the secret properties of plants is probably occult.

It is because Faust has turned away from God that all he touches becomes tainted and suspect. When P.F. describes him as a 'wordly man', he is probably mistranslating the German word used at this point: 'Weltmensch'. The original author meant his readers to see Faust as a 'natural philosopher', the secular equivalent of the divine in terms of the dignity and profundity of his learning, but subordinate to the divine in that he is concerned with the physical world rather than the metaphysical which lies behind it and makes it work. But P.F.'s phrase recalls the tradition of the foolish scholar. Here, then, natural philosophy may be seen as a rival to divinity, absurdly threatening to usurp its position at the unassailable apex of all knowledge. When the wordly man looks upwards, he sees the heavens, not Heaven. He sees the stars and tries to work out their movements by his mathematics and their operations by his astrology, with a view to exploiting this knowledge for worldly gain; whereas the divine, or merely the pious observer, sees the intricate and mysterious dance of the celestial bodies as a symbol of God's inscrutable providential designs. The folly of astronomers was, in fact, proverbial.[7] The art of physic is caught up in this suspicion because it is just as much a branch of natural philosophy as astrology since it requires a knowledge of the secrets of nature.

In an intellectual world less strongly dominated by divinity, natural philosophy might still be regarded as an innocent pursuit of knowledge hidden to most but not all. But in the world of the early Faust tradition, such enquiries are branded as 'speculation'. P.F. tells us that soon after Faust took his degree in divinity, he 'fell into such fantasies and deepe cogitations, that he was marked of many, and of the most part of the Students was called the *Speculator*' (sig. A2r, p. 92). A 'speculator' was one who was unsatisfied with the usual explanations and preferred to make up his own much more abstruse hypotheses. In the language of the Reformation, a speculator was primarily one who deviated from the teaching of the Bible; and the Faust Book goes on to note how, once addicted to speculation, Faust 'would throw the Scriptures from him as though he had no care of his former profession'. This is why the Faustus we meet in the opening pages of the Faust Book seems so curiously unmotivated; he has no ardent thirst for knowledge and power, but is idly discontent with theology. Even with P.F.'s addition of his 'naughty minde', Faust, we feel, should have better reasons – or just more reasons – for taking up the infernal arts.

But Marlowe dramatises his source by breathing life into Faustus. This is not to say that the prose Faust is entirely lifeless; but he is a listless fellow who shuffles from episode to episode without much sense of urgency. Particularly, Marlowe gives Faustus a much greater sense of motivation in the all-important opening scene. In the Faust Book, Faust has already started trifling with sorcery before he takes his degree in divinity, which is merely a tedious formality as far is he is concerned; once it is over, he returns to deeper study of necromancy and conjuration. In the play, he comes to sorcery only after completing his study of divinity, which is presented in a much more positive light. It is the 'fruitfull plot of Scholerisme' (line 16); and when the Chorus tells us that Faustus passed his degree by 'Excelling all, whose sweete delight disputes / In heavenly matters of *Theologie*' (lines 18–19), we may assume that Faustus enjoyed these intellectual pleasures as well as the next man. His pursuit of knowledge is often represented as a sort of physical appetite, and the Chorus observes that after a while, 'glutted now with learnings golden gifts, / He surfets upon cursed Negromancy. / Nothing so sweete as magicke is to him' (lines 23–5). We may not wish to approve his appetitive and concupiscent nature, but it turns Faustus into a full-blooded and 'lusty' dramatic character very different from his thin and exiguous prose counterpart.

Faustus is hungry, indeed greedy, for knowledge, and this becomes abundantly clear as soon as we set eyes on him in his study, surrounded by his books. We know, because we have just been told by the Chorus, that Faustus has already given himself over to magic, or, will do so in the course of the act. In fact, Faustus's long first speech (sixty lines) appears to re-enact this decision in a rather comic dismissal not only of divinity, but also of philosophy, physic and law. The speech works like a kind of routine: each of the four arts is represented by a single book, which is itself represented by a line or two of Latin supposedly taken from its pages, and each is passed over for the next with a humorous quip. The outcome is already pretty certain from the very start (lines 29–41):

Settle thy studies Faustus, and beginne
To sound the deapth of that thou wilt professe:
Having commencde, be a Divine in shew,
Yet levell at the end of every Art,
And live and die in Aristotles workes:
Sweete *Analutikes* tis thou hast ravisht me,
Bene disserere est finis logices,
Is to dispute well, Logickes chiefest end,

Affords this Art no greater myracle?
Then reade no more, thou hast attain the end:
A greater subject fitteth *Faustus* wit,
Bid *on cai me on* farewell, Galen come:
Seeing, *ubi desinit philosophus, ibi incipit medicus.*

The implied sequence of studies is a little disordered here. Faustus is already
a divine, but he speaks as if he has opened Aristotle's *Analytics* for the first
time, as if this is a new area of science which has 'ravisht' him with its
novel charms, like a new mistress. Moments later, Faustus reveals that he
can already dispute well, so need not concern himself further with the art of
philosophical logic. Disputation, of course, was the means by which candid-
ates for academic examinations were tested; and the Chorus has already
told us that Faustus is one of those 'whose sweete delight disputes / In
heavenly matters of *Theologie*'. But Faustus would have learnt how to dispute
by reading Aristotle, so must have made his mind up long ago about the
unremarkably mundane character of the syllogism, which he now regards
as contemptible. Here he rehearses that earlier rejection as a comic device,
no doubt leering at the book to suggest his first attraction to it, then throw-
ing the *Analytics* away with a melodramatic gesture of disgust – only to pick
up Galen instead. Physic, law, and finally divinity also come in for the same
treatment. Faustus scoffs each one away with a bumptiousness which verges
on recklessness. His well-known misconstruction of passages from the Bible
is a provocative parody of the official Calvinist doctrine of predestination:
'What doctrine call you this, *Che sera, sera*, / What wil be, shall be? Divinitie,
adieu' (lines 75–6).

The introduction of the secular sciences – what Euphues calls 'humayne
wisedome' as opposed to 'devine knowledge' (*Euph.*, pp. 286–7) – adds a
new dimension to Faustus's fall into sorcery. Faustus seems to have considered
the pursuit of these sciences as the way to a professional career. Philosophy
of the logical kind represented by Aristotle's *Analytics* was the mainstay of
the English universities, especially Oxford, owing to the crucial importance
of disputation. But physic and law would have taken Faustus out into the
wider world. Indeed, we know that he has already practised medicine: 'Is
not thy common talke sound Aphorismes?' (line 47). This detail is taken
from the Faust Book, but since Marlowe's Faustus uses divinity not physic
as the cover for his sorcery, it is a detail which might have been discarded.
However, Marlowe puts it to good use. Physic is held out as the royal road
to the things which most ordinary men want from life: 'Be a physition
Faustus, heape up golde, / And be eternizde for some wondrous cure' (lines
42–3). Money and fame are held out for a moment, then, but only to be
snatched away when Faustus considers the lawyer instead: 'His study fittes

a mercenary drudge, / Who aimes at nothing but externall trash, / Too servile and illiberall for me' (lines 62–4). The pursuit of money, then, turns out to be inglorious, making men slaves not kings. It is only when we come to magic that we learn of what truly attracts Faustus: 'O what a world of profit and delight, / Of power, of honour, of omnipotence, / Is promised to the studious Artizan?' (lines 81–3). Traditionally, ritual magic of the kind practised by Faustus was aimed mainly at discovering hoards of hidden gold.[8] Marlowe's Faustus, however, has more heroic aspirations. He wishes to 'Chase the Prince of Parma from our land, / And raigne sole king of all our provinces' (lines 121–2). In fact, he does nothing of the kind; he spends his twenty-four years playing pranks. In this he follows the Faust of the *Historia*, where the point is made that the pursuit of magic is trivial in the light of the one true knowledge, which is knowledge of God's will. The same point is carried over into the play in the comic middle scenes written by A. But Marlowe provides an interesting and characteristic variation on the theme by replacing prankishness with the pursuit of pleasure, especially love poetry. Here it is that the *litterae humaniores* make their presence felt; but Marlowe (if not Faustus) is still keenly aware that these stand in an ultimately sinister relationship to divinity and to salvation.

Marlowe and Musaeus

'Tis Magicke, Magicke that hath ravisht mee'. So says Faustus to his instructors Valdes and Cornelius. In this mood of excited exultation, his mind turns to past as well as future glories (lines 139–46):[9]

> Then gentle friends ayde me in this attempt,
> And I that haue with concise sylogismes
> Graveld the Pastors of the Germaine Church,
> And made the flowring pride of W[it]tenberge
> Swarme to my Problemes as the infernall spirits
> On sweet Musaeus when he came to hell,
> Will be as cunning as Agrippa was,
> Whose shadowes made all Europe honor him.

These lines trace a movement from divinity to magic: Agrippa was even more famous than Faustus, and acts as a model for Marlowe's character (Roberts, 1996). But between these poles Faustus places an image of Musaeus in hell. This makes sense in that Faustus can only make the transition from divine to magician with the help of 'infernall spirits' such as Mephistopheles (and in the Faust Book he actually visits hell himself). However, Musaeus is no magician, but a poet.

When, in the sixth book of Virgil's *Aeneid*, Aeneas goes down to the underworld with the Sibyl, in search of the spirit of his father, he at length comes to the 'blessed seates of soules' (6.638–9; trans. Phaer, 1558, p. 138). Here is the final destination of heroes, priests, philosophers and 'prophets [*vates*, i.e. bards] pure of life' (6.660, p. 139): 'Elysium' (as later ages would name the place). But only one of these blessed spirits is named: Musaeus – 'for he inclosed is in throng / With numbers great of soules, and him they kéepe alwaies among, / Bresthigh above them all, and all to him their heads incline'. This is the scene that Faustus has in mind when he boasts to Cornelius and Valdes of his reception by the flowering pride of Wittenberg. Where Virgil has Musaeus stand head and shoulders above the other spirits, Faustus seems to see these lifting him up on their own shoulders in the time-honoured manner of celebrating the victor's triumph. Still, the point is made. Faustus, then, at the very moment where he fully reveals his aspirations, remembers a well-known piece of verse from his schooldays. He compares himself, indeed, with a poet who held a special interest for Marlowe himself. Musaeus is a mythical poet: the son or pupil of Orpheus. But his name also indicates a direct connection with the Muses themselves. Like Orpheus, Musaeus was regarded as a true *vates*: a 'seer'. The *vates* was able to see things that were invisible to the ordinary eye: the past and the future, for example, but also the secrets of creation. Hence Musaeus does have an affinity with the magician in his access to occult knowledge. However, the only poem by Musaeus known to the Renaissance was of a rather different nature: the erotic epyllion called *Hero and Leander*. And Marlowe himself translated this poem.

Of course, *Hero and Leander* is not really by Virgil's Musaeus. It seems to be the work of a Greek schoolmaster of the fifth century AD (and a Christian one too): 'Musaeus Grammaticus'. In other words, the author of *Hero and Leander* was not the semi-divine son of Orpheus, but what Harington and Hume would have called a humanist. Elizabethan writers were not aware of the true identity of this Musaeus, but they had their doubts that it was the poet singled out by Virgil in the *Aeneid*. After all, *Hero and Leander* is hardly vatic. It is a sentimental account of the tragic affair between two young lovers, a tale not dissimilar to *Romeo and Juliet* in tone and detail. So Renaissance poets and scholars like George Chapman, who continued Marlowe's translation in 1598, were surprised that the great *vates* should have composed such a dainty piece on 'so trifeling a subject, which yet made the first Author, divine Musaeus, eternall' (p. 513). The vatic poet writes trivial love poetry; this is exactly what Harvey had in mind when he uses the word 'humanist' in his marginal comments in his Chaucer and his Periegetes.

Chapman writes of 'divine Musaeus', but the real Musaeus's *Hero and Leander* belongs to the secular and witty world of sophisticated *humanitas*.

Marlowe's temperament was very different from Chapman's. It was precisely the trivial and erotic aspects of Musaeus's poem which attracted him, since it was these aspects which he amplified in his own translation, or rather, rewriting of the poem. His version shies away from the original after only a line or two in order to riot in an exorbitantly sophisticated and sensual description of the two young lovers. But we are immediately led back to a properly vatic mixture of metaphysics and high sentence by the 'sterne Muse' of George Chapman's continuation of Marlowe's poem in 1598 (3.4). In other words, when Faustus describes Musaeus as 'sweet', he is probably thinking of him as the suave author of *Hero and Leander*, rather than as the sternly vatic figure admired by Virgil and Chapman. Such an idea adds an interestingly ambiguous inflection to his picture of 'sweet Musaeus when he came to hell'.

It may seem to us unpropitious that Faustus should compare himself to Musaeus 'when he came to hell'. But at this point in the play, Faustus does not seem to believe in the Christian view of hell as a stinking pit of eternal torment: 'This word damnation terrifies not him, / For he confounds hell in Elizium. / His ghost be with the olde Philosophers' (lines 294–6). Faustus does not deny that there is a place under the ground reserved for the spirits of the dead, but he seems to prefer the pagan view to the Christian. He would have read in his Virgil that the underworld had a place where spirits were terribly punished as well as one where they lived in eternal bliss: Tartarus and Elysium. Christian cosmology keeps the place of punishment down below as 'hell', but raises paradise to a place above the earth in 'heaven'. But Faustus 'confounds hell in Elizium', which seems to mean (though it is by no means certain) that he thinks that what the Christian divines call by the name of 'hell' is really a misrepresentation of Elysium. A little later, he chaffs Mephistopheles for apparently upholding the orthodox Christian view that hell is a place of torment: 'Thinkst thou that Faustus is so fond, to imagine, / That after this life is any paine?' (lines 565–6). When Mephistopheles insists that he is damned and in hell here and now, Faustus rounds on him in derision: 'How? now in hell? nay and this be hell, Ile willlingly be damnd here: what walking, disputing, &c.' (lines 570–1). Faustus's mind is running on the Elysium of the 'olde philosophers' at this point. After he himself has 'come to hell' like Musaeus, he will (so he thinks) spend his time gravelling Plato and Aristotle with his syllogisms.

However, we know differently. Whatever personal religious convictions we may bring to *Doctor Faustus*, we are certain that its 'hell' is not Elysium, but Tartarus; the presence of the devils proves it. These, surely, are the 'infernall spirits' who surround Musaeus when he reaches hell, not the shades of the great poets and philosophers as in Virgil. They have not 'swarmed' around him in order to hear his sweet verses, but because they 'flye, in hope to get his glorious soule' (line 284). Faustus does not believe this, of course; but Marlowe may have wished us to pause at the image more thoughtfully. It is as if Musaeus is revealed as the trivial love poet, not the mythic *vates*, approaching hell as if it really were Elysium, but soon to be seized on by the devils, and to learn too late that his poetry will not charm then into obedience, as Orpheus's music is said to have placated the infernal demons when he visited the underworld. For all Faustus's learning, he is still a *dilettante* when it comes to wisdom. When he thinks of hell, his mind goes back to his grammar-school reading, to provide his conceit with a flattering image of himself as the great Musaeus; but Marlowe, mischievously, uses the same curriculum of *litterae humaniores* to set up Faustus's hellish fall.

Faustus and Paris

Poetry does not lead to damnation, of course, especially in the Calvinist context of predestination. But an addiction to poetry could be regarded as a sign of reprobation, and thus as an indication of the likely final resting place of the soul. Poetry provides pleasure on earth, but too great a love for this kind of pleasure may be a token of damnation.[10] However, Marlowe's Faustus on several occasions seeks to use ancient poetry to divert his mind from the thought of perdition, after he begins to have second thoughts about the wisdom of his pact with Lucifer and tries to repent. But he lacks the resolution to repent in the face of threats by the infernal powers, who try to persuade him to despair instead, offering him 'swordes and knives, / Poyson, gunnes, halters, and invenomd steele' (lines 633–5) with which to dispatch himself:

> And long ere this I should have slaine my selfe,
> Had not sweete pleasure conquerd deepe dispaire.
> Have not I made blinde Homer sing to me
> Of Alexanders love, and Enons death,
> And hath not he that built the walles of Thebes,
> With ravishing sound of his melodious harp
> Made musicke with my Mephastophilis?

It is to the old epic and vatic poets, rather than the old philosophers, to whom Faustus turns when he requires 'sweete pleasure'. However, Homer is not called upon to sing fierce wars, but to recall an episode of the matter of Troy which, though sad, is sweetly sad: a lyrical interlude in the epic narrative. The Alexander to whom Faustus here refers is Paris, who courted the nymph Oenone, then abandoned her in favour of Helen. She then refused to help Paris when he was brought to her suffering from a wound that only she could cure; he died, and she killed herself in remorse. The action is tragic, but not epic: it takes place well away from the epic action of the main story. Properly, it belongs to pastoral, since Paris was a shepherd; and the story is partially represented in George Peele's pastoral play *Arraignment of Paris* (1584). In other words, it is the sweeter poetry that Faustus seeks; not that which will make him feel more valiant and resolute, which would be much more appropriate to his situation. As a matter of fact, he is consoled by what Homer and the mythical Theban poet Amphion sing to him: 'Why should I dye then, or basely dispaire? / I am resolu'd Faustus shal nere repent'. But it is 'sweete pleasure' that leads him on. There is a sort of generic reduction here. The epic figure of Alexander the Great, whom the collaborator A's Faustus conjures up for the delight of the German emperor in the middle scenes of the play, is replaced with a pastoral and erotic 'Alexander the Little', as it were, just as the vatic Musaeus has his trivialised namesake in the Greek schoolmaster.[11] Marlowe's Faustus may be regarded as a Paris figure in his turning away from his earlier heroic aspirations and settling for the pleasures of lover instead. But the figure is not without tragic pathos, as we can see by comparing the scenes with Helen of Troy in the prose-book and the play.

In the Faust Book, Helen of Troy appears at the end of a sequence of chapters dealing with Faustus's escapades on his return to academic life (of a kind) at Wittenberg. These are mainly of a gourmandising character. Day after day he invites his friends from the university to sumptuous meals at which large amounts of wine are consumed: 'Doctor Faustus was himself the God Bacchus, who having well feasted the Studentes before with daintie fare, after the manner of Germanie, where it is counted no feast except all the bidden guests be drunke' (sig. H3v, p. 158). Here is festivity of a rather exorbitant kind. The detail on compulsory drunkenness is not in the German *Historia*, of course, but added by the Englishman P.F.; at any rate, they are a far cry from the elegant and moderate pleasures enjoyed by the company at Crassus's villa in the *De oratore*. Moreover, despite the fact that Faust is entertaining a company of scholars, there is no attempt made at humane conversation. Instead: 'Doctor Faustus began to play his olde prankes' (sig. I1r, p. 161). Cup dances with pot, apes and monkeys caper, a calf's head speaks on its platter. Only once does the entertainment rise above this coarse revelry. Faust and the students have been drinking: 'and being merry, they began some of them to talke of the beauty of women, and every one gave foorth his verdit what he had seene and what he had heard' (sig. I1v, p. 162). And so the scene is set for one of the rare moments in which the spirit of *humanitas* and the *litterae humaniores* flickers briefly and dimly in the Faust Book. One of the students expresses a desire to see Helen of Troy, noting that her beauty must be splendid indeed, 'there was for her recovery so great blood-shed'. Faust recalls his old grammar-school studies in humanity and gives the students a brief identification of Helen such as one might find in a dictionary: 'that famous pearle of Greece, fayre Helena, the wife of King Menelaus, and daughter of Tindalus and Laeda, sister to Castor and Pollux, who was the fayrest Lady in all Greece'. In fact, this information can be traced verbatim (in the German) to just such a text: Petrus Dasypodius's *Dictionarium Latino – Germanicum et vice versa Germanico – Latinum* ('A Latin–German and German–Latin Dictionary': 1565; cit. Füssel and Kreutzer, 1988, p. 309). And to such pedantry, we may add a certain coarseness in the treatment of Helen, who is represented as a flirtatious courtesan: 'shee looked round about her with a rouling Haukes eye, a smiling & wanton countenance, which neere hand inflamed the hearts of the students' (sig. I2r, p. 163). Faust even gives the students pictures of Helen to take home with them and gaze at in their beds.

In the play, Helen is treated with much greater respect, even veneration. The context in which she is presented to our eyes is more elevated. True, a faint echo of the old moral scandal of the Faust Book still survives. The final movement in the play is introduced by Wagner's puzzled comments on his master's behaviour: Why is he giving himself up to revelry when his end is near? Wagner thinks Faustus should be praying, not indulging in 'such belly-cheere, / As Wagner nere beheld in all his life' (lines 1243–4). But Faustus's supper is a more dignified occasion than the riotous drinking-parties of the Faust Book. He makes the scene a testament to beauty. In the Faust Book, we feel that there is an element of ribaldry in the students' enquiry; but here it is refined into a 'conference about faire Ladies' (lines 1246–7). Nor are the students interested merely in Helen's beauty. Other qualities are also admired, such as her 'majesty'. Moreover, Faustus spares us the pedant's commentary, and places Helen in a more dramatic context (lines 1258–61):

> You shall behold that pearelesse dame of Greece,
> No otherwaies for pompe and majestie,
> Then when sir Paris crost the seas with her,
> And brought the spoiles to rich Dardania.

We have moved from one kind of humanism to the other in this detail. The stock-in-trade gloss of the professional pedant has been replaced with the excitement of the amateur of *belles lettres*.

Helen appears: '*Musicke sounds, and Helen passeth over the Stage*'. The students are deeply moved; and Marlowe increases the dignity of the scene by making it resonate to Homer's ancient melody (lines 1263–5):

> *2. Sch.* Too simple is my wit to tell her praise,
> Whom all the world admires for majestie.
> *3. Sch.* No marvel tho the angry Greekes pursude
> With tenne yeares warre the rape of such a queene,
> Whose heavenly beauty passeth all compare.

These lines recall the symbolic importance of Helen of Troy in the humanist tradition. She is the archetypal *causa belli*: 'the cause of war'. Conflict is the enemy to *humanitas*, and war throws down the quiet country houses where Cicero's speakers conduct their elegant conversations. How, then, could the Greeks and Trojans go to war for such a trifle as the abduction of a single woman? The answer was simple: Helen was so beautiful. This *causa belli* was also a *causa bella*: 'a beautiful cause'. This answer was given as early as the *Iliad* itself. Early in the poem, a group of Trojan elders, too old to fight and now given over to gossiping, look down on Helen from the tower where they sit, 'as in well-growne woods, on trees, cold spinie Grashoppers / Sit chirping' (3.146; trans. Chapman, 1598–1611, 1.78) As she approaches the tower they murmur: 'What man can blame / The Greekes and Troyans to endure, for so admir'd a Dame, / So many miseries, and so long? In her sweete countenance shine / Lookes like the Goddesses' (3.155–8).

Of course, Marlowe's Helen is not a 'goddess'. Spirit or demon, she is a citizen of hell and instrument of perdition. Yet she is so extremely lovely that we almost forget this, even in the second Helen scene, despite Marlowe's mischievous hints. Faustus meets the Old Man, and is persuaded to consider repentance; but once again Mephistopheles threatens him, Faustus collapses immediately and applies himself to his usual means of oblivion: romantic fantasy. He begs Mephistopheles to supply him with 'That heavenly Helen which I saw of late' (lines 1319, 1322). Helen enters, and Faustus speaks what are surely the lines Marlowe is most famous for (lines 1328–1350):

> Was this the face that lancht a thousand shippes?
> And burnt the toplesse Towres of Ilium?
> Sweete Helen, make me immortall with a kisse:
> Her lips suckes forth my soule, see where it flies:
> Come Helen, come give mee my soule againe.
> Here wil I dwel, for heaven be in these lips,
> And all is drosse that is not Helena: *Enter old man.*
> I wil be Paris, and for love of thee,

Insteede of Troy shal W[it]tenberge be sackt,
And I wil combate with weake Menelaus,
And weare thy colours on my plumed Crest:
Yea I wil wound Achillis in the heele,
And then returne to Helen for a kisse.
O thou art fairer then the evening aire,
Clad in the beauty of a thousand starres,
Brighter art thou then flaming Jupiter,
When he appeard to hapless Semele,
More lovely then the monarke of the skie
In wanton Arethusaes azurde armes,
And none but thou shalt be my paramour.

This is all Marlowe's invention, from the merest of hints in the Faust Book. Much depends on its success on the stage. On the one hand, we must know (as the students in the Faust Book do) that when Faustus kisses Helen, he is really kissing a spirit or even a demon. However one looks at the situation, the 'sweete imbracings' (line 1322) he looks forward to enjoying are deeply deviant. Yet Helen must be portrayed as beautifully as possible for the earlier scene with the students to work its full effect. When Faustus kisses Helen, we must be convinced that she might indeed be a woman. It is not that Marlowe is trying to seduce his audience into the sin of demoniality, but rather an exercise in his own powers as a poet and dramatist to draw us into a particularly spellbinding scenic moment. More than any other moment in the play, Marlowe is writing in his most intensely glamorous manner.

Yet this speech is shot through with ironies of a subtler kind than we usually encounter in this play. On the one hand, we still meet with the overt provocations of a line like: 'Sweete Helen, make me immortall with a kisse'. So lovers speak. But what are we to think when Faustus says that Helen's kiss steals his soul away: 'see where it flies'. He is surely playing, but the entrance of the Old Man moments later reminds us of the serious implications of Faustus's dalliance. Perhaps it is really Marlowe who is playing here. The famous lines about Helen's face and the thousand ships are taken from the satirical *Dialogues of the Dead* by the Graeco-Syrian satirist Lucian of Samosata. The cynical philosopher Menippus is taken to the underworld by Mercury, where he sees what happens to the great and powerful after they have died. At one point he picks up a skull, to be told that it was Helen's. Menippus retorts: 'And was it then for thys that all Graecia manned her thowsand shyppes?' (5.409). Marlowe 'saw the skull beneath the skin', as T.S. Eliot said of John Webster. Dr Faustus can never quite bid divinity adieu as carelessly as he would wish, surrounding himself with the beauties of *litterae humaniores* as symbolised by Helen of Troy, for these beauties are revealed again and again to disguise the darker face of death and despair.

Notes

1. It is interesting to note that the author of the original *Historia* was also chiefly interested in the beginning and the end of his story (Füssel and Kreutzer, 1988, p. 332).

2. The dates of all these works are hard to ascertain. Possibly they are all early pieces, dating from the mid- or late 1580s.

3. Cf. Füssel and Kreutzer: 'There is quite certainly no connection to be made between the Faustus of the *Historia* and the historical tradition of German humanism' (1988, p. 334).

4. In the pages that follow, the prose-book figure is called 'Faust' and the dramatic one 'Faustus'.

5. For the early dating of these texts, see Jones, 1994, pp. 52–71. The first *extant* edition of the *Damnable Life* dates from 1592, which accordingly gives a late date to *Doctor Faustus* (Marlowe died in 1593). But there is other evidence to suggest that the earlier date is more likely.

6. The *Damnable Life* uses the word 'humanity' only once, in the usual sense of 'courtesy', when Faustus scolds a rude and unfriendly country clown as a 'voyde of all humanitie' (sig. I2v, p. 164). This is a moderated version of the expression used by the German Faust: 'worthless scum [*nichtswerdiger Unflat*' (p. 99). Faustus himself here behaves boorishly, one feels.

7. 'To look at the stars and fall into a ditch' (Tilley, 1950, S827). This proverb must have been in everyone's mouth in 1589, when *Doctor Faustus* was written, since 1588 had been predicted by many astrologers – including Richard Harvey – as a year of great calamity for England, whereas, in fact, it had seen the defeat of the Spanish Armada. Lyly uses the proverb in his play *Galatea*, performed at court in 1588, where a vainglorious astronomer makes absurd predictions (3.3).

8. See Butler, 1949, *passim*, and esp. 'The Faustian School' (pp. 154–294).

9. The A Text has 'Wertenberge', but this is changed to 'Wittenberg' in the B Text, which makes more sense as the cradle of Lutheran Protestantism. But see Marcus, 1989.

10. For the radical critique of poetry in the English Renaissance, see Fraser, 1970.

11. Plutarch relates how Alexander, when he visited the ruins of Troy, scorned the opportunity to see Paris's harp, but longed to see Achilles' instrument, to

which he sang 'all the famous acts done by valiant men in former times' ('Alexander', 15.5; trans. North, 1579: 7.22). It is worth noting that Lyly had also called up Alexander and another of his beauteous paramours in his first play, *Campaspe* (1583, pr. 1584). Here, too, the context is trivial. The prologue explains that they have called up Alexander's spirit to 'seeke only who was his love' (lines 11–12). See Pincombe, 1996, pp. 46–8.

CHAPTER TEN

Imitations of Humanity:
William Shakespeare's
Hamlet, Prince of Denmark

'What a peece of worke is a man!' Hamlet's celebrated expression (2.2.1245) has long been a *locus classicus* for the 'philosophical' interpretation of Renaissance humanism which is so often associated with Marlowe's Faustus. He goes on: 'how noble in reason, how infinit in faculty, in forme and mooving, how expresse and admirable? in action, how like an Angell? in apprehension, how like a God'. Here is that seductive *superhumanitas* which did indeed lead on many thinkers of the Renaissance to aim at an heroically transcendental conception of humanity. But to Hamlet man is merely a 'Quintessence of dust'. The *heros* – half man, half god – is a mythical creature. In the grave-yard scene, he wryly observes that even the greatest of the heroes of human history, such as Alexander the Great, glorified by Marlowe's collaborators as by so many other Renaissance writers, merely 'returneth into dust' (5.1.3175–6). His remains are used for corks in beer barrels. Hamlet is no transcendentalist, then; rather he inclines towards the 'grotesque' aspects of humanity, those which do not easily conform to the set of normative con-ceptions which generally operate as a kind of ideal, such as those expressed in the 'What a piece of work' passage. Indeed, Hamlet announces his intention to explore the grotesque when he tells Horatio at the end of the first act that he will 'put an Anticke disposition on' (1.5.790) in order to provide cover for his investigations into the claims made by the apparition claiming to be his father's ghost. This word 'antic' is very interesting. It commonly referred to an actor who wore an ugly mask and hopped and capered (hence our modern 'antics').[1] In other words, Hamlet intends to present himsef as a grotesque travesty of humanity by acting as if he were suffering from some kind of mental 'deformity'. Yet the word 'antic' also has an association with the normative conception of humanity which is sometimes described as 'classical'.[2] It is a by-form of the word 'antique', and is thus mysteriously connected with the world of what we call 'classical antiquity'. In fact, this description of ancient Greek and Roman culture is already shaped by a 'classicism' which has selected certain aspects of that culture to value and imitate. What is left is dismissed as 'primitive', 'aberrant', 'decadent', because it does not conform to the classicist's ideal. In terms of the master-narrative of Renaissance humanism, then, these 'grotesque' elements turn out to be 'Gothic'; and we shall end this chapter by examining the relationship between neoclassical humanism and the northern vernacular tradition in terms of Rome and Denmark. But I also wish to suggest that for Shakespeare, this relationship is played out in terms of his own profession as a man of the theatre. In his instructions to the players, Hamlet tells them not to overact when performing *The Murder of Gonzago*, since he has seen tragic actors who have 'so strutted & bellowed, that I have thought some of Natures Jornimen had made men, and not made them well, they imitated humanitie so abominably' (3.2.1759–62). This 'imitation of humanity' principally refers to human form and gesture, of course, but Hamlet's remarks may also be interpreted in the light of the *translatio humanitatis* from Greece and Rome to the Gothic North, to Denmark, but also to Elizabethan England. Let us begin, then, by looking at Hamlet as a literary humanist.

Hamlet the humanist

We have seen that literary humanism tends to have a scholarly and a courtly aspect, and that these are often set in opposition by those who regard themselves as principally courtly writers. Shakespeare uses the same scheme in *Hamlet*, where the two aspects are represented by Polonius and Hamlet and their views on tragedy and the drama in general. Both men seem to have considerable experience of the drama. Polonius once played Julius Caesar 'i'th Universitie' (3.2.1822). Perhaps Hamlet has played at Wittenberg; he is certainly well acquainted with the popular drama purveyed by 'the Tragedians of the Citty' (2.2.1259). Indeed, he consistently relies on theatrical metaphors to make sense of his situation. But it is when the tragedians arrive at Elsinore that he and Polonius exercise their critical opinions in most detail. Let us begin with the older man.

Polonius's notoriously nonsensical list of the kinds of play the company can perform marks him out as a pedant: 'Tragedie, Comedie, History, Pastorall, Pastorall Comicall, Historicall Pastorall, Tragicall-Historicall, Tragicall-Comicall-Historicall-Pastorall' (2.2.1327–30). The final category exposes the futility of the schoolmasterly passion for classification when applied to traditional vernacular drama. But there are other and more subtle indications of Polonius's essentially pedantic approach – for example, his praise for Hamlet's recital of the speech of Aeneas on the murder of Priam: 'Foregod my Lord well spoken, with good accent and good discretion' (2.2.1598–9). This is the sort of praise which Elizabethan schoolmasters gave to pupils who did well when reading out passages from classical poetry, or acting in plays written in Latin: putting the accent on the right syllable is no easy matter when you are standing in front of the class or your parents and other important people. You needed 'audacity' – and this is how the school drama was usually defended when its opponents made their periodic attacks on transvestism or sodomy or whatever.

Polonius, then, seems disposed to regard dramatic performance as an extension of rhetoric, and the delivery of dramatic speeches of one kind and another had been used as exercises in formal rhetorical instruction since the days of Cicero. This schoolroom emphasis may also explain why Polonius impatiently interrupts the player's tirade against Fortune with the laconic comment: 'This is too long' (2.2.1430). Such tirades are a stock component of Tudor tragedy, not only in stage-plays, but in the less familiar narrative form which preceded the tragic drama in England, as exemplified in the poems first published in the monumental *Mirror for Magistrates* in 1559, and then expanded several times over the next sixty years. Such poems generally use a first-person narrator who exclaims against the operations of Fortune in his or her own downfall, often at some length, and usually with only minor variations on the same basic rhetorical material. Here is one reason why Polonius finds the tirade tedious; but we may also presume that the complaint was used as a declamation exercise in the schools. We recall how Jacques first encounters Touchstone in *As You Like It*: '[He] rail'd on Lady Fortune in good termes, / In good set termes, and yet a motley foole' (2.7.939–49). The point here is that Touchstone, though a mere jester, can improvise with such expertise on the old theme in 'good set terms': the terms taught at school and university.

It is at this point that Hamlet taunts Polonius with his lack of artistic appreciation: 'he's for a Jigge, or a tale of bawdry, or he sleepes' (2.2.1432–4). Hamlet accuses Polonius of vulgar tastes, then, against which his own more sophisticated preferences are to be opposed. The player continues; and so does Hamlet's baiting of Polonius:

1. Player. But who, o who, had seene the mobled Queene –
Hamlet. The mobled Queene.
Polonius. That's good: Mobled Queene is good.
1. Player. Runne barefoote up and downe . . .

This is clearly meant to be a particularly passionate and tragical moment, but the word 'mobled' gets in the way. The word (whatever it means) is and was rare. That is why Hamlet draws attention to it. Perhaps he wants to tease Polonius with a choice verbal titbit in order to provoke him to another outburst. Certainly, Polonius approves, and no doubt for the usual pedantic reasons: schoolboys learning Latin were instructed to seek out such words and phrases – the *elegantiae* which provided Valla with the title of his immensely influential compendium of such items. Why is it choice? That is difficult to say, because we do not really know what the word means. But it seems that the first recorded instance of this mysterious word is *Hamlet*. If so, Hamlet teases Polonius by making him comment on a word which he might not know – yet still approves.

One the other hand, Hamlet may well be genuinely interested in the word 'mobled'. Polonius, one feels, is probably not very sensitive to details of diction, but Hamlet certainly is, as demonstrated most obviously in the scene with Osric, who is represented as excessively devoted to *elegantiae* in the shape of words which have been wrested to senses slightly other than the one which they are normally given. Hamlet easily outwords him in a dizzyingly contrived eulogy of Laertes, which clearly baffles Osric (M. 15–24):[3]

> *Ostricke.* Your Lordship speakes most infallibly of him.
> *Hamlet.* The concernancy sir, why doe we wrap the gentleman in our more rawer breath?
> *Ostricke.* Sir[?]
> *Horatio.* Is't not possible to understand in another tongue, you will too't sir rarely.
> *Hamlet.* What imports the nomination of this gentleman[?]
> *Ostricke.* Of Laertes[?]
> *Horatio.* (*aside to Hamlet*) His purse is empty already, all's golden words are spent.

The two university men tease Osric for trying to speak a finer language than he is able to sustain for more than a few lines. Osric is a 'chough' (2.2.3357). He is at once a 'chuff', or 'wealthy peasant': 'spacious in the possession of dirt'; and also a garrulous jackdaw ('chough'). Both senses of the word fix him squarely in the lower reaches of humanity. Hamlet remarks: 'let a beast be Lord of beasts, and his crib shall stand at the Kings messe'.

Hamlet mocks Osric for his diction because he feels fine speech really belongs to educated men such as himself, and degrades him as 'inhumane' in order to dismiss him as a provincial rival. But, really, Hamlet is rather foppish in his penchant for elegancy as well. What are we to make of the passage where he reminds the player of the speech he wishes him to recite (2.2.1366–79):

> I heard thee speake me a speech once, but it was never acted, or if it was, not above once, for the play I remember pleasd not the million, t'was caviary to the generall, but it was as I receaved it & others, whose judgements in such matters cried in the top of mine, an excellent play, well digested in the scenes, set downe with as much modestie as cunning. I remember one sayd there was no sallets in the lines, to make the matter savory, nor no matter in the phrase that might indite the author of affectation, but cald it an honest method, as wholesome as sweete, & by very much, more handsome then fine: one speech in it I chiefly loved, t'was Aeneas tale to Dido, & there about of it especially where he speakes of Priams slaughter.

Hamlet's comments are couched in the familiar language of Elizabethan humanism. How many times have we heard the claim that a poet should write for the few and not for the many? But there are some details here which need examining. One is Hamlet's allusion to 'savoury matter' – what we would call 'spice'. He seems to be suggesting that *risqué* erotic material has found its way into popular tragedy. This was certainly true of some Elizabethan plays, and we may perhaps detect a reference to some of the more wanton episodes in Marlowe's *Dido, Queen of Carthage* (?1587, pr. 1594), to which the play described by Hamlet seems to bear some kinship.[4] There we see Jupiter dandling Ganymede on his knee, and the grotesque wooing of tiny Cupid by an infatuated crone. But Hamlet praises the Danish Dido play because of a certain stylistic 'chasteness'. The qualities he admires are again typical of a certain kind of humanism: modest, unaffected, honest, wholesome, sweet: 'by very much more handsome than fine'. One almost hears the voice of Gabriel Harvey praising Ascham and Sidney and the others in *Pierce's Supererogation*. Hamlet here speaks like a 'silly humanitian of the old world . . . which . . . esteemed every thing fine, that was neat, & holesome' (sig. T1v). And the nostalgic element is important. Modern taste, Hamlet seems to imply, is too 'fine': too much concerned with exquisite artifice. Yet there is a thin line to be drawn between his speech and Osric's.

Still, Hamlet's emphasis on modesty and delicacy may seem a little misplaced when applied to tragedy, where one would expect more forcible qualities to be singled out for praise. But Hamlet has to appeal to these values because he knows that tragedy is inimical to *humanitas*. According to the usual Renaissance definitions, tragedy dealt with miserable slaughters. In other words, it dealt with 'man's inhumanity to man'. But tragic inhumanity also has linguistic and stylistic consequences, since the dramatic imitation of tragic actions seems to require a decorously 'inhumane' kind of speech for tyrants and other characters driven by extreme passion towards a kind of madness (*furor*). For Hamlet, this need not be so much a question of diction as of delivery, as his instructons to the player makes very plain (3.2.1):

> Speake the speech, I pray you, as I pronounc'd it to you, trippingly on the tongue, but if you mouth it as many of your Players do, I had as live the towne cryer had spoke my lines, nor doe not saw the ayre too much with your hand thus, but use all gently, for in the very torrent tempest and as I may say, whirlwind of your passion, you must acquire and beget a temperance that may give it smoothnesse, ô it offends mee to the soule, to hear a robustious perwig-pated fellowe tere a passion to totters, to very rags, to spleet the eares of the groundlings, who for the most part are capable of nothing but inexplicable dumbe showes and noyse: I would have such a fellow whipt for ore-doing Termagant, it out Herods Herod, pray you avoyde it.

Hamlet's complaint is that even when extreme passions are to be represented, they must be delivered delicately: 'trippingly' and 'gently' and 'smoothnesse' are all words which belong to the vocabulary of *humanitas*. The player must cultivate a 'temperance' which is very close to urbanity, and which will inform his delivery even at moments of extreme emotion. He must remain in rational control of the emotions he imitates, not give into them. It is still a little odd, however, to imagine the actor playing a tyrant speaking his lines so mildly. We can see why Hamlet wishes the player to avoid falling into the old-fashioned excesses of medieval stage-tyrants such as Herod and Termagant, but it is not clear that the suavity he recommends in a passionate speech is really an improvement.

The reason Hamlet errs in the direction of overmuch delicacy is that he is anxious about the grotesque aspects of tyrannical delivery. He tells the player 'the purpose of playing . . . is, to holde as 'twere the Mirrour up to nature'; but the naturalistic style must still observe the rules of decorum:

> Now this over done, or come tardie off, though it makes the unskilfull laugh, cannot but make the judicious greeve, the censure of the which must in your allowance ore-weigh a whole Theater of others. O there be players that I have seene play, and heard others prayse, and that highly, not to speake it prophanely, that neither having the accent of Christians, nor the gate of Christian, Pagan, nor no man, have so strutted & bellowed, that I have thought some of Natures Jornimen had made men, and not made them well, they imitated humanitie so abominably.

Why does Hamlet make so much of this point? It is partly because he has a horror of vulgarity. Sound and fury is what the 'groundlings' like. Presumably Hamlet has witnessed their applause on visits to the plays performed by the tragedians of the city. But the main reason is that he feels compelled to obey the ghost of his father (if such it is) and act the part of the avenger in his own revenge-tragedy. This is why his mind turns to the speech in which Aeneas 'speakes of Priams slaughter'. Priam is slain by Pyrrhus as an act of vengeance for the death of his father Achilles. It is not an exact analogy, because Priam has not personally killed Achilles; but Hamlet is perhaps most interested in the image of Pyrrhus towering over the helpless Priam with his sword sweeping down to slay him, suddenly arrested by the sound of the walls of Troy falling about him, so that 'Pirrhus stood / And like a newtrall to his will and matter, / Did nothing' (2.2.1412–13). This matches Hamlet's own situation very closely; and a few scenes later he himself will stand above the praying Claudius with his sword raised but still unable to do the deed (3.3). What prevents him at this point is, according to his own testimony, the worry that he might send Claudius's soul to heaven rather than hell; but there is another reason why Hamlet prevaricates so consistently throughout the play. In the following section I argue that Hamlet regards vengeful murder not so much as a 'crime against humanity' (he seems to have few real moral qualms about it) but an offence against *humanitas*. To play the part of the avenger is too much like taking on the role of a ham actor in a vulgar revenge-tragedy.

Hamlet the avenger

What most offends Hamlet about bad tragic actors is that they produce so much noise. However, *clamor* had been a highly respectable feature of tragedy since at least the Middle Ages. As Chaucer's Monk declares in *The Canterbury Tales* (7.2761–4: my italics):

Tragediës noon oother maner thyng
Ne kan in syngyng *crie* ne *biwaille*,
But that Fortune alwey wole assaille
With unwar strook the regnes that been proude.

Clamorous complaint against the operations of Fortune was certainly a salient part of the older narrative tradition – poems telling the story of the 'fall of princes' – from Chaucer to the *Mirror for Magistrates*. This latter work also provided a link with the new developments in dramatic tragedy, especially those influenced by the study of the plays of Seneca, in that its tragedies are related by the ghosts of their protagonists, as in Chaucer's original model, Boccaccio's *De casibus illustrium virorum* (1363–73).[5] The various tragedies in the *Mirror for Magistrates* are connected by prose passages in which readers are asked to imagine they see the ghost of the English noble-man whose fall is to be recounted, who then relates his own tale in the first person, with much crying and bewailing at Fortune's strokes. These ghosts were distant relatives of those who appear in 'Senecal' tragedy.[6]

In fact, Seneca used the ghost relatively sparingly in his own plays; and the Elizabethans seem to have thought he should have made more of the figure. For example, when Jasper Heywood inaugurated the great series of Elizabethan translations of Seneca's plays with his version of *Troas* in 1559, he included as a sort of prologue to the second act a speech by 'The sprite of Achilles added to the tragedie by the translatour' (lines 578–9). In the Latin original, the apparition is only mentioned; but Heywood helps himself as he pleases to the text, adding a ghost because he wishes, presumably, to make capital of the opportunity to indulge in a great rhetorical set-piece: the description of the horrors of hell. Heywood's 'spright' is based on a character from Seneca: Tantalus in *Thyestes* (which Heywood translated in 1560). But there is a difference: Tantalus is driven up from hell to infect his grandson Thyestes with the same madness that drove his grandfather to commit a terrible crime against the gods (he fed them his own son at a banquet). But Tantalus does not seek revenge; it is the fury Megaera who goads him on stage and makes him an unwilling agent in the gods' revenge against the family of the Tantalids. But Heywood's Achilles seeks revenge against the Trojans for the sly way in which he was killed by Paris 'in Appolloes church . . . Wherof the hell will now just vengeance have' (lines 613–14). And the figure of the vengeful ghost rising clamorously from hell to seek revenge became a stock figure of later Elizabethan tragedy.

The most memorable example is the ghost of Don Andrea in Thomas Kyd's *Spanish Tragedy* (c. 1587, pr. 1592). But this ghost is rather unusual: he is not vengeful at the start of the play, but only as it proceeds is he gradually possessed by the spirit of Revenge, who accompanies him on his journey from hell to earth. More typical is the ghost of Gorlois in a play written at the same time as Kyd's tragedy: *The Misfortunes of Arthur* (1587) by Thomas Hughes and others. Gorlois was killed by Arthur's father, Uther Pendragon, and now his ghost ascends from hell to 'Glutte on revenge' (1.1.9). But the device seems to have become too familiar a convention, and eventually was treated with a degree of ridicule by some writers. For example, the anony-mous author of the tragedy *A Warning for Fair Women* (1599) – a play which Shakespeare seems to have had in mind when writing *Hamlet* – does not take tragic ghosts very seriously. This play opens with a curious induction in which female figures representing Tragedy, Comedy and History, scold one another. Comedy complains that the volume at which tragedy is conducted is generally much too high. The Chorus no longer speaks with grave passion, but 'comes howling in, / And tels us of the worrying of a cat' (sig. A2v). The Elizabethans knew that tragedy was marked by clamorous lamentation – but not 'howling'. Comedy goes on to deplore how 'a filthie whining ghost, / Lapt in some fowle sheete, or a leather pelch, / Comes skreaming like a pigge halfe stickt / And cries *Vindicta*, revenge, revenge'. The ghost's swinish shriek, then, is very far removed from the urbane ideals of *humanitas*.

However, the most important ghostly precursor of *Hamlet* is a play which has not come down to us but which Shakespeare certainly knew: the so-called ur-*Hamlet*. This is an earlier treatment of the same material that Shakespeare used in his play; probably the author was Thomas Kyd. This attribution depends on a famous passage in the preface 'To the Gentlemen Students of Both Universities' attached by Thomas Nashe to Robert Greene's novella *Menaphon* (1589). Here Nashe refers scornfully to a certain contemporary author who has evidently made some mark as a writer of tragedies: 'hee will affoord you whole Hamlets, I should say handfuls of Tragicall speeches' (p. 315). Here is our play, then, and when Nashe a line or two later compares its author to 'the Kid in Aesop' (p. 316), the case for Thomas Kyd is confirmed. Further evidence for Kyd's authorship are to be found in the following passage, which seems to allude to Kyd's training as a 'scrivener', or legal copyist:

> It is a common practise now a dayes amongst a sort of shifting companions, that runne through every Art and thrive by none, to leave the trade of *Noverint* [i.e. scrivening], whereto they were borne, and busie themselves with the indevours of Art, that could scarcely Latinize their neck verse if they should have neede; yet English Seneca read by Candlelight yeelds many good sentences, as *Blood is a begger*, and so forth; and if you intreate him faire in a frostie morning, hee will affoord you whole Hamlets, I should say handfuls of Tragicall speeches.

Nashe's comments reveal more about himself than about Kyd (or whomever). But these prejudices are familiar tokens of the more exclusive kind of Elizabethan humanism: an uneducated man should not attempt to meddle with *litterae humaniores*. The allusion to professional writers reminds us of Sidney's scorn, and the general tone is reproduced in the attitude Hamlet displays, less patently, towards Osric.

Unfortunately, despite valiant (or quixotic) attempts to 'reconstruct' this play, we know hardly anything at all about it. But the one thing we do know is that it contained a ghost. In 1596, Thomas Lodge, a university man and himself the author of a tragedy called *The Wounds of Civil War* (1588, pr. 1596), turned his pen to a general satire on the vices of his devil-ridden age called *Wit's Misery and the World's Madness*. Here Lodge describes a demon called Hate-Virtue who 'walks for the most part in black under a colour of gravity, & looks as pale as the Visard of the ghost which cried so miserably at the Theat[e]r like an oisterwife, *Hamlet, revenge*' (sig. H4v). This black-clad malcontent reminds us of Hamlet; but what mainly concerns us here is the allusion to the apparition of the Ghost of the old ur-*Hamlet*.

Lodge's comparison of the Ghost in the ur-*Hamlet* with an oysterwife may well have some basis in actual performance: a loud and high-pitched wail might have sounded like the cry of a female street-vendor. For we should not dismiss these derisive descriptions of the sound made by the ghost as merely fabricated. There is evidence to suggest that ghosts really did 'shriek' on the Elizabethan stage. Horatio, for example, recalls that when Julius Caesar was about to be murdered, ghosts did 'squeake and gibber in the Roman streets' (*Hamlet*, A.9). But the emphasis on volume is still important and inextricably bound up with the kind of theatre in which plays like the ur-*Hamlet* and *Women beware Women* were performed. The public playhouses were large spaces, and since they were open to the air, sound was lost as it was produced; moreover, sounds from outside the playhouse could also be heard in the background. In other words, actors would have to project their voices more powerfully than in the closed halls associated with the privileged drama in the private playhouses, or at school and university – or at court.

In any case, the miserable cry of the ghost in the old ur-*Hamlet* seems still to have echoed in Shakespeare's ears when he wrote his new version of the story. The phrase *Hamlet, revenge!* was, in fact, such a cliché that it was still in parodic use years after the original play was written in the late 1580s. In Thomas Dekker's *Satiromastix* (1602), written about the same time as *Hamlet*, the absurd Captain Tucca, who is represented as a man whose head is filled with scraps of plays and poems which had come to be regarded as quaint and old-fashioned by the turn of the century, exclaims: 'my name's Hamlet revenge' (4.1.121). On the other hand, it seems that Shakespeare's new tragedy had an immediate impact on London audiences. Gabriel Harvey observes to himself that it had much to 'please the wiser sort' in a note which he must have written earlier than the spring of 1601 (*Marg.*, p. 232). But it had not yet usurped the place of the ur-*Hamlet* in the memory of the playgoer. Indeed, Shakespeare must have consciously written *against* this old play in order to make room for his own.

Shakespeare's Ghost is a far more dignified figure – and far quieter. What is most striking about the first scene of *Hamlet* is not so much the mere apparition of the Ghost, though that is very well handled, but, rather, it is the fact of the Ghost's silence. Shakespeare here follows a well-known folkloric tradition: ghosts cannot speak to you until you first speak to them. Thus he makes a break with the well-worn dramatic tradition of the clamorous apparition. Indeed, silence makes Shakespeare's Ghost seem all the more eloquent. Certainly, nobody could accuse it of the sort of bombastic excesses associated by the sophisticated critic with the howling, squeaking, screaming, gibbering ghosts of the popular stage.

Shakespeare may have thus protected himself from the sorts of charge that were being made at the time against the stage-ghost. But Hamlet is still very sensitive on the issue of tragic revenge rhetoric. We have seen how he exclaims against its excesses, and how he associates it with vulgar audiences and 'the eares of the groundlings, who for the most part are capable of nothing but inexplicable dumbe showes and noyse' (3.2.30). Hamlet imagines a grotesque scene peopled by clamour-makers: town criers, robustious periwigs, Herods, Termagants, bellowing like bulls. But he himself all too easily falls into this kind of rhetoric when he gives way to the fits of vengeful passion which occasionally overtake him. For example, after the rehearsal scene, when Hamlet is vexed that a mere actor should be able to pretend grief more feelingly than a genuinely grieved party such as himself, his blood suddenly rises in disgust at his own inactivity. Hamlet breaks out into a blaze of violently 'tragical' rhetoric: 'bloody, baudy, villaine, / Remorsless, trecherous, lecherous, kindlesse villaine' (2.2.1511–12). Then his fury collapses into a self-disgust which is even more unpalatable, since it is now mixed with self-mockery:

> Why, what an Asse am I, I sure, this is most brave,
> That I the sonne of the deere murthered,
> Prompted to my revenge by heaven and hell,
> Must like a whore unpacke my hart with words,
> And fall a cursing like a very drabbe,
> A scullyon, fie uppont, foh!

No sooner than Hamlet injects a little tragical forcibleness into his style, he catches a glimpse of himself, as it were, strutting and bellowing in the mirror of his own grandiloquence, and reverts to his usual bitter humour.

Hamlet's critical sense is well informed. His imprecations hardly soar up to the properly elevated style required by Elizabethan theoreticians of the drama in a tragedy: 'stately speeches and well sounding Phrases, clyming to the height of Seneca his stile', as Sidney puts it in his *Apology* (pp. 196–7). An insult comes to Hamlet's lips and he amplifies it in the manner all Elizabethan grammar boys learnt to master at school. The word 'bloody' produces 'remorseless' and 'treacherous'; and its alliterative partner 'bawdy' gives us 'lecherous' and 'kindless' (i.e. unnatural, incestuous). The symmetry is neat; but these rhetorical schemes were almost habitual with Elizabethan writers. Alliteration is so common in ordinary unpremeditated speech that it hardly seems artful at all. This is not in itself a defect in Elizabethan aesthetics. From Cicero and Quintilian, Elizabethan writers learnt that it was desirable to become so fluent by constant practise in rhetorical techniques of all kinds, that not only did you seem to be talking naturally, but you actually could turn art into a kind of second nature. On the other hand, once you start to rely on extempore skills, little quirks tend to creep unnoticed into your speeches. Did Hamlet really intend that the word 'lecherous' should rhyme so neatly with the 'treacherous' that immediately precedes it? It seems more likely that, in the heat of the moment, Hamlet loses rational control of words, thus allowing all the naturally playful musical properties of the English language to assert themselves.

But this is not the end of the matter. It is not merely that Hamlet falters because he notices, too late, that he has accidentally used a rather ridiculous figure in what should be a very solemn and stately speech. The gravity of his intention has also been overthrown by the anxious reflection that he has been speaking not like a prince – such as he is, and such as should be the speaker of stately speeches according to the theory – but like the very lowest of the low: 'a cursing like a very drabbe, / A scullyon'. The last word should perhaps read 'stallion': a male prostitute to go with the female 'drab'. But whether we are dealing here with household menials or the whores of the street, the point of Hamlet's self-accusation is the same: he has broken the first rule of *humanitas* by lapsing into vulgarity.

Why does Hamlet delay? It is an old question; but one reason is that playing the part of the avenger, at least as that character was portrayed on the popular stage, offended his sense of personal and princely dignity. Whenever Hamlet seems to be visited by the passion he requires to take up his sword against Claudius, the rhetorical explosion in which this passion is partially expressed deflates his spirit of vengeance, so vulgarly does it sound in his ears. Hamlet cannot help comparing himself to the ham actor he despises because he imitates humanity so ludicrously, as if he, like Hamlet only unwittingly, had put on an 'antic disposition'. Truly to imitate humanity, or rather, *humanitas*, would be to put on an '*antique* disposition'. But was it possible for a people to do so who lived, as did the Danes, on the periphery of Europe, so far removed from the central Mediterranean region, where the *studia humanitatis* had its origins and revival? In the final section, we explore the spectre of northern barbarism that stalks 'Hamlet the Dane'.

Hamlet the Dane

Hamlet's outbursts of tragic passion remain private embarrassments until the final act of the play, when, stirred to emulation by Laertes' rhetoric and gesture as he leaps into Ophelia's grave, Hamlet comes out of hiding and jumps in with his rival (5.1.3218–26):

> *Laertes.* Now pile your dust upon the quick and dead,
> Till of this flat a mountaine you have made,
> To'retop old Pelion, or the skyesh head
> Of blew Olympus.
> *Hamlet.* (*comming forward*) What is he whose griefe
> Beares such an emphesis, whose phrase of sorrow
> Conjures the wandring starres, and makes them stand
> Like wonder wounded hearers, this is I
> Hamlet the Dane.

With these words, Hamlet finally comes into his kingdom. Twice elsewhere in the play is the phrase 'The Dane' used as the title of the King of Denmark; in both cases it refers to Claudius (1.1.16, 1.2.44). Now Hamlet takes back the title usurped by his uncle, restoring it, as it were, to the name of his father. But Hamlet also comes into his inheritance as a Dane like any other Dane. Against the classicising rhetoric of Laertes, with its reference to the distant and almost legendary topography of the ancient Mediterranean, Hamlet opposes himself as a man of the northern lands that the ancient Greeks knew only by hearsay. He also, I suggest, claims his Gothic inheritance.

It is a complex claim, partly because Hamlet's words have a classical ring to them. Such statements are common in Seneca and Senecal tragedy as an expression of absolute and uncompromising tragic selfhood. But it is significant that Hamlet makes the claim when he is taken unawares by a moment of extreme passion, in which he also falls prey to the tragic rhetoric he despises; for let it be noted that Hamlet puts words into Laertes' mouth when he says he has conjured the stars – Laertes has talked only of more earthly matters. But Hamlet cannot help rehearsing the repertory of tragic bombast (as he sees it). It reduces him to a state of absurd rivalry with Laertes (5.1.3242–5):

> S'wounds shew me what th'owt doe:
> Woo't weepe, woo't fight, woo't fast, woo't teare thy selfe,
> Woo't drinke up essil, eate a Crocadile,
> Ile doo't.

It is important to note that once he has been interrupted by Hamlet in the midst of his rather conventional tragic tirade, Laertes does not attempt to pick up the thread; but Hamlet cannot stop ranting. Here his 'Anticke disposition' takes control of him. Laertes' leaping into the grave is not without dignity; but Hamlet's crazily emulative remarks about drinking vinegar and eating crocodiles are grotesque. Hamlet clearly means these words to be taken as parodic, but they represent an extreme overreaction to what Laertes has actually said. Really, they reveal Hamlet's obsession with the kind of rhetoric, behaviour and identity that he despises – and yet must eventually recognise as part of his own 'destiny'. Hamlet is aware that the events in which he takes part are those of a tragedy, but he is unhappy with the role allotted to him: 'The time is out of joynt, ô cursed spight / That ever I was borne to set it right' (1.5.806–7). But he cannot help becoming an avenger, however badly he may perform his role, and he must also become more-or-less the same kind of avenger that Shakespeare had inherited from his Elizabethan predecessors: loud, unruly, and, to his own courtly taste, insufferably vulgar. In this final section, I wish to argue that, despite this initial flurry of 'Anticke disposition', 'Hamlet the Dane' does, however, achieve a kind of tragic catharsis. It is not only that Hamlet finally purges himself of the melancholy madness that has possessed him for most of the play, but also that Shakespeare provides us with a return to a 'stately style' which is purified of the worst excesses of Elizabethan popular tragedy. Let us begin, however, with the nightmarish prospect that the Danish (and, by implication, their northern cousins the English) are incorrigibly 'inhumane'.

To the Elizabethans, the Danes were egregiously heavy drinkers.[7] Thomas Nashe puts the standard view in his satirical pamphlet *Pierce Penniless his Supplication to the Devil* (1592). Like Lodge's *Wit's Misery*, this work is structured around the scheme of the Seven Deadly Sins, but Nashe's comments on Danish drunkards come in his remarks on pride rather than in those on gluttony. Nashe tells us that all the nations are vistited by pride, but especially France, Italy and Spain – a quite conventional view in his time. Then he breaks new ground: 'The most grosse and sencelesse proud dolts (in a different kind from all these) are the Danes' (p. 177). The Spaniard is a fairly simple braggart, but according to Nashe, the Italian and the Frenchman pride themselves on their exquisite finesse and courtesy: on their *humanitas*. However, the Danes stand on 'their unweldy burliboand soldiery'. But Nashe goes on to suggest that all his coarsely military swagger is to no avail because the Dane is perpetually drunk: 'he . . . stamps on the earth so terrible, as if he ment to knocke uppe a spirite, when (foule drunken bezzle) if an Englishman set his little finger to him, he falles like a hogs-trough that is set on one end' (p. 178).

Scholars are fairly sure that Shakespeare had read *Pierce Penniless*. It is not only that he makes Claudius and the Danish court heavy drinkers; even the phrasing of Hamlet's criticisms of his uncle's carousing seems to owe much to Nashe's at several points. For example, Hamlet complains (B.1–4):

> This heavy headed reveale east and west
> Makes us tradust and taxde of other nations,
> They clip us drunkards, and with Swinish phrase
> Soyle our addition.

The words 'heavy headed' and 'Swinish', though perfectly appropriate to the context, both happen to occur in Nashe's account of the Danes in *Pierce Penniless*. But it is also possible to argue that Shakespeare took much more from Nashe than the mere allegation of heavy drinking. Immediately after comparing the drunken Dane to a hog-trough, Nashe goes on, somewhat inconsequentially (p. 178):

> Therefore I am the more vehement against them, because they are an arrogant Asse-headed people, that naturally hate learning, and all them that love it: yea, and for that they would utterly roote it out from among them, they have withdrawen al rewards from the Professours thereof. Not Barbary it selfe is halfe so barbarous as they are.

Nashe goes on to assert that the Danes set no value by school learning because society is so rigidly organised that there is no place for advancement and therefore no need for intellectual self-improvement except '[f]or fashion sake' (p. 179).

He also insists that drunkenness is closely related to the lack of good letters in Denmark (p. 180):

> The Danes are bursten-bellied sots, that are to bee confuted with nothing but Tankards or quart pots, and Ovid might as well have read his verses to the Getes that understood him not, as a man talk reason to them that have no eares but their mouths, nor sense but of that which they swallowe downe their throates. God so love me, as I love the quicke-witted Italians, and therefore love them the more, because they mortally detest this surley swinish generation.

Did the Italians hate the Danes? Probably they did not; but Nashe is spinning out a plausible scenario from the materials of Renaissance humanism. The theme was in Shakespeare's mind when he wrote *As You Like It* a year or so before *Hamlet*. There we recall how Touchstone compares himself to 'Ovid ... among the Gothes' (3.3.1571–2). Here, though, the brutish element is supplied by the 'swinish' Danish descendants of the Goths (Nashe's 'Getes'); and the word, as we have seen, makes its presence felt in Hamlet's complaints about his countrymen's – and his king's – heavy drinking in Shakespeare's play.

Nashe's tirade against the Danes, though it is to be found in his remarks against pride, naturally leads on to his comments on English drunkenness in the section on gluttony. Nashe records that attitudes towards drunkenness have undergone a great change in recent years. It is a 'sinne, that ever since we have mixt our selves with the Low-countries, is counted honourable: but before we knew their lingring warres, was held in the highest degree of hatred that might be' (p. 205). The Dutch were also infamous as great drinkers; and Nashe implies that it was a result of English soldiers serving in the Dutch Wars of the last thirty years, and perhaps also the example of Dutch refugees in England and especially London, that heavy drinking has become a social custom in his own country. In other words, England is in the process of a kind of barbarisation from the Gothic North. Holinshed says that the same had happened in the reign of King Edgar (955–79), when many Danes settled in England; and Nashe praises Edgar's attempts to prevent the spread of the custom. He provides a geographical explanation for the propensity to drink of the 'Germaines and lowe Dutch' (p. 206). It is because their heads have been turned by 'the foggie aire and stinking mistes that arise out of their fennie soyle'. In the South, the sun is hot enough to evaporate this excess water, but in the North it only turns to mist and fog.

Such ideas are commonplace in Elizabethan literature. Even now we would accept that a person's temper is affected by the weather; and Renaissance thinkers saw climate as having a determinative effect on the 'character' of nations. Shakespeare would have believed it, too. This is one reason why *Hamlet* abounds with the imagery of bogs and fens and low, smelly places. It is a sign that the particular climatic influences against which northen countries must strive threaten to reclaim the Danish nation. But it is also a sign that the nation is sinking downwards beyond the lower limits of humanity into bestiality. The human body was supposed to have less water in it than did those of other animals. Hence, excessive drinking meant that you became more watery, and more like a brute beast.

Here is the nightmare perspective, but it is not allowed to go unchecked. Hamlet focuses his misgivings about Danishness on Claudius, but in his own father he presents a figure in which the Gothic North meets and fuses with the classical South. The comparison is made early on in the play, when Hamlet muses on the inexplicability of his mother's remarriage. How could she contemplate turning from one to the other: 'So excellent a King, that was to this / Hiperion to a satire' (1.2.295–6). Old Hamlet is like the sun-god Hyperion: a *heros*. But Claudius is the very antithesis of the *heros*: half man and half beast. Hamlet dismisses him as a satyr because he regards him as a lecher (Old Hamlet was by contrast 'loving'). But Claudius is also the familiar goatish demon of Elizabethan humanism. Hamlet turns to the theme once more when he confronts Gertrude with her choice and makes her compare the pictures of his father and his uncle (3.4.2267–80):

> See what a grace was seated on this browe,
> Hiperions curles, the front of Jove himselfe,
> An eye like Mars, to threaten and command,
> A station like the herald Mercury,
> New lighted on a heaven-kissing hill,
> A combination and a forme indeed
> Where every God did seeme to set his seale
> To give the world assurance of a man,
> This was your husband, looke you now what followes,
> Here is your husband like a mildewed eare,
> Blasting his wholsome brother, have you eyes,
> Could you on this faire mountaine leave to feede,
> And batten on this Moore, ha, have you eyes?

Old Hamlet is a mountain to Claudius's 'Moore'. This word is not to be interpreted as an upland heath, since that would defeat the point of Hamlet's contrast between high and low. It is used in the old sense of a marsh. Gertrude is like a sheep who has strayed from the mountain to the moor, where no sheep should properly feed because the ground is unhealthy (sheep get foot-rot in low-lying wetlands). It is the excess water that leads to this condition, just as it is damp which leads to mildew. Claudius's drinking makes his body marshy, of course; but it is also a sign of his concupiscently satyrish nature. The satyr, as we have seen, is the enemy of the shepherd, and Claudius is in this role just as inimical to the pastoral ethos as he is in his role as a 'Moore'.[8]

In contrast, Old Hamlet provides us with a picture of a Danish king who embodies the traditions of both North and South. He renews his comparison of his father to the celestial gods who occasionally descend to earth to mate with mortal women: Hyperion, Jupiter, Mars and Mercury. (Presumably this makes Hamlet a *heros* in his own imagination.) Old Hamlet gives Nashe's slanders the lie. Nashe had represented the Dane as a tiresome but drunken and pusillanimous martialist. But the first thing we hear about Old Hamlet is his military vigour, when Horatio and Marcellus see the ghost in the same armour 'when in an angry parle / He smote the sleaded pollax on the ice' (1.1.60–1). Here is an interesting crux. Should the word here spelt 'pollax' be interpreted as 'Polacks' (or 'Poles') or as 'pole-axe'? Modern editors prefer the first reading; but we recall Nashe's ludicrous image of the Dane with his battle-axe at his girdle, stamping on the floor 'as if he ment to knocke uppe a spirite' – as Hamlet will do a few scenes later to call up the Ghost. It is as if Shakespeare had Nashe's image of the drunken Dane firmly in his mind when he wrote *Hamlet*, using certain elements without alteration in his characterisation of Claudius, whilst reversing certain others in his depiction of Old Hamlet.

The positively heroic reputation and appearance of the Ghost of Hamlet's father is matched by the dignity of his speech. He calls for revenge, but not in the bloodthirsty manner of Achilles, Andrea, Gorlois and the rest. Of his sojourn in purgatory, he tells Hamlet: 'I could a tale unfolde whose lightest word / Would harrow up thy soule, freeze thy young blood, / Make thy two eyes like stars start from their spheres' (1.5.632–5). However, he does not; any other Elizabethan ghost, one feels, would not pass over the chance to dwell in detail on the torments of the underworld, one of the great rhetorical set-pieces of Senecal tragedy; but not so Old Hamlet. Instead, he calmly tells the story of his posioning in the orchard by Claudius, with one single anguished outcry: 'O horrible, ô horrible, most horrible' (1.5.697). The effect of the tale on Hamlet is considerable: his heart races, and his limbs grow weak and faint; and yet the Ghost's speech has been very measured. Indeed, the Ghost has spoken as Hamlet would have his tragic actor speak. He relates a tale calmly, without bombastic exclamation, but to powerful effect, just as Aeneas does in the second book of Virgil's *Aeneid*, and as he does in the play which Hamlet likes so much.[9]

In generic terms, the Ghost deploys a style which is closer to epic narration than to the sort of tragic rhetoric the Elizabethans were used to. We can see a similar process taking place in Hamlet's development away from his 'Anticke disposition'. His final burst of bombast is followed in the next scene by a remarkably unruffled account of his discovery and deflection of the plots laid against him whilst on board the ship carrying him to England to be executed. It is in this exchange with Horatio that Hamlet reveals a new and unexpected trust in providence: 'Ther's a divinity that shapes our ends, / Rough-hew them how we will' (5.2.3277–8). Horatio replies: 'That is most certaine'. This laconic remark should remind us how, earlier in the play, Hamlet has told Horatio that he admires him because of his indifference to Fortune (3.2.1790–3):

> ... for thou hast been
> As one in suffring all that suffers nothing,
> A man that Fortunes buffets and rewards
> Hath tane with equal thanks.

Horatio's Stoicism is the very antidote to the tradition in early English tragedy which gave such prominence to clamorous complaint against Fortune's wiles and blandishments.

However, even Horatio is susceptible to tragic gestures. When Hamlet, dying, asks him to make sure his tale is told aright, in other words, to assume the role of a calm narrator of the events as they happened, Horatio cries: 'I am more an anticke Romaine then a Dane' (5.2.3561). This is a paradoxical moment. Horatio means to kill himself by drinking what is left of the poison in the cup; and suicide was an accepted means of coming by death according to the Stoics (Seneca himself committed suicide). But Stoic suicide was calm and deliberate, not an act of impulse, as it would be in Horatio's case. Horatio seeks to die 'after the high Roman fashion', but in the heat of the moment he reverts to 'Danishness'.[10] It is as if he fails to be an 'antique Roman', then, and can manage only a travesty of the real thing: an 'antic Roman'. However, Horatio is here being used as a foil to Hamlet, who dies calmly and with dignity, without wailing and gnashing of teeth, or threats and imprecations after the manner of the old stage-tyrant. He has turned away from the world of words: 'the rest is silence'.

Notes

1. The word 'antic' was applied to ludicrous or grotesque stage-types as early as the 1560s (*Oxford English Dictionary*, under 'antic', 4a). The humorous effect of this character lay in his travesty of human form and action, a convention which was so well established that Shakespeare can vary it in *The Tempest*, when the shipwrecked courtiers are presented with a feast by 'severall strange shapes' who deck the table and 'dance about it with gentle actions of salutations' (3.3.1367 SD). The point is made that these odd-looking creatures – Sebastian calls them a 'living Drolerie', or puppet-show – display greater humanity than the human beings they wait upon. The good Gonzalo observes: 'though they are of monstrous shape, yet note / Their manners are more gentle, kinde then of / Our humaine generation you shall find / Many, nay almost any'.

2. Roman baths were often, it seems, decorated with fantastic murals in which human, animal, vegetable and other forms were bizarrely intermingled. When these were excavated during the Renaissance, such art was described as *grottesco*, with reference to their subterranean location (*grotto*: 'cave'). But it was also called *antico*, because these murals were antique; and the two words seem to have been more-or-less interchangeable in sixteenth-century Italy. In Tudor England, however, there was only the word 'antic', with 'grotesque' appearing

in the following century (see *OED*, under 'antic', headnote). This casts a very interesting light on the neoclassicism of the Renaissance.

3. The Oxford editors use the quarto of 1604/5 as their copy-text, but have excerpted certain passages and included them in an appendix of 'additions'.

4. The exact relation between the two texts is difficult to establish. See Jenkins, 1982, pp. 478–81.

5. The best modern study of the development of English medieval tragedy is Kelly (1997).

6. See Farnham, 1963, and Baker, 1939.

7. For drinking reputations, see Martin, 1999.

8. Perhaps there is a pun on the 'moor' as a blackamoor, such as Othello, who is likewise regarded by Iago and others in Shakespeare's plays as bestially lustful.

9. What would Hamlet have made of Marlowe's exorbitantly sensational treatment of this episode in his *Dido*. A few lines may serve to reveal the character of the writing: 'the franticke Queen leapt on his face, / And in his eyelids hanging by the nayles, / A little while prolong'd her husbands life: / At last the souldiers puld her by the heeles, / And swong her howling in the emptie ayre' (lines 539–43). As Dido says: 'O end Aeneas, I can heare no more'.

10. So says Cleopatra, another non-Roman, in *Antony and Cleopatra* (4.16.2575).

CONCLUSION

This book began with a conscientious declaration to the effect that it would not attempt to 'define' the word 'humanism'. But it may be useful nonetheless to conclude by briefly returning to the two main points which (I trust) have emerged from this study. Most of the late sixteenth-century texts we still read today were touched in one way or another by Elizabethan humanism, so it is worth trying to formulate what we mean when we use the term. The essays in the second part of this study have each tried to apply to various texts aspects of the loosely articulated formulations of the chapters making up the first part. The same formulations could be used to explore and illuminate other texts, of course, and it is my hope that readers will try them out in their approaches to Thomas Kyd or Robert Greene or Lady Mary Sidney – or whomever.

Two main points seem especially important. In the first place, we should think of humanism as a 'discourse'. This word has acquired several specialised literary-theoretical meanings in recent years, but here it is intended to refer to a lexicon or even a rhetoric of words, phrases, examples, anecdotes, myths, and so on, which centre around the term 'humanity' or *humanitas*. Elizabethan humanism was never a well-organised and well-regulated literary and cultural programme which everyone knew about and some people actually followed. Grammar schools may have operated on that principle, but humanism was not confined to grammar, nor even, as we have seen, to any other obviously discernible grouping of disciplines such as the influential but questionable Kristellerian pentad of grammar, poetry, rhetoric, history and moral philosophy. Rather it was a more-or-less loose set of associations with the words 'humanity' and *humanitas* acting as a semantic and ideological centre of gravity. Some of these associations operate more powerfully than others, and I have tried to give an account of these in the first part of this book: the 'ascent of man' from brutishness to civilisation; the lapse from humanity to ferocity; the importance of leisure, wit and charm; the will-o'-the-wisp of universal learning – all of these go back to Cicero and may be found again and again in the works of Elizabethan writers. There are also non-Ciceronian elements in Elizabethan humanism, of course; the important mythology of muses, nymphs, shepherds and satyrs, derives largely from late-medieval French and Italian sources. But the discourse of humanity was sufficiently flexible and capacious to accommodate all kinds of new material. For the same reasons, the discourse is really a plurality of discourses; and we have seen how different inflections of Elizabethan humanism – for example, the scholarly and the courtly kinds – can come into conflict. They share a good deal of common ground, but they can disagree on important details. This leads me to my second point.

Elizabethan humanism was essentially 'exclusive' in character. One might think that any humanism should be 'inclusive': humanity should be a property of all human beings, not one of an exclusive minority. But this is not the case in late sixteenth-century England. Ciceronian humanism is also exclusive, but not so eagerly or anxiously exclusive as its Elizabethan descendant. Elizabethan humanism dwells almost obsessively on the line which separates the truly humane from the boorish, the barbaric, the brutal or bestial – or even the demonic. There are many reasons for this. The situation of secular learning reflects the exclusiveness of salvation according to the Calvinist divines whose teachings provided the main tenets of the Elizabethan settlement in religion. Christ died on the cross to save the elect few, not the reprobate many. More importantly, most of the men we now recognise as humanists came from families whose circumstances placed them on or near the line where the lower ranks of the gentry met the upper ranks of the common people. These men picked up their humanism at grammar school and many were clearly determined to use it as a means of improving their social position. Hence they tend to patrol the limits of *humanitas* very aggressively in their own writings. This led in turn to a strange fixation on the image which I have chosen to illustrate the cover of this book: a woodcut from Spenser's 'Sonnets' (1569). The brutish incursion of the satyrs in the dainty paradise of the *mouseion* cannot be easily rewritten in terms of the routine activities of the humanists themselves, since it was not so much direct attack from an ignorant and hostile public they had to fear, but indifference and neglect. But the image nevertheless neatly captures the sense of deep anxiety which underlies much humanist writing and undercuts its more rhapsodical effusions.

Paradoxically enough, it may be that this anxiety is what makes the Elizabethan humanist a more congenial figure to the modern reader than some of his later Ciceronian cousins. For example, when, in *A Sicilian Romance* (1790), Anne Radcliffe came to describe what she would no doubt have thought of as the 'Gothic' education of the daughters of the Marquis of Mazzini at 'the close of the sixteenth century', she makes a distinction between two kinds of conversation: 'the familiar and the sentimental' (p. 7). She explains: 'It is the province of the familiar, to diffuse cheerfulness and ease – to open the heart of man to man, and to beam a temperate sunshine upon the mind'. Here, then, is a generously inclusive version of Ciceronian *humanitas*. Anyone, it is hinted, can speak like this. But 'sentimental conversation' is more difficult (and to us by now more 'familiar' in the ordinary sense):

> To good sense, lively feeling, and natural delicacy of taste, must be united an expansion of mind, and a refinement of thought, which is the result of high culture. To render this sort of conversation irresistibly attractive, a knowledge of the world is requisite, and that enchanting ease, that elegance of manner, which is to be acquired only by frequenting the higher circles of polished life.

This is the kind of conversation Gabriel Harvey tried to reproduce when he was presented to the court at Audley End. Thank goodness he failed. Radcliffe's sentimental conversation is impervious to self-doubt in its smugness and superiority; whereas the very vulnerability of our Elizabethan humanist, even when it is revealed in its darker and more hostile aspect, always reassures us that these humanists were, at least, human.

WORKS CONSULTED

Abbreviations

EETS   Early English Text Society
ELR   *English Literary Renaissance*
JCWI   *Journal of the Courtauld and Warburg Institutes*
JHI   *Journal of the History of Ideas*
LCL   Loeb Classical Library
MSR   Malone Society Reprints
NQ   *Notes and Queries*
RES   *Review of English Studies*
Smith   G. Gregory Smith, ed. *Elizabethan Critical Essays*. Oxford, 1904
RenD   *Renaissance Drama*
STC   *Short-Title Catalogue*

Primary texts

Ascham, Roger. *Toxophilus* (1545). Ed. William Aldis Wright, *Roger Ascham: English Works*. Cambridge, 1904. Except otherwise stated, all references to Ascham's works are to this edition.

Ascham, Roger. *The Schoolmaster* (1570).

Ascham, Roger. *A Report and Discourse of the Affairs and State of Germany* (1570).

Ascham, Roger. *The Whole Works of Roger Ascham*. Ed. J.A. Giles. London, 1864–5.

Ascham, Roger. *Letters of Roger Ascham*. Trans. Maurice Hatch, ed. Alvin Vos. New York, 1989.

Aulus Gellius. *Noctes Atticae*. Ed. Peter K. Marshall. Oxford, 1968.

Aylett, Robert. *Peace with her Four Guarders*. London, 1622. *STC* 1002.

Barclay, Alexander, trans. [Domenicus Mancinus] *The Mirror of Good Manners*. London, 1518. *STC* 18205.

Barclay, Alexander. *Eclogues* (1530; 3rd edn 1570). Ed. Beatrice White. Oxford, 1928 (EETS).

Beroaldus, Philip [Filippo Beroaldo], ed. *M.T. Ciceronis oratio pro A. Licinio Archia poeta*. Lyons, 1517.

Blennerhasset, Thomas. *The Second Part of the Mirror for Magistrates* (1578). Ed. Lily B. Campbell, *Parts Added to The Mirror for Magistrates*. Cambridge, 1946.

Bolerus, Martin, ed. *M.T. Ciceronis pro A. Licinio Archia poeta oratio*. Paris, 1541.

Bond, R. Warwick. See Lyly, *Euphues*.

Bradshaw, Henry. *The Life of St Radegund*. London, 1525. *STC* 3507.

Castiglione, Baldessare. *The Book of the Courtier*. Trans. Sir Thomas Hoby (1561), ed. Virginia Cox. London and Vermont, 1994.

Caxton, William, trans. [Jacobus de Voragine] *The Legend Named in Latin Legenda Aurea*. London, 1483. *STC* 24873.

Chapman, George. *Hero and Leander* (1598). Ed. C.F. Tucker Brooke, *The Complete Works of Christopher Marlowe*. Oxford, 1910.

Chapman, George. See also Homer, *Iliad*.

Chaucer, Geoffrey. *The Canterbury Tales*. Ed. F.N. Robinson, *The Complete Works of Geoffrey Chaucer*. 1933; 2nd edn Oxford, 1957.

Chettle, Henry. *Kind Heart's Dream*. London, 1593. *STC* 5123.

Cicero, Marcus Tullius. *De officiis*. Latin text ed. M. Winterbottom. Oxford, 1994. English text trans. Nicholas Grimald as *Cicero's Three Books of Duties* (1556), ed. Gerald O'Gorman. Washington, 1990.

Cicero, Marcus Tullius. *De oratore*. Ed. Augustus S. Wilkins. Oxford, 1895.

Cicero, Marcus Tullius. *Pro Archia poeta*. Ed. Helmuth and Karl Vretska. Darmstadt, 1979.

Cicero, Marcus Tullius. *De divinatione*. Ed. Armstrong Pease. Urbana, IL, 1920.

Cicero, Marcus Tullius. *Disputationes Tusculanae*. Latin text ed. J.E. King as *Tusculan Disputations* (LCL). London and New York, 1971. English text trans. John Dolman as *Those Five Questions which Mark Tully Cicero Disputed in his Manor at Tusculanum*. London, 1561. *STC* 5317.

Civil and Uncivil Life. London, 1579. *STC* 15589.

Clyomon and Clamydes (1599). Ed. W.W. Greg. Oxford, 1913 (MSR).

Cooper, Thomas. *Thesaurus linguae Romanae et Britannicae*. London, 1565. *STC* 5686.

Dasypodius, Petrus. *Dictionarium Latino Germanicum et vice versa Germanico Latinum* (1565). Eds Füssel and Kreutzer, 1988 (Faust Book).

Dekker, Thomas. *Satiromastix* (1602). Ed. Fredson Bowers, *The Dramatic Works of Thomas Dekker*. Vol. 1. Cambridge, 1958.

Dolman, John. See Cicero, *Disputationes Tusculanae*.

Elyot, Sir Thomas. *The Book Named the Governor* (1531). Ed. Foster Watson. London, 1907.

Elyot, Sir Thomas. *The Image of Governance* (1541). Facs. ed. in *Four Political Treatises* by Sir Thomas Elyot (introduced by Lillian Gottesman). Gainseville, FL, 1967.

Faust Book. *Historia von D. Johann Fausten* (1587). German text ed. Stephan Füssel and Hans Joachim Kreutzer. Stuttgart, 1988. English text trans. P.F. as *The History of the Damnable Life and Deserved Death of Doctor John Faustus* (reference by signature). London, 1592. *STC* 10711. Ed. John Henry Jones as *The English Faust Book* (reference by page). London and New York, 1994.

Fisher, John. *Three Dialogues*. London, 1558. *STC* 10917.

Fleming, Abraham, trans. *The Bucolics of Publius Virgilius Maro*. London, 1575.1 *STC* 24816.

Fleming, Abraham, ed. *A Bright Burning Beacon Forewarning All Wise Virgins*. London, 1580. *STC* 11037.

Fleming, Abraham, trans. *The Bucolics of Publius Virgilius Maro*. London, 1589. *STC* 24817 (printed with item below).

Fleming, Abraham, trans. *The Georgics of Publius Virgilius Maro*. London, 1589. *STC* 24817 (printed with item above).

Florio, John. *A World of Words*. London, 1598. *STC* 11098.

Gascoigne, George. *The Glass of Government* (1575). Ed. John W. Cunliffe, *The Complete Works of George Gascoigne*. Vol. 2. Cambridge, 1907–10.

Gellius. See Aulus Gellius.

Giles, J.A. See Ascham, *Whole Works*.

Golding, Arthur. See Ovid, *Metamorphoses*.

Greville, Fulke. *A Treaty of Humane Learning*. Ed. Geoffrey Bullough, *The Poems and Dramas of Fulke Greville, First Lord Brooke*. Vol. 1. Edinburgh, 1939.

Harington, Sir John. 'Preface, or Brief Apology for Poetry' to his trans. of Arisoto's *Orlando Furioso* (1591). In Smith, Vol. 2.

Harington, Sir John. *The Metamorphoses of Ajax* (1596). Ed. Elizabeth Story Donno. London, 1962.

Harvey, Gabriel. *Ciceronianus* (1577). Ed. Harold S. Wilson, trans. Clarence A. Forbes. Lincoln, NE, 1945.

Harvey, Gabriel. *Smithus; vel Musarum lachrymae*. London, 1578. *STC* 12905.

Harvey, Gabriel. *Gratulationes Valdinenses* (1578). Ed. and trans. Thomas Hugh James. Unpublished dissertation, Yale, 1938.

Harvey, Gabriel. *Three Proper and Witty Familiar Letters* (with Edmund Spenser: 1580). Eds J.C. Smith and E. de Selincourt, *The Poetical Works of Edmund Spenser*. London, 1912.

Harvey, Gabriel. *Pierce's Supererogation* (1593). Facsimile reprint, Menston, 1970.

Harvey, Gabriel. *Gabriel Harvey's Letter-Book A.D. 1573–1580*. Ed. Edward John Long Scott. London, 1884.

Harvey, Gabriel. *Gabriel Harvey's Marginalia*. Ed. G.C. Moore Smith. Stratford upon Avon, 1913.

Harvey, John. *A Discursive Problem Concerning Prophecies*. London, 1588. *STC* 12908.

Harvey, Richard. *A Theological Discourse of the Lamb of God and His Enemies*. London, 1590. *STC* 12915.

Henryson, Robert. *The Testament of Cresseid* (1532). Ed. Charles Elliott, *Robert Henryson: Poems*. 1963; 2nd edn Oxford, 1974.

Heywood, Jasper. Trans. Seneca, *Troas* (1559). Ed. H. de Vocht, *Jasper Heywood and his Translations of Seneca's* Troas, Thyestes, *and* Hercules furens. Louvain, 1913.

Hill, Adam. *The Defence of the Article: Christ Descended into Hell.* London, 1592. *STC* 13466.

Hoby, Sir Thomas. See Castiglione.

Holland, Philemon, trans. Suetonius, *The History of Twelve Caesars.* London, 1606. *STC* 23422.

Homer. *Iliad.* Trans. George Chapman as *The Iliads of Homer* (1598–1611), ed. Allardyce Nicoll. Vol. 1. London, 1957.

Hughes, Thomas. *The Misfortunes of Arthur* (1587). Ed. John W. Cunliffe, *Early English Classical Tragedies.* Oxford, 1912.

Humphrey, Laurence. Latin text: *Optimates.* London, 1560. English text trans. anon. as *The Nobles.* London, 1563. *STC* 13964.

Kempe, William. *The Education of Children in Learning* (1588). Ed. Robert D. Pepper, *Four Tudor Books on Education.* Gainesville, FL, 1966.

Lodge, Thomas. *Wit's Misery and the World's Madness.* London, 1596. *STC* 16677.

Lucian. *Dialogues of the Dead.* Eds A.M. Harmon and M.D. McLeod, *Lucian* (LCL). Vol. 7. London and New York, 1913–67.

Lyly, John. *Euphues: The Anatomy of Wit* (1578). Ed. R. Warwick Bond, *The Complete Works of John Lyly.* Vol. 1. Oxford, 1902. All references to Lyly's works are to this edition.

Lyly, John. *Euphues and his England* (1580). Vol. 2.

Lyly, John. *Campaspe* (1584). Vol. 2.

Lyly, John. *Pap with an Hatchet* (1589). Vol. 3.

Lyly, John. *Midas* (1592). Vol. 3.

Mantuan, see Spagnuoli.

Marlowe, Christopher. *Tamburlaine* (1590). Ed. C.F. Tucker Brooke, *The Works of Christopher Marlowe.* Oxford, 1910. All references to Marlowe's work are to this edition.

Marlowe, Christopher. *Dido, Queen of Carthage* (1594).

Marlowe, Christopher. *Doctor Faustus* [A Text] (1604).

Maunsell, Andrew. *The Second Part of the Catalogue of English Books.* Printed with *The First Part [etc.].* London, 1595. *STC* 17689.

Maximus. See Valerius Maximus.

Moryson, Fynes. *An Itinerary.* London, 1617. *STC* 18205.

Nashe, Thomas. Preface 'To the Gentlemen Students' to Robert Greene's *Menaphon* (1589). Ed. Ronald B. McKerrow, *The Works of Thomas Nashe* (1906–10), Vol. 3; rpt. and ed. F.P. Wilson. Oxford, 1958. All references to Nashe's works are to this edition.

Nashe, Thomas. *Four Letters Confuted* [a.k.a.: *Strange News of the Intercepting of Certain Letters and a Convoy of verse*] (1592). Vol. 1.

Nashe, Thomas. *Pierce Penniless his Supplication to the Devil* (1592). Vol. 1.

Nashe, Thomas. *Christ's Tears over Jerusalem* (1593). Vol. 2.

Nashe, Thomas. *Have With You to Saffron Walden* (1596). Vol. 3.

Nice Wanton. London, 1560. *STC* 5016.

Norton, Thomas, and Thomas Sackville. *Gorboduc* (1565; 2nd edn 1571). Ed. John W. Cunliffe, *Early English Classical Tragedies*. Oxford, 1912.

Olney, Henry. Address 'To the Reader' to his edition of Sidney's *Apology for Poetry* (1595). Ed. Smith, Vol. 1.

Ovid. *Metamorphoses*. Latin text ed. Frank Justus Miller. 1916; 2nd edn London and New York, 1921 (LCL). English text trans. Arthur Golding as *Metamorphosis* (1564–7), ed. W.H.D. Rouse as *Shakespeare's Ovid: Being Arthur Golding's Translation of the Metamorphoses*. London, 1961.

Ovid. *Epistulae heroidum*. Latin text ed. Grant Showerman, *Ovid: Heroides and Amores* (LCL). London and New York, 1921. English text trans. George Turberville as *The Heroical Epistles*. London, 1567. *STC* 18940.

Phaer, Thomas. See Virgil, *Aeneid*.

Plato. *Gorgias*. Ed. Gonzalez Lodge. Boston and London, 1891.

Plutarch, *Lives*. Ed. Bernadotte Perrin, London and Cambridge, MA, 1921 (LCL). Trans. Sir Thomas North (1579), ed. W.H.D. Rouse. London, 1908.

Puttenham, George. *The Art of English Poesy* (1589). Ed. Smith, Vol. 2.

Quintilian. *Institutio oratoria*. Ed. Michael Winterbottom. Oxford, 1970.

Radcliffe, Anne. *A Sicilian Romance* (1790). Ed. Alison Milbank. Oxford and New York, 1998.

Rhodes, Hugh. *The Book of Nurture* (1577). Ed. F.J. Furnivall, *The Babees Book* [etc.]. London, 1868 (EETS).

Sackville, Thomas. See Thomas Norton.

Shakespeare, William. *A Midsummer Night's Dream* (1600). All references to Shakespeare are taken from the original-spelling edition of *William Shakespeare: The Complete Works*. Ed. Stanley Wells *et al*. Oxford, 1986.

Shakespeare, William. *Hamlet, Prince of Denmark* (1604).

Shakespeare, William. *Antony and Cleopatra* (1623).

Shakespeare, William. *As You Like It* (1623).

Shakespeare, William. *The Tempest* (1623).

Sidney, Sir Philip. *An Apology for Poetry* (1595). Ed. Smith, Vol. 1.

Smith, Sir Thomas. *A Discourse of the Commonweal of This Realm of England* (ms 1565). Ed. Elizabeth Lamond. Cambridge, 1893.

Smith, Sir Thomas. *De recta et emendata linguae Anglicae scriptione dialogus* (1568). Ed. Bror Danielsson, *Sir Thomas Smith: Literary and Linguistic Works*. Vol. 3. Stockholm, 1983.

Smith, Sir Thomas. *De recta et emendata linguae Graecae pronuntiatione dialogus* (1568). Ed. Bror Danielsson, *Sir Thomas Smith: Literary and Linguistic Works*. Vol. 2. Stockholm, 1978.

Spenser, Edmund. 'Epigrams' (1569). Eds J.C. Smith and E. de Selincourt, *The Poetical Works of Edmund Spenser*. London, 1912. All references to Spenser's works are to this edition.

Spenser, Edmund. *The Shepherd's Calendar* (1579)

Spenser, Edmund. *Three Proper and Witty Familiar Letters* (1580: with Gabriel Harvey).

Spenser, Edmund. *The Fairy Queen* (1590–1609).

Spenser, Edmund. *Tears of the Muses* (1591).

Stanyhurst, Richard. 'The History of Ireland'. Ed. Raphael Holinshed, *The First Part of the Chronicles of England, Scotland, and Ireland*. London, 1577. *STC* 13568.

Sturmius, John [Johann Sturm]. *De nobilitate litterata* (1549), trans. Thomas Browne as *A Rich Storehouse or Treasury for Nobility and Gentlemen*. London, 1570. *STC* 23408.

Suetonius. *De grammaticis et rhetoribus*. Ed. J.C. Rolfe, *Suetonius* (LCL). Vol. 2. London and Boston, 1970.

Sylvius, Francis, ed. *M.T. Ciceronis pro A. Licinio Archia poeta oratio*. Paris, 1541.

Turberville, George, trans. *The Eglogues of the Poet B. Mantuan Carmelitan*. London, 1567. *STC* 22990.

Udall, Nicholas, trans. *Apophthegms Gathered by Erasmus* (1542). Ed. Robert Roberts. Boston, 1877.

Valerius Maximus. *Facta et dicta memorabilia*. Latin text ed. D.R. Shackleton Bailey as *Memorable Doings and Sayings* (LCL). Cambridge, MA, and London, 2000. English text trans. Samuel Speed as *The Acts and Sayings of the Romans*. London, 1678.

Varro. *De lingua Latina*. Ed. Roland G. Kent as *On the Latin Language* (LCL). Cambridge, MA, and London, 1938.

Virgil *Bucolics*. Ed. H. Rushton Fairclough, *Virgil*. Vol. 1. 1916; rev. edn. Cambridge, MA, and London, 1935. All references to Virgil's works in Latin are to this edition.

Virgil *Aeneid*. Trans. Thomas Phaer (1558), ed. Steven Lally, *The Aeneid of Thomas Phaer and Thomas Twyne*. New York, 1987.

Vos, Alvin. See Ascham, *Letters*.

Warning for Fair Women, A. London, 1599. *STC* 25089.

Webbe, William. *A Discourse of English Poetry* (1586). Ed. Smith, Vol. 1.

Wilson, Robert. *The Cobbler's Prophecy* (1594). Ed. A.C. Ward. Oxford, 1914 (MSR).

Wotton, Henry, trans. [Jacques Yver] *A Courtly Controversy of Cupid's Cautels*. London, 1578. *STC* 5647.

Secondary texts

Attridge, Derek. *Well-weighed Syllables: Elizabethan Verse in Classical Metres*. Cambridge, 1974.

Baker, Howard. *Induction to Tragedy: A Study in the Development of Form in* Gorboduc, The Spanish Tragedy, *and* Titus Andronicus. Lafayette, LA, 1939.

Baldwin, T.W. *William Shakspere's Small Latine and Less Greeke.* Urbana, IL, 1944.

Bates, Catherine. *The Rhetoric of Courtship in Elizabethan Language and Literature.* Cambridge, 1992.

Bevington, David, and Eric Rasmussen, eds. *Christopher Marlowe: Doctor Faustus.* Manchester and New York, 1993.

Binns, J.W. *Intellectual Culture in Elizabethan and Jacobean England: The Latin Writings of the Age.* Leeds, 1990.

Bloomer, W. Martin. *Valerius Maximus and the Rhetoric of the New Nobility.* London, 1992.

Bonner, Stanley F. *Education in Ancient Rome: From the Elder Cato to the Younger Pliny.* London, 1977.

Boyancé, Pierre. *Études sur l'humanisme cicéronien.* Brussels, 1970.

Bryson, Anna. *From Courtesy to Civility: Changing Codes of Conduct in Early Modern England.* Oxford, 1998.

Bushnell, Rebecca W. *A Culture of Teaching: Early Modern Humanism in Theory and Practice.* Ithaca and London, 1996.

Butler, Elizabeth M. *Ritual Magic.* 1949; rpt. Stroud, 1998.

Carlson, David R. *English Humanist Books: Writers and Patrons, Manuscripts and Print, 1475–1525.* Toronto, 1993.

Caspari, Fritz. *Humanism and the Social Order in Tudor England.* Chicago, 1954.

Cooper, Helen. *Pastoral: Mediaeval into Renaissance.* Ipswich and Totowa, 1977.

Crane, Mary Thomas. *Framing Authority: Sayings, Self, and Society in Sixteenth-century England.* Princeton, 1993.

Curtis, Mark H. *Oxford and Cambridge in Transition, 1558–1642: An Essay on the Changing Relations between the English Universities and English Society.* Oxford, 1959.

Curtius, Ernst Robert. *European Literature and the Latin Middle Ages* (1948). Trans. Willard R. Trask. London, 1953.

Davies, Tony. *Humanism.* London and New York, 1997.

Dewar, Mary. *Sir Thomas Smith: A Tudor Intellectual in Office.* London. 1964.

Duncan-Jones, Katherine, & Jan A. van Dorsten, eds., *The Miscellaneous Prose of Sir Philip Sidney.* Oxford, 1973.

Duncan-Jones, Katherine, ed. *Sir Philip Sidney: A Critical Edition of the Major Works.* Oxford and New York, 1989.

F., P. See Faust Book.

Farnham, Willard. *The Medieval Heritage of Elizabethan Tragedy.* Oxford, 1963.

Fletcher, John. 'The Faculty of Arts'. In James McConica, ed. *The Collegiate University.* Oxford, 1986 (Vol. 3 of *The History of the University of Oxford*).

Fraser, Russell. *The War Against Poetry.* Princeton, NJ, 1970.

Füssel, Stephan, and Hans Joachim Kreutzer, eds. *Historia von D. Johann Fausten: Kritische Ausgabe.* Stuttgart, 1988.

Giustiniani, Vito D. 'Homo, humanus, and the meanings of "humanism"', *JHI* 46 (1985), pp. 167–95.

Grafton, Anthony. 'The world of the polyhistors: humanism and encyclopaedism', *Central European History* 18 (1985), pp. 31–47.

Grafton, Anthony, and Lisa Jardine. *From Humanism to the Humanities: The Institutionalising of the Liberal Arts in Fifteenth- and Sixteenth-century Europe.* Cambridge, MA, 1986.

Grafton, Anthony, and Lisa Jardine. '"Studied for action": How Gabriel Harvey read his Livy', *Past and Present* 129 (1990), pp. 30–78.

Gray, Hannah H. 'Renaissance humanism: the pursuit of eloquence', *JHI* 24 (1963), pp. 497–514.

Greaves, Margaret. *The Blazon of Honour: A Study in Renaissance Magnanimity.* London, 1954.

Greenlaw, Edwin, Charles Grosvenor Osgood, Frederick Morgan Padelford and Ray Heffner, eds. *The Works of Edmund Spenser: A Variorum Edition.* Baltimore, 1933–43.

Helgerson, Richard. *The Elizabethan Prodigals.* Berkeley, 1976.

Hunt, H.A.K. *The Humanism of Cicero.* Melbourne, 1954.

Hunter, G.K. *John Lyly: The Humanist as Courtier.* London, 1962.

Jardine, Lisa. 'Encountering Ireland: Gabriel Harvey, Edmund Spenser, and English colonial ventures'. In Brendan Bradshaw, Andrew Hadfield and Willy Maley, eds, *Representing Ireland: Literature and the Origin of Conflict, 1534–1660.* Cambridge, 1993, pp. 60–75.

Jenkins, Harold. ed. [William Shakespeare] *Hamlet.* London and New York, 1982.

Jensen, Kristian. 'The humanist reform of Latin and Latin teaching'. In Jill Kraye, ed., *The Cambridge Companion to Renaissance Humanism.* Cambridge, 1996, pp. 63–81.

Jones, Howard. *Master Tully: Cicero in Tudor England.* Nieuwkoop, 1998.

Jones, John Henry, ed. *The English Faust Book.* Cambridge and New York, 1994.

Kaster, Robert A. *Guardians of Language: The Grammarian and Society in Late Antiquity.* Berkeley, CA, 1988.

Kearney, Hugh F. *Scholars and Gentlemen: Universities and Society in Pre-industrial Britain 1500–1700.* London, 1970.

Kelly, Henry Ansgar. *Chaucerian Tragedy.* Cambridge, 1997.

Kohl, Benjamin G. 'The changing concept of the *studia humanitatis* in the early Renaissance', *Renaissance Studies* 2 (1992), pp. 185–209.

Kristeller, Paul Oskar. *Renaissance Thought: The Classic, Scholastic, and Humanist Strains.* New York, 1955.

Leader, Damian Riehl. *The University to 1546.* Cambridge, 1988 (Vol. 1 of *A History of the University of Cambridge*).

Lewis, C.S. *English Literature in the Sixteenth Century Excluding Drama.* Oxford, 1954.

Major, John F. *Sir Thomas Elyot and the English Renaissance.* Lincoln, NE, 1964.

Marcus, Leah. 'Textual Indeterminacy and Ideological Difference: The Case of *Doctor Faustus*'. *RenD* 20 (1989), pp. 1–29.

Marrou, H.-I. *A History of Education in Antiquity* (1948). Trans. George Lamb. London, 1956.

Martin, A. Lynn. 'National Reputations for Drinking in Traditional Europe'. *Parergon* (n.s.) 17 (1999), pp. 163–86.

Martindale, Joanna, ed. *English Humanism: Wyatt to Cowley*. London, 1985.

McCarthy, Penny. 'E.K. was only the postman'. *NQ* 47 [245] (2000), pp. 28–31.

McConica, James Kelsey. *English Humanists and Reformation Politics under Henry VIII and Edward III*. Oxford, 1965.

McConica, James., ed. *The Collegiate University*. Oxford, 1986 (Vol. 3 of *The History of the University of Oxford*).

McKerrow, Ronald B., ed. *The Works of Thomas Nashe* (1906–10). Rpt. and ed. F.P. Wilson, Oxford, 1966.

Moore Smith, G.C., ed. *Pedantius: A Latin Comedy Acted at Trinity College, Cambridge*. Louvain, 1905.

Mueller, Janel. *The Native Tongue and the Word: Developments in English Prose-style 1380–1580*. Chicago and London, 1984.

North, John David. *Chaucer's Universe*. Oxford and New York, 1988.

Nussbaum, Martha. *Cultivating Humanity: A Classical Defense of Reform in Liberal Education*. Cambridge, MA, and London, 1997.

Pincombe, Michael. 'Some sixteenth-century records of the words humanist and humanitian'. *RES* (ns) 44 (1993), pp. 1–15.

Pincombe, Michael. 'Lyly's *Euphues*: Anatomy or Peepshow?'. In Wolfgang Görtschacher and Holger Klein, eds, *Narrative Strategies in Early English Fiction*. Lewiston and Salzburg, 1995, pp. 103–14.

Pincombe, Michael. *The Plays of John Lyly: Eros and Eliza*. Manchester, 1996.

Ramage, Edwin S. *Urbanitas: Ancient Sophistication and Refinement*. Norman, OK, 1973.

Reeve, Michael D. 'Classical scholarship'. In Jill Kraye, ed. *The Cambridge Companion to Renaissance Humanism*. Cambridge, 1996, pp. 20–46.

Rieks, Rudolf. *Homo, humanus, humanitas: Zur Humanität in der lateinischen Literatur des ersten nachchristlichen Jahrhunderts*. Munich, 1967.

Roberts, Gareth. 'A new source for John Lyly's *Euphues and his England*'. *JCWI* 42 (1979), pp. 286–9.

Roberts, Gareth. 'Necromantic works: Christopher Marlowe, Doctor Faustus, and Agrippa of Nettesheim'. In Darryll Grantley and Peter Roberts, eds, *Christopher Marlowe and English Renaissance Culture*. Aldershot, 1996, pp. 148–71.

Schleiner, Louise. 'Spenser's 'E.K.' as Edward Kent (Kenned/of Kent): Kyth (Couth), Kissed, and Kunning–Conning', *ELR* 20 (1990), pp. 374–407.

Shearman, John. *Mannerism*. Harmondsworth, 1967.

Shepherd, Geoffrey, ed. *Sir Philip Sidney: An Apology for Poetry*. Manchester, 1965.

Skinner, Quentin. *The Foundations of Modern Political Thought*. Cambridge, 1978.

Stern, Virginia. *Gabriel Harvey: His Life, Marginalia and Library*. Oxford, 1979.

Stewart, Alan. *Close Readers: Sodomy and Humanism in Early Modern England*. Princeton, NJ, 1997.

Tilley, M.P. *A History of the Proverbs in England in the Sixteenth and Seventeenth Centuries*. Ann Arbor, MI, 1950.

Wilson, Katherine. 'Revenge of the Angel Gabriel: Harvey's "A Nobleman's Suit unto a Country Maid"'. In Mike Pincombe, ed., *The Anatomy of Tudor Literature: Proceedings of the First International Conference of the Tudor Symposium (1998)*. Aldershot and Burlington, VT, 2001, pp. 79–91.

INDEX